Aggravation, Mitigation and Mercy
in English Criminal Justice

For my wife,
who has put up with this sort of thing
for sixty years

Aggravation, Mitigation and Mercy in English Criminal Justice

Nigel Walker

BLACKSTONE
PRESS LIMITED

First published in Great Britain 1999 by Blackstone Press Limited,
Aldine Place, London W12 8AA. Telephone 0181-740 2277
www.blackstonepress.com

ISBN: 1 85431 943 4

British Library Cataloguing in Publication Data
A CIP catalogue record for this book is available from the British
Library

Typeset by Style Photosetting Limited, Mayfield, East Sussex
Printed by Livesey Ltd, Shrewsbury, Shropshire

. . . For we ought always, for love and fear of God, to doom and prescribe more lightly to the feeble man than to the strong; because we know full well that the powerless cannot raise a like burthen with the powerful, nor the unhale a like with the hale; and therefore we ought to moderate, and discreetly distinguish between age and youth, wealth and poverty, freedom and slavery, hale and unhale. And both in religious shrifts and secular dooms these things ought to be discriminated. Moreover in many a deed, when anyone is an involuntary agent, then is he the better deserving of protection, because he did what he did from necessity: and if anyone do a thing unwillingly, it is not at all like that which he does wilfully.

From Thorpe's translation (1840) of the laws of Cnut, about 1020 AD

Contents

Preface

In 1877 Edward Cox, Recorder of Falmouth, published the first English textbook on sentencing, *The Principles of Punishment*. It preached a Benthamite version of utilitarianism, in which the only important consideration was the need for deterrence in some kinds of case, and the absence of this need in other kinds.

Reformation was treated with scepticism. There were brief chapters on aggravation and mitigation, but none on mercy. Most remarkable, however, was the absence of any attention to retribution, let alone 'just deserts'. Today, as we shall see, it is impossible to write about aggravation and mitigation in sentencing without taking notice of the strong undertow of retributivism which tugs at modern judges.

The modern literature of sentencing is almost entirely devoted to courts' powers and procedures. Some textbooks list sentencers' aims briefly and with the implication that they present no real problem. Few deal with their chances of achieving those aims, or with the conflicts between them. Hardly any deal systematically with the considerations that seem to persuade courts to pursue their aims with leniency or severity in individual cases.[1] Yet the legislation of the nineties, with its emphasis on proportionality, aggravation and mitigation, has increased their importance. This book is an effort to fill all these gaps.

The subject makes it hard to avoid sententiousness, although I have done my best. An example is calling sentencing an art, as many a judge has done. When meant literally – as it usually is – this is both sententious and pretentious. The aims of sentencing are neither aesthetic nor original. If all that is meant is that it cannot be taught by mere rules, that is true, at least of modern British sentencing; but it is also true of skills which we would not seriously call arts, such as playing bridge. In fact sentencing is now more, not less, rule-bound than it was. English sentencers' freedom to follow their own policies is far more limited, both by statute and by case-law, than it was a quarter of a century ago.

Yet there is still room for individuality, not to say idiosyncrasy; and judges defend the need for it. In *De Havilland's* case (1983) the Court of Appeal (Criminal Division) deplored the increasing tendency to cite its sentencing decisions as if they were precedents. It emphasised that the choice of sentence was, with exceptions, still at judges' discretion:

> It follows that decisions on sentencing are not binding authorities in the sense that decisions of the Court of Appeal are binding both on this Court and on lower courts. Indeed they could not be, since the circumstances of the offence and the offender present an almost infinite variety from case to case . . . The vast majority of decisions of this Court are concerned with the particular facts and circumstances of the case before it, and are directed to the appropriate sentence in that case. Each case depends on its own facts.

That was in 1983. Whether 'the De Havilland doctrine' really represents the present position of the Court of Appeal – and whether it ever did – is a question best left for the final chapter.

Another awkwardness which must be faced is that lower courts often mitigate sentences for reasons – or to an extent – which the Court of Appeal would reject. An example is leniency for women, which is demonstrated by statistical research but long ago condemned by the Court of Appeal: see chapter 12. It is only when a sentence seems to the Attorney-General to have been excessively lenient that it is referred to the Court of Appeal. The same, *mutatis mutandis*, can be said of cases in which the lower court has ignored aggravating considerations. Most cases of this kind do not appear in the law reports, but are occasionally noticed by the news media. Although reports in the daily papers lack the authority (and often the accuracy) of the Criminal Appeal Reports (Sentencing) I have sometimes had to cite them for want of properly reported examples.

As for statute law, it is only in recent legislation that Parliament has attempted to provide guidance on one or two aspects of aggravation or mitigation. The relevance of previous record or of a plea of guilty are examples, and even then the guidance is vague. The statutes hardly ever say that this or that consideration must not be taken into account by way of mitigation, although, as we shall see, they limit the scope for aggravation.

Consequently the reader who expects to find certainties in the law will not find many in this book. Inconsistencies abound, and although some could be resolved by a certain amount of ingenuity the Court of Appeal does not always make the effort, and when it has not it would be presumptuous of me to do so.

As this book is meant to be readable I have tried to avoid pedantries. I refer to the Court of Appeal (Criminal Division) as 'the Court of Appeal', or 'the Court'. I use 'he' to include 'she'. (Some authors nowadays use 'she' to include 'he' when writing of offenders, but I am never sure whether they are prompted by fear or humour.) I identify cases by name and date only, leaving readers to look up the full reference in the Table of Cases. I call offences 'imprisonable', meaning 'punishable with imprisonment or its juvenile equivalent', which is no worse than calling them 'summary'.

I write 'aggravations' and 'mitigations' where a pedant would insist on 'aggravating (or mitigating) considerations'; and I have also interpreted aggravation and mitigation rather widely, discussing not only pleas of the kind which are offered after conviction but also pleas of a similar kind which can lead to an acquittal or a less serious conviction. For instance the chapter on mental disorder deals (briefly) with 'insanity' and 'diminished responsibility' as well as disorders of the kind which are relevant only to sentencing. Nor have I ignored considerations which are likely to persuade the Crown Prosecution Service to decide that it is 'not in the public interest' to bring the offender to court. 'Mercy' on the other hand I have tried to distinguish very sharply – *pace* the Court of Appeal – from both mitigation and expediency.

The chapter on mercy is an expanded version of my article in *Philosophy*. It is not meant to insert a soft centre into the book, but is a hard-headed attempt to distinguish mercy from justified leniency. The chapter on superior orders and staleness is a revised version of my article on Colonel Priebke's trials in the *New Law Journal*.

Finally, it would be ungracious and ungrateful not to mention the help I have had from impromptu discussions with David Thomas, as well as from his publications. It was he, for example, who drew my attention to Edward Cox's nineteenth-century textbook. He is not responsible for my critical comments on draftsmen, sentencers or the Court of Appeal. I owe thanks to Loraine Gelsthorpe for her comments on early drafts of chapters 9 and 12. I am grateful as always for the helpfulness and tolerance of the staff of my Institute's library.

NOTE

1. An exception is David Thomas's three-volume *Current Sentencing Practice*, which by no means ignores what the Court of Appeal has said about aggravation and mitigation. I also feel bound to mention Joanna Shapland's 1981 study of a sample of pleas in mitigation. It was a pioneering piece of sociology, but was not designed to distinguish pleas which have an effect from those which do not.

Nigel Walker
The Institute of Criminology,
The University of Cambridge,
April 1999

Table of Cases

Table of Statutes

PART I
JUSTIFYING PENALTIES

Chapter 1
Desert

The reasoning which underlies decisions to mitigate penalties, to aggravate them or to exercise mercy is based on retribution, utility, expediency or humanity, so that this book must begin with short discussions of them. The deliberate infliction of harm on unconsenting people needs justification. We justify dragging children to the dentist, or compulsorily treating the mentally disordered, by the belief that it is for their good. Clubs and other organisations justify painful or humiliating initiation rituals by claiming that they induce *esprit de corps*, loyalty or some other desirable attitude. The rules of most games involve penalties in order to give point to competition or to discourage cheating. The rules of professions, trade unions, educational establishments, armed services, police forces are designed to enforce discipline, ensure efficiency or preserve prestige. Their function is useful, and their justification is what is called 'utilitarian'. Utility has always been the main aim of law-enforcement; but in the last two centuries retributivism has made such claims and created so many complications that it needs to be discussed before the problems of utilitarianism can be clearly seen.

Principles of Retribution

Retributivism asserts two principles. The negative one is that the innocent should not be penalised. This raises two sorts of problem.

How sure must courts be that the defendant is guilty before penalising him? Absolute certainty has never been demanded, only absence of a 'reasonable doubt'[1]. An exception was the death penalty, which used to be commuted if, in the view of the Home Office, there was 'a scintilla of doubt'. Since the condemned man had already been found guilty beyond reasonable doubt a scintilla must set a higher standard; but no examples were ever made public. More relevant to the subject of this book is the problem which arises when the normal sentence would inflict suffering not only on the defendant but also on innocent members of his family: examples of sentencers' solutions will be discussed in chapter 8.

The second principle has varied. Traditional retributivism holds that when a penalty is deserved (whatever that means) there is a *duty* to impose it. Modem retributivism merely asserts a *right* to do so, which need not always be exercised. Both kinds assume that the duty or right is created by culpability. It is this relationship between blameworthiness and punishing which retributivism does not find it altogether easy to explain.

Superstitious Retributivism

In some early cultures the penalising of grave offences was intended to placate supernatural beings, or to purify the community. Even as late as the eighteenth century Kant, who attached such value to human rationality, said that a state which was about to surrender its independent existence ought first to execute every murderer in its gaols, since otherwise it would share their 'blood-guilt' (*blutschuld*). This is interestingly superstitious and irrational. It would have been more logical to say that the state would be guilty of neglect of its duty, but hardly of being an accomplice in the crime.

Kantian Retributivism

When Kant was being more rational he offered a justification which was not superstitious but metaphysical. Human beings are creatures of a special kind. They have a 'noumenal' self, which can formulate, understand and follow moral rules. When they choose to follow moral rules they are exercising free will. They are 'autonomous', self-regulating, and morally responsible. This led Kant to the conclusion – although he did not explain how it follows – that this special nature must be recognised by making people suffer punishment for infractions of the criminal law. He called this 'treating them as ends in themselves'; and he was strongly opposed to this theory's contemporary rival – that penalties are justified by their effectiveness, which he called treating people as means: that is, as mere instruments for a practical purpose. He did not say that they must not be treated as means; but that they must never be treated *only* as means. Metaphysical as Kant's picture of human beings was, it is still influential: a modern exponent was C S Lewis (1953). It underlies many people's belief that criminals 'deserve' to suffer loss or harm: a doctrine that is sometimes called 'just deserts'. Kantian retributivism holds that the state has a *duty* to punish *all* criminals and *only* criminals.

Intuitions of Desert

Kant was probably at heart an 'intuitionist'. He seems to have believed that we are simply aware of the fact that law breaking deserves punishment, much as we are aware of the intentional nature of people's actions. Certainly this is the view of a modern intuitionist. 'Culpability is no less a natural property of persons than is intentionality, voluntariness, and so on' (Moore, 1987). Both the wording and the analogy are careless. It is actions, not persons, which are intentional. More important, inferring from observation that an action is intentional is not the same thing as inferring that it is culpable. To infer the latter we need to know the circumstances, and in particular whether there was any excuse for the action. Moore also appeals to people's guilt about their own actions, which 'generates a judgment that we deserve the suffering that is punishment'. Yet guilt is notoriously a product of upbringing and culture. In some families and some cultures people feel no guilt about deliberate cruelty to animals. More important, it is possible to feel guilty without feeling that one needs punishment. Moore's version of retributivism lacks the same bridge as Kant's: it does not say why culpability makes the infliction of punishment morally necessary. Obviously culpability incurs *blame* by others; but one can blame without thinking it necessary to inflict punishment. The Japanese approach to law breaking (as described by Macfarlane, 1995) is at least as moralistic as ours, but sees more need for confession of guilt than for retribution. Penalties are seen as correctives rather than deserved punishments.

Primates' Behaviour

Intuitionists and Kantians should be more interested than they are in the fact that non-human animals do not seem to behave retributively. Psychologists sometimes describe them as 'punishing' each other, but use the word to refer to their attempts to discourage behaviour while it is taking place. An important feature of genuinely retributive punishment is that it can be delayed without being regarded as unjustified. Yet it is extremely doubtful whether delayed retaliation takes place even among chimpanzees or bonobos, our closest non-human kin. De Waal (1982) for instance describes only one example in his colony of chimpanzees; and the chimpanzee was at most avenging an earlier injury to herself. I have come across no description of primate aggression which could be interpreted as delayed retaliation on behalf of the group. On the other hand, De Waal's chimpanzees frequently exhibited *reconciliatory* behaviour some time after fights. Intuitionists and Kantians would no doubt argue that this is evidence that human beings have perceived something about themselves which is peculiar to their species. *Homo sapiens* has been credited with various sorts of behaviour which were believed to distinguish him from other animals: politics, social interaction, language, tool-making, aesthetic appreciation. It certainly seems that one sort which is peculiar to the species is its propensity for delayed retaliation. The possibility cannot be excluded that the propensity, though not inborn, is the product of its culture – or rather cultures. Some cultures, and some religions within cultures, are more retributively minded than others. Man's long memory and superior reasoning power may have made delayed retaliation nearly as effective as immediate retaliation in discouraging undesired behaviour. If this is one of the assumptions of a culture it is likely to be inculcated at an early age, and the result may be adult intuitionists. An evolutionary explanation of the intuition, however, would weaken intuitionists' position. For them the rightness of inflicting desert is something as eternal as the truths of arithmetic. If the intuition of its rightness were merely the result of generations of human appreciation of the benefits of delayed retaliation this would make it a mere utilitarian justification, and what is more a justification which could cease to justify – for example if more effective ways of dealing with antisocial behaviour were discovered.

Expressive Retribution

Most 'just deserters', however, have felt the need to offer something more than intuition to explain why culpability calls for punishment. Sometimes the explanation is metaphorical: for example that punishing an offender symbolises the 'annulment' of his crime, or at least is a reassertion of the rights of others which his offence infringed. This may seem to come close to 'treating people as means' to achieve a useful purpose; but there is an interesting version which seems free of this taint. Nozick (1981) suggests that punishing criminals is the best way (or the only way; but he does not say so explicitly) of 'connecting' them to the community's values which they have flouted. He concedes that by so doing we *may* have a beneficial effect on their conduct; but holds that this is merely a bonus, and that even if punishment does not have this useful effect it is justified as a message to the offender. This is the purest version of what can be called 'expressive retributivism'. It is tempting to borrow E M Forster's famous phrase and call it the 'only connect' version. It raises interesting issues. The best way of showing an offender how he has flouted his community's values may well be to do to him what he did to his victim if that is possible, and if not to do the nearest thing to it. This would suggest a return to what are called 'talionic' penalties – the kind favoured by Kant. Talionic means 'of the same kind', and is linked etymologically to 'retaliation'. An obvious example is the death penalty for murder, although Nozick himself sits on this very pointed fence, and does not propose that penalties should be talionic. If penalties are not to be talionic it is not clear what is to determine their severity; but as we shall see proportionality is a problem for any theory of punishment. More crucial, perhaps, is the question whether an offender who fully appreciates (perhaps as a result of instruction) that he has flouted the community's values, and is as remorseful as Nozick would want him to be, should be excused punishment altogether because its message is unnecessary. Nozick, who does not disapprove of the useful functions of penalties, might well answer that the usual penalty, even if not needed to 'connect' the offender to proper values, should be inflicted if it would contribute to general deterrence or respect for the law; but he should face the fact that there will be cases which are most unlikely to receive any publicity, so that no deterrent or educative purpose would be served. His version of retributivism, however, can be put to good use, as we shall see in chapter 8, by those who want to justify punishing unsuccessful attempts more leniently than successes.

Desert as Debt

A version which used to be fashionable, and has been revived by Burgh (1987), regards punishment as justified because it compels the offender to compensate society for 'social harm'. This is reminiscent of the way in which prisoners used to be said – sometimes still are said – to be 'paying their debt to society'. Its advocates often point out that *retributio* meant 'repayment', which is certainly a pointer to the origins of the notion, but not to its moral justification. Nowadays it is obviously no more than a metaphor, and not a very good one, since it implies an analogy which breaks down as soon as it is examined. Punishing someone by imprisoning him *costs* society. Only fines and community service can be regarded as a positive contribution, and even they often cost more to enforce than they contribute. Again, the analogy of a debt breaks down when we consider attempts at crimes. If my attempt to borrow from you is refused I owe you nothing; but to a retributivist an attempt to commit a crime is punishable whether it succeeds or not.

Evening the Score

Another version of retributivism regards offences as taking unfair advantage of those who obey the law, and sees punishment as a way of evening the score (see for example Davis, 1983). This is a version which could be proposed only by someone familiar with the concept of a game, which seems a good reason for distrust. In any case it raises questions of an awkward kind. One concerns unsuccessful attempts again. More serious is the question whether 'evening the score' can be achieved without talionic punishments. A third objection is that it implies that offences against moral or criminal codes are always *competitive*: that the offender is always doing what a law-abiding person would be tempted to do were it not forbidden. It is true that even rare types of offence – such as paedophile molestation – do tempt some people who nevertheless refrain from them, while some yield to temptation. But to regard the refrainer rather than the victim as a competitor who needs to be compensated seems artificial in the extreme.

Rule-following

However that may be, it does seem undeniable that genuinely retributive behaviour is not possible without an ability to think in terms of a rule. This suggests a version of retributivism which seems free of most, perhaps all, of the problems to which I have drawn attention, even if it lacks the superstitious, metaphysical, metaphorical or symbolic mystiques of the older versions. Another distinctive feature of human beings is that they are rule-making, rule-following animals. Their behaviour, unlike that of other animals, is largely dictated by rules, so much so that they feel discomfort, even resentment, when they see rules broken. Language itself is an example of an inbuilt capacity to make, understand and follow rules. In this sense human beings *are* special, as Kant himself believed. Human groups – families, clans, organisations, societies – use rules of conduct to minimise conflict or misunderstanding. Sometimes these rules are simply conventions, which may even be unconscious, as ethnomethodologists have demonstrated, and make no provision for the consequences of infringement, leaving it to members of the group to express condemnation or ridicule (the rules of grammar are an example). Rules are more likely to be obeyed, however, if they prescribe penalties for infringements, and these prescriptions create the feeling that an infringement *ought* to involve the infringer in a penalty. Otherwise yet another rule has been broken. Hence the feeling of discomfort emphasised by intuitionists. This account offers not only a logical version of retributivism, free of superstition, metaphysics and metaphor, but also a psychological explanation of the feeling that infringements of formal rules should be penalised. Retributivists who want an explanation which does more, and is morally persuasive, find it disappointing; but disappointment is not an argument. 'Rule-retributivism' is a version of traditional retributivism that can be defended: perhaps the only one that can.

Modern Retributivism

Many modern penal codes, however, are not drafted so as to make specified penalties obligatory. They allow sentencers considerable freedom of choice, and merely specify the maximum severity permitted. This reflects the difference between traditional, Kantian, retributivism and its latter-day form. Traditional retributivism regarded punishment as a duty: Hegel (and C S Lewis) even thought that offenders had a right to be punished, and that they were wronged if denied this right. A right, of course, is something that the possessor can claim or disclaim; and most offenders would not claim it (C S Lewis would have retorted 'But they ought to'). Modern retributivism does not regard punishment as a duty: only as a right, but a right of the state, not the offender; and the state is not obliged to exercise it, or exercise it fully, in every case. The offender has given the state the right to punish him, provided that it does not exceed a limit; but whoever deals with him on the state's behalf is free to choose how to do so within that limit (see, for example, Longford, 1961). The sentence may be chosen in the hope that it will correct the offender, or serve some other useful purpose. (Kant would have condemned this as treating the offender only as a means.) It has been claimed that this sort of retributivism has biblical authority,[2] and that the Pentateuch's slogan 'an eye for an eye, a tooth for a tooth' merely lays down a limit to the severity of retaliation; but nobody who has looked at chapter 24 of *Leviticus* could believe this:

> And he that killeth any man shall surely be put to death; and if a man causeth a blemish in his neighbour, as he has done, so shall it be done to him: breach for breach, eye for eye, tooth for tooth . . .

That is talionic punishment, Kant's *jus talionis*, the law of like for like.

Whatever the origin of modern retributivism it provided a rationale for penal codes such as England's, which – with a few exceptions – do not prescribe the quantum of punishment, merely its upper limits for the type of offence in question. Yet it is worth noting that, when the type of offence in question arouses enough public alarm or indignation, the statutory limits turn out to be alterable, and are frequently increased as a political response. Sentencers seldom resort to the maximum, and increasing it often has little effect on their policies; but the gesture has a pacifying effect.

Humanitarian Limits

An interesting question, in passing, is whether limits to the severity
of penalties need be retributive. A social historian could point out that
some penalties have become controversial and have eventually been
outlawed not because they were regarded as undeservedly severe but
for a subtler reason. There is a tradition, traceable to the Stoic
philosophers, which asserts that there are some things which human
beings ought not to do to each other because, as the European
Convention on Human Rights put it, they are 'inhuman or degrading'.
This is one of the arguments used to discredit capital punishment,
castration, limb-amputation, branding, pillorying and corporal punishment, and it is quite distinct from arguments about desert or utility. It
seems to be humanity rather than desert which underlies such notions
as the 'totality principle', discussed in chapter 7.

'Natural Punishment'

Another contribution from humanity is the notion of 'natural punishment'. The orthodox retributivist assumes that punishment must be
deliberately inflicted, not accidental. This is one of the many similar-
ities between desert and revenge; but philosophers manage to distinguish the two by insisting that the punisher must have been entrusted
with the duty of punishing by his society (even if some societies
recognise revenge as a duty). However that may be, we shall see in
chapter 8 that sentencers sometimes forgo a penalty because the
accidental consequences of the offence seem 'punishment enough';
and in chapter 10 the principle is traced back to Roman law. This does
not worry utilitarians so long as the consequences seem likely to
deter; but it troubles retributivists.

Modern Retributivism and Culpability

Another feature of modern retributivism which is reflected in the
criminal law is its greater refinement in assessing culpability and
desert. Intention is increasingly important. Harm attempted, for
example, is now viewed as severely and can be punished as heavily.
as harm actually done, even if in practice sentencers – and some
philosophers – tend to be more old-fashioned, as we shall see in

chapter 8. Excuses used to be either complete or irrelevant, as intoxication is officially; but some partial excuses are now accepted. Provocation was the first: infanticide and diminished responsibility are twentieth-century examples. Excuses which used to be snubbed are recognised, sometimes under another name, as happened to necessity when it was called 'duress of circumstances'. What was really the case is being replaced here and there by what the defendant believed to be the case. The defendant is less often required to have the self-control or good sense of 'the reasonable man' and sometimes allowed to have 'characteristics' which make him vulnerable to such temptations as provocation. Sentencers are expected to take account of offenders' circumstances to an extent that, within living memory, would have been considered quite unnecessary.

Proportionality

Both traditional and modern retributivism – but particularly the traditional kind – have to cope with the problem of proportionality. Talionic punishment avoided this: the penalty was simply made as similar as possible to the crime, as in *Leviticus*. Nor did the problem arise when it was thought sufficient to pay compensation to victims, although there could be arguments about its form or amount. But the notion that the severity of the penalty must be what the offender deserved, or at least not exceed it, instantly raises the question 'How is the degree of severity to be determined?'. In practice it is determined by sentencers within limits set by legislators; but it still makes sense to ask whether the determination is guided by intuition, by reasoning or simply by reaction to events and public opinion. The problem of retributive proportionality has troubled philosophers and jurists. Hegel (1854) revived a mediaeval neurosis:

> Injustice is done at once if there is one lash too many, or one dollar or one cent, one week in prison or one day too many or too few.

Cross (1971) reasoned simply that more heinous offences should be punished more severely than less heinous ones, and thought that this was as far as reasoning could take one. Von Hirsch (1993), however, believes it possible to construct scales which will indicate rather more precisely the sorts of penalties appropriate to most of the common

types of crime. He concedes that scales will differ from one society
to another. In some the maximum will be death: in others long
imprisonment. Minima too may differ. But between the 'anchor
points' at extremes it will be possible to assign places to different
types of offence. The severity of the penalties will be partly justified
by their deterrent or incapacitative effect, partly by the harm done,
attempted or risked, but chiefly by the way in which the penalties
convey 'censure' of the offence:

> The structure of my proposed justification for punishing is also one
> in which the blaming function has primacy. A condemnatory
> response to injurious conduct . . . can be expressed either in a . . .
> symbolic mode, or else in one in which the reprobation is expressed
> through the visitation of hard treatment. The criminal sanction is a
> response of the latter kind. It is preferred to the purely symbolic
> response because of its supplementary role as a disincentive. The
> preventive function thus operates only *within* a censuring frame-
> work.

The problem is that blame varies with the circumstances of each
particular offence. No doubt murder should top the list; but some
rapes are more blameworthy than some murders. A printed scale can
hardly reflect degrees of blame. And to whom is the censure being
conveyed? To the offender certainly: but see what has been said earlier
about Nozick. To potential offenders, too, so that they may be deterred
or at least made aware of the reprehensibility of the offence, although
that is mere utility, as von Hirsch concedes. Yet a retributive
proportionalist who, like von Hirsch, wants a scale to reflect degrees
of blame with something like precision must accept that it would have
to have such a huge number of detailed subdivisions that its utility as
a way of conveying messages would be zero. A notice in society's
shop-window must be simple and clear, with no small print. Propor-
tionalists can try to achieve either desert or discouragement, but not
both, unless they are prepared to forget the terms of the notice when
a customer enters the shop. Until recently sentencing statutes paid
regard to proportionality only when they laid down maxima for fines
and custodial sentences. Sentencers of course had their own estimates
of what were proportional penalties for different offences and circumstances; and when the Court of Appeal reduced a sentence it was

usually on the ground that it was disproportionate to the offence. The Criminal Justice Act 1991, however, put proportionality on a more formal footing when it required the lengths of custodial sentences to be 'commensurate with the seriousness of the offence, or the combination of the offence and one or more offences associated with it' (s. 2(2)(a)). It allowed the sentence to be mitigated or aggravated, or to be longer than commensurate when this seemed necessary to protect the public from serious harm; but commensurateness was central. The same is true when the penalty is a community sentence. Its 'restrictions on liberty shall be such as in the opinion of the court are commensurate with the seriousness of the offence, or the combination of the offence and one or more offences associated with it' (s. 6(2)(b)). When the penalty is a fine, however, the statute (s. 18(2)) uses different language. 'The amount . . . shall be such as, in the opinion of the court, *reflects* the seriousness of the offence' (my italics). All three sections are in the same Act, and all refer to the 'seriousness of the offence', so that avoidance of the word 'commensurate' where fines are concerned must be either inadvertent or deliberate. A possible reason for it is offered in chapter 8, under 'Financial harm'.

The most important feature, however, of sections 2 and 6 of the Act is that they seem to proclaim the classical rather than the modern version of retributivism. Sentencers are no longer free, when using imprisonment or community penalties, to choose between desert and utility. The length of the custodial sentence, or the community penalty's restrictions on liberty, '*shall* [not 'may'] be commensurate with the seriousness of the offence'. This sounds more rigid, however, than it really is. It does not mean that the court *must* impose a commensurate custodial (or community) sentence: only that *if* such a sentence is imposed it must be commensurate. And what seems commensurate prima facie may be aggravated or mitigated, for reasons some of which are specified in statutes, some not.

Consistency

Unfortunately neither the 1991 Act nor any official guidance told sentencers how to work out what sentences are 'commensurate'. Until this problem is solved the most that can be achieved is the less ambitious aim of consistency. Utilitarians are not worried by inconsistencies unless they provoke enough grievances or public disapproval to interfere with the criminal justice system. For a retributivist, however, there is something wrong if two similar offences by similar offenders are dealt with differently. Wrong because it would mean that at least one of them, and perhaps the other too, was being punished too leniently or severely. Consistency does not of course guarantee proportionality. A consistent sentencing policy could be consistently disproportionate. (In the late nineteenth century mothers who killed their new-born babies were consistently sentenced to death and their sentences were consistently commuted to five years' penal servitude.) Moreover the ideal of consistency requires the sentencer to know whether two crimes or two criminals are *relevantly* similar. Does it matter whether A's attempt to rob was successful and B's was not? Or whether A is a man and B a woman? As we shall see, the Court of Appeal is unhappy about the occasional inconsistency between accomplices' sentences, especially if it is likely to be resented as an injustice by one or other of them. When two offences are unconnected inconsistencies are sometimes relied on in appeals, but often dismissed with what, in the Preface, I called 'the De Havilland doctrine': that no two cases are exactly similar. I shall return to the subject in the final chapter.

Attempts to Standardise

There have been occasional attempts to standardise English sentences. In 1901 a committee of Queen's Bench judges drew up a *Memorandum of Normal Punishments in certain Kinds of Crime*, but it was not even distributed to Quarter Sessions, and was rapidly forgotten.[3] One of the benefits expected from the creation of the Court of Appeal in 1908 was the reduction of disparities in sentences.[4] In the early case of *Woodman* (1909) the Court of Appeal said:

> Of course no invariable tariff can ever be fixed, for it is impossible to classify guilt so nicely as to indicate it, even approximately, by names given to the various crimes [an early version of the De Havilland doctrine]. But with time it is to be expected that the revision of sentences by this court will tend to harmonise the views of those who pass them, and so ensure that varying punishments are not awarded for the same amount of guiltiness.

Unfortunately the Court soon made it clear that it was not going to interfere with lower courts' sentences merely because it would have been somewhat more lenient – only when the sentences seemed quite wrong. This policy was probably designed to shelter the Court from a hail of appeals; but one effect has been to prevent it from achieving a greater degree of 'harmonisation'. Another attempt to discourage excessive penalties was made, at the Home Office's instance, by the Advisory Council on the Penal System (1978), but its report, like the 1901 Memorandum, was not endorsed officially, and was as quickly forgotten.

The Worst Possible Case

The Court of Appeal has always been chary of formulating principles, preferring to interfere with individual sentences, and then only if they seem substantially wrong. What it made clear quite early in its career, however, was that the statutory maximum sentence should be reserved for the 'worst possible case', even when the maximum was as low as two years (as it was in *Harrison's* case (1909)). Since it is nearly always possible to conceive of a case that would be worse than the one in question, this encouraged appeals against sentences which applied the maximum. In one such case (*Ambler* (1976)) the Court of Appeal irritably urged judges not to 'use their imaginations to conjure up unlikely worst possible kinds of case' but to consider 'the worst type that comes before the court'. Even so, the effect has been that courts seem to operate within a range of sentence-lengths for each type of offence, which reaches as far as the statutory maximum only when this is very low. This has been called 'the tariff', which gives a misleading impression of price-fixing. The Lord Chief Justice called it a 'bracket' in the case of *L and H* (1997), two young girls who had been convicted of manslaughter:

> while there is no such thing as a mathematically right sentence, every sentence must fall within a bracket . . . The appropriate bracket in the present circumstances was one of two to three and a half years.

Modern preoccupations with desert and proportionality, however, should not be allowed to obscure what was emphasised at the beginning of this chapter: that utility[5] has always been the main objective of penal legislation. It has its own problems, which the next chapter will discuss.

NOTES

1. For judicial attempts to define 'reasonable doubt' see *Blackstone's Criminal Practice* (ed P Murphy, 1999).

2. It is often said that the New Testament does not preach retributivism; but that is an oversimplification. People *are* punished – usually by sudden death – as for example Ananias and Sapphira were in *Acts*, for lying about their property.

3. Until R M Jackson unearthed and published it in 1967.

4. See David Thomas (1979).

5. Sentences which are intended to have beneficial consequences, such as discouraging or preventing offending, can be loosely called 'utilitarian', on the assumption that reducing the frequency of any sort of offence is a positive contribution to general happiness or welfare. Since it is not always clear that this is so – for instance in the case of victimless offences – it would be more precise to use the professional philosopher's term 'consequentialist', which does not involve this assumption; but in the context of sentencing there is little harm in using the familiar terms 'utility' and 'utilitarianism'.

Chapter 2
Utility

Most of the crimes and offences in the common law or the statutes got there not so much because of moral disapproval as because they threatened the peace. There were exceptions, especially where biblical views of sexual behaviour were concerned, but they were in the minority, and some were dealt with by ecclesiastical, not secular, courts. Whatever the reason for proscribing the behaviour the penalties were intended to prevent or discourage it. Morality intervened – rather belatedly – with its increasing insistence on the need to be certain that suspects were genuinely guilty. Proportionality in the severity of penalties was a comparatively late notion: capital punishment was used until the early nineteenth century for offences ranging from murder to poaching. Nineteenth-century transportation was crudely graded, with different terms for different offences. So were fines, penal servitude and imprisonment. Legislators, however, were more concerned with maxima than proportionality, and until the passing of the 1991 Act tended to leave the latter to the discretion of sentencers. It was utility, too, that prompted concessions such as shorter prison sentences for giving 'Queen's evidence' against accomplices, or for saving trouble by pleading guilty. Until recently legislators have been guided by assumptions about the effectiveness of penalties rather than by organised experience – that is, by research.

Capital punishment was simply assumed to be more effective than any
lesser penalty, until research showed that – at least where homicide is
concerned – the prospect of death deters no more people than the
prospect of 'life'. It was assumed, too, that flogging deterred robbers,
until a follow-up of violent robbers after release from their prison
sentences found that those who had also been sentenced to a flogging
were just as often reconvicted of robbery as those who had not
(Cadogan, 1938). Later research brought other disillusionments. There
is not room here for a detailed review of the literature, but it is
possible to sum up, without too much oversimplification, the present
state of knowledge – or, to be more precise, of research and
commonsense.

General Deterrence

The use of publicised sentences to discourage potential imitators is
not as effective as it was believed to be in the days before research,
but is not totally ineffective, as has been claimed by some penal
reformers (including a former Director of the Howard League). What
can be said, a trifle weakly, is that *some* kinds of penalty, of *some*
degrees of severity, will for *some* lengths of time deter *some* kinds of
people from *some* sorts of behaviour in *some* situations. But

(a)   Increasing the probability of detection and conviction seems
more effective.
(b)   Some offenders are not deterred and unlikely to be because of
very strong motivation (e.g. some terrorists), extreme confidence in
their skill, enjoyment of risk-taking (e.g. 'joy-riders'), or circumstances so desperate that imprisonment holds no terrors (e.g. 'dossers').
(c)   Law-abiding people overestimate the risks of detection, conviction and severe penalties to a greater extent than do experienced
offenders.
(d)   Murders apart, few members of the public remember what
sentences were passed, even in well-publicised cases.
(e)   Well-publicised innovations designed to improve detection
rates (e.g. breathalysers) have an impact, but a temporary one.
(f)   The stigma of conviction for some types of offence (e.g.
dishonest or sexual offences) is feared by potential offenders, but
much less by those already stigmatised. Some kinds of offence (e.g.

violence at football matches or dangerous driving) do not stigmatise
the offender in the eyes of his associates.

Correction

When a sentenced offender has apparently refrained from reoffending
it is not always possible to be sure whether he has really refrained, and
if so whether this was the effect of the conviction or the sentence, and
if of the sentence, whether it simply deterred or reformed in some
subtler way. Fines can hardly do anything but deter, and their deterrent
effect is weakened by efforts to adjust them to offenders' financial
situations. Supervisory measures are more likely than incarceration to
help offenders to find law-abiding work, and sometimes even to
improve their attitudes to offending. 'Correction' is a term which begs
no questions about what has taken place (if it has taken place). When
follow-ups make allowances for variables associated with differing
reconviction rates (e.g. gender, age, type of offence, previous records)
the rates following custodial and non-custodial sentences are remarkably similar. Part of the explanation seems to be that what corrects (or
fails to) is not the sentence but the *regime* to which the sentence hands
over the offender. Sentences are not like physicians' prescriptions
which deal out identical doses. One probation officer's way of handling
his probationers will not be the same as another's. No two institutions
subject their inmates to identical regimes. Offenders' personalities,
too, make a difference. One may respond well to Probation Officer A
but badly to B, who may nevertheless be more effective than A with
another sort of probationer. The same, *mutatis mutandis* is true of
institutions. So comparing reconviction rates after different *sentences*
obscures these effects. It is true that some research has identified
regimes with special features which seem to be effective, especially
with the young. Unfortunately the effectiveness often depends on the
skills of a special member of staff, which are not easy to pass on to
others. The old question 'What works?' ought to be 'What sort of
personal interaction works, and with what sorts of offender?'.

Moral Education

One result of disillusioning research has been to drive utilitarians –
like retributivists – to somewhat desperate resorts. Among them is the

claim that sentencing at least has a beneficial effect on public attitudes to offences: what Marsh and I (1984) called 'the Sargeant effect' because of Lord Lawton's *dictum* in *Sargeant* (1974). This is a traditional belief of lawyers, traceable at least as far back as the first half of the eighteenth century. To our surprise it had never been tested properly. Our experiment with faked newspaper reports of crimes and sentences found no evidence to support it. Even when questioned about real cases reported in newspapers only 58 per cent of respondents remembered details of a single case, and only 39 per cent of them (about 23 per cent of the whole sample) could recall the sentence. Yet the belief dies hard among lawyers.

Expressing Outrage

Perhaps the most desperate of utilitarian resorts is the argument that sentences at least give public expression to the outrage which people experience when they learn of serious crimes (for an example see Gross, 1992). This gives them some degree of satisfaction, which can be regarded as utility of a sort. The argument would of course at most justify the penalising of publicised crimes: the penalising of unpublicised crimes would have to be justified by the victims' satisfaction or by an appeal to consistency. In any case, surveys of opinions find that *dissatisfaction* with the leniency of sentences is the attitude of the majority of English respondents (79 per cent in the report by Hough and Roberts, 1998). This does not rule out the possibility that there are jurisdictions whose penalties are Draconian enough to satisfy their constituents; but even the Athenians were somewhat embarrassed by Draco.

Prevention

Preventive measures are less disappointing. The efficacy of detention is demonstrable. As we shall see in chapter 6 we cannot expect non-custodial measures such as disqualifications to be very effective, but incarceration is plainly effective. It fails only when the offender escapes or commits his offences against staff or fellow-inmates. In a sense it also fails when he is released and reoffends in a similar way, either because the sentence was too short or because decision-makers took a risk. On the whole, however, utilitarians can claim prevention as achievable. It is only in recent years that it has been criticised as penalising offenders not for what they have done but for what they may or may not do – a criticism which is discussed in chapter 5.

Penalising the Innocent

An even more serious accusation is that utilitarianism has so little respect for desert that it will on occasion tolerate the penalising of the innocent. In one academic scenario (see Ten, 1987) a sheriff of a small American community is faced with a rape which has allegedly been committed by a black man. Unless someone is convicted there will be an inter-racial riot, and probably lynchings. To prevent this he arranges for the conviction of a man he knows to be innocent. If utilitarians agree that this would be intolerable, is it because they acknowledge that penalties must be deserved? Not necessarily, said Herbert Hart (1968). They could argue that life in a society which allowed the deliberate punishment of the innocent would be intolerably full of apprehension. Law-abiding people would not be able to order their lives with any confidence in the future.

A similar but not quite identical issue is raised when it is proposed to alter rules of evidence, or to lower standards of proof, so as to reduce the number of acquittals of guilty suspects. An unwanted but unavoidable by-product would of course be an increase in the percentage of convicted innocents. Similar but again slightly different is the proposal of a Home Office working group in 1998 for confiscating assets that seem to have been acquired by crimes which are unlikely to be identified or prosecuted successfully. This would be done by civil forfeiture, requiring only proof on a 'balance of probabilities', and not 'beyond reasonable doubt'. The working group argues that the forfeiture would not have a punitive function; yet its value would exceed that of most fines. Although the safeguards would be such that innocent property-owners would be unlikely to suffer, the possibility is already being used as a powerful objection. The issue is complicated by the fact that such proposals do not involve deliberately penalising a few people who are known to be innocent – merely increasing slightly the risk that an occasional innocent will suffer, which may not seem as objectionable as the cynical behaviour of Ten's sheriff. Even criminal proceedings are bound to involve the occasional sentencing of innocents, so that the question is not whether to create a new risk but how great an existing risk must be to amount to a moral objection, to which the answer must depend on the harmfulness of the crime and the penalty.

Retroactivity

Another area where utilitarians have to walk warily is penal legislation which is retroactive. Chapter 6 describes examples of recent legislation – by both Conservative and Labour Governments – which imposes objectionable requirements on sexual offenders whose offences were in many cases committed long before the legislation. The justification for the requirements is that they are expected to reduce the likelihood that an offender will repeat his offence. The question is whether they breach a principle. Retributivists say that a penalty is unjust if it was not allowable when the offence was committed. The rationale seems to be that it would be just only if the offender knew that he might incur it, and therefore chose to risk it. A sounder objection is that this line of reasoning treats penalties not as deserts but as threats, and as such meaningful only if the offender was aware of them. It is also arguable, as we shall see, that the measures in question are not penalties, although penalties are provided for non-compliance. As it was, Parliament raised no objection to the retroactivity of the measures in question. Had they involved compulsory detention it almost certainly would have.

Staleness

As we shall see in chapter 13 courts in some jurisdictions deal leniently with offences which were committed a long time ago, while the English Court of Appeal is disinclined to take 'staleness' into account. It is not too difficult for a utilitarian to argue the relevance of staleness, but very difficult for a retributivist.

Expediency

A somewhat sordid kind of utility is expediency. An example is the need to encourage offenders to assist the machinery of law-enforcement. 'Oiling the conveyor belt', as it has been called, is just as utilitarian as trying to satisfy the public, and often more realistic. If every defendant – or even one in every three defendants – pleaded 'not guilty' the wheels of justice would grind to a halt. It is for this reason that a timely plea of guilty earns a reduction of a custodial sentence, and not because it is naively assumed to be a sign of remorse, although credulous sentencers sometimes see it as such. This, and similar considerations of expediency, will be discussed in chapters 4 and 7.

Utilitarian Proportionality

As we saw in the first chapter, retributivists are concerned about the proportionality between culpability and penalty. Utilitarians need not have so much concern, at least in theory. In practice legislators and sentencers must have some regard for the views of desert-minded journalists and their readers. That consideration apart, Bentham (1789) offered two principles. One was 'frugality': no more severity than is needed to deter. The other restraint was cost: 'the greater the mischief of the offence the greater is the expense which it may be worthwhile to be at, in the way of punishment'. To take a modern example, a short term of imprisonment might suffice to deter both dangerous drivers and litter-droppers, but litter is not a great enough mischief to justify the cost. There is a practical problem, however. Most types of crime are like most types of disease: hard to eradicate completely. What frequency of bad driving is the irreducible minimum, the reaching of which would call a halt to increases in the severity of the deterrent? A Benthamite approach has been suggested by Braithwaite and Pettit (1990). The severity of the normal penalty for each type of crime could be reduced step by step until the stage is reached at which that type of crime begins to become more frequent. The idea has its difficulties and at least one oddity. The political problem is obvious; but less obvious is the uncertainty as to whether a fluctuation in, say, the frequency of burglary in year N is attributable to a reduction in the average custodial sentence for it in year $N-1$ (or perhaps in year $N-2$ or $N-3$: we do not know how long it takes for changes such as this to be appreciated by potential burglars). The oddity is the proposal's assumption that we cannot do better than adjust the penalty for burglary so that its frequency does not increase. Most utilitarians would hope to find a level of severity which would at least reduce its prevalence. (The explanation is that

Braithwaite and Pettit's aim is of a rather special kind: they want to minimise interference with the 'dominion' – i.e. freedom – of all members of society, including its offenders.) Nevertheless what such proposals, with all their difficulties, do show is that the notion of utilitarian proportionality is not nonsensical, even if in real life legislators and sentencers must respect, or at least have regard to, the voter's notion of proportionality.

Eclecticism

It is not surprising that the problems of utilitarianism have encouraged just deserters to claim that it is easier to be sure that retributive aims are achieved. This inadvertently relegates just deserts to the status of a *pis aller*. It also claims a little too much. It is easier to be sure that prevention is achieved than it is to be sure that the severity of a penalty is exactly suited to the culpability of an individual offender. Just deserters can make sure that offenders are receiving deserts of a sort, but not that the deserts are just. There are solutions which are less crude. One is eclecticism: allowing sentencers to reason in retributive or utilitarian ways according to the nature of the case. There are, of course, two kinds of eclectic: the emotional and the principled. The emotional eclectic thinks retributively when the features of a case outrage his moral sense. The result is inconsistency. The principled eclectic has rules to tell him when utility should take priority over desert, or vice versa. But what should the rules be? The traditional distinction between what is wrong in itself and what is wrong merely because forbidden (*malum in se* and *malum prohibitum*) would be useful, but the demarcation line is now too disputable. (Is consensual bigamy *malum in se*, for instance?) I have not come across a set of rules expressly designed to discriminate in a principled way.

A Third Way?

At a crossroads there is a tendency to look for a 'third way', and recent writers – for example Bottoms (1998) – view 'expressive retributivism' (see chapter 1) in this light. Yet most of its exponents seem to expect that signifying moral condemnation will have some beneficial effect, whether on the offender or on others; and this can hardly be distinguished from utilitarianism. Only Nozick seems able to maintain that his justification, 'connecting the offender to society's values', is not utilitarian. Like Nozick, von Hirsch (1993), from whom I quoted in chapter 1, holds that the primary justification for sentences is that they signify censure, but unlike Nozick he concedes that punishment 'is preferred to the purely symbolic response because of its supplementary role as a disincentive'. Censure has taken the place of desert, and the reason for preferring penalties as a way of expressing it is utilitarian; but it is no clearer why censure *has to be* expressed. Von Hirsch could argue that expressing it gives satisfaction to victims and others in a ceremonial way, rather as a funeral does to the bereaved, and that the satisfaction is so limited and temporary as not to deserve being called 'utility': but he does not. Like Kant and Moore he fails to cross the gap between blaming and penalising. There is still a bridge too few. In any case 'thirdwaymen' who disclaim retributivism have to face an awkward question which I have often posed but never seen adequately answered. Would it be sufficient if those who are outraged by a crime were merely led to believe that the offender had been adequately penalised? If so, that would make sentencing a 'symbolic response'.[1] If on the other hand the sentence must actually be carried out, can some non-retributive, non-utilitarian reason for doing so be given?[2] It is worth noting – though not often noted – that Kant himself offered one such reason, albeit in an *obiter dictum* and *per incuriam*. If the state does not punish it shares the guilt. It does not matter, for the moment, that this was an illogical overstatement, as I pointed out in chapter 1. What matters is that avoiding the sharing of guilt is not the same as obeying a duty to inflict desert, and is scarcely utility.

The accepted 'third way', however, is the compromise which I called' modern retributivism' in chapter 1. It regards the infliction of proportional penalties not as a duty but as a right, so that they become maxima and not a tariff. It justifies them only when they are both deserved and efficacious. It allows sentencers to choose penalties with utilitarian aims in mind so long as they do not exceed deserved severity, and so long as they do not collude in the penalising of the innocent. Desert is thus relegated to a limiting role. Obviously this does not solve the problem of retributive proportionality, but neither does any other compromise. And modern retributivists (as we shall see in chapter 5) are still unhappy about precautionary sentences which exceed the maxima.

Statutory Guidance

The sentencing statutes of the late nineteenth century and twentieth century seem to be based on modern retributivism. Only for treason, murder and piracy were the penalties fixed by law. For other offences maximum penalties were prescribed, but sentencers were free within those limits (or any lower limits laid down by the Court of Appeal). They were not told how to reason. There were exceptions. Special powers were provided in special circumstances for sentences or other methods of disposal expressly intended to protect the public from 'serious harm' (see chapters 5 and 6). Courts dealing with juvenile offenders were required to 'have regard to their welfare' (see chapter 9). Sentencers were encouraged – sometimes obliged – to consider pre-sentence reports which were usually concerned with utilitarian aspects of the case. Otherwise, however, they were left to speculate as to the aims they were meant to have in mind: they could if they wished be 'modern retributivists'. The silence was deliberate. Where legislation is concerned the fewer ideologists who are provoked the sooner the Bill will get through its Parliamentary stages. Ambiguity was the best policy.

The Conservative Government's Criminal Justice Act 1991 was a departure from this tradition, requiring custodial and community sentences to be 'commensurate with the seriousness of the offence or the combination of the offence and other offences associated with it' (s. 2). Other sections (3 and 29) made it clear that sentences could be aggravated or mitigated, in ways that will be discussed in later chapters. The aim, however, was clearly just deserts, although clothed in the persuasively unobtrusive term 'commensurate'. Only Lord Longford offered an amendment designed to restore sentencers' freedom to consider the effect on the offender; and he was unsupported.

In sharp contrast – at first sight – was the clearly utilitarian section of the Labour Government's Crime and Disorder Act 1998 which deals with the aim of 'youth justice' (s. 37):

(1)   it shall be the principal aim of the youth justice system to *prevent* offending by children and young persons.
(2)   In addition to *any other duty* to which they are subject, it shall be the duty of all persons and bodies carrying out functions in relation to the youth justice system to have regard to that aim. (my italics)

But does this mean that youth justice is to be exempt from the retributive approach of the 1991 Act to custodial sentences? Or is that 'another duty'? The Government's intention will be discussed in chapter 9.

NOTES

1.   The point is not altogether fanciful. Some sentences *are* virtually symbolic. Examples are reprimands in military courts and admonitions in Scottish courts. Suspended prison sentences are a neat combination of symbolism and utility: the offender is sentenced to imprisonment, but after a pause the sentence is converted into a mere threat.

2.   A pedantic utilitarian might argue that even if the public could be deceived into believing that an offender had been penalised it would always mean a sacrifice of utility, since the offender himself would know the truth and would not be corrected. In fact a lot of offenders are not corrigible by the most severe sentences that society feels justified in inflicting, while others are so shocked by what they have done that they need no correction.

Chapter 3
Sentencing for What?

What we have been considering are rival views about what Herbert Hart (1968) called 'the general justifying aim of punishment' – the 'why?' of sentencing. But that does not answer the question 'What is an offender being sentenced for?'.

Kant, Hume and Fletcher

To a retributivist the answer may seem too obvious to justify the question. An offender is being sentenced for criminal behaviour. Yet it has been plausibly argued that this oversimplifies, and that he is really being sentenced for his character. This was probably not Kant's view,[1] but another eighteenth century philosopher, David Hume (1750), believed that we blame (or approve) actions 'so far only as they are indications of the internal character'; and this view has been reinforced by Fletcher's 'theory of excuses', in *Rethinking Criminal Law* (1978). Excuses excuse because they tell us that what the offender did cannot be assumed to be 'in character'. It was an accident; he was threatened; it was necessary; he got the facts wrong; he was out of his mind; he was asleep; he was acting under orders; it was a long time ago. If so, suggests Fletcher, he is excused because his act or omission is not enough to justify the inference that 'he is like that'. Nor is it only complete excuses which support 'character theory'. As we shall see in the chapters on aggravation and mitigation, sentencers and the Court of Appeal sometimes increase or reduce the severity of sentences for reasons which suggest that they have in mind the presumed or inferred character of the offender as well as his offence. 'Character', however, is an imprecise word. When a court hears evidence of 'good character' it is often told merely that the defendant has not previously been convicted. It may be told that he has a job, or that he looks after his family: in short that he is respectable. Occasionally, as we shall see, the court may be told not merely that he is not deviant but that he has done meritorious deeds – for example saved a drowning child (see chapter 7). Retributivists can regard this as relevant by resorting to 'moral bookkeeping', utilitarians by hoping that the deeds are symptoms of conformity. Sometimes, however, 'character' is an imprecise way of referring to a disposition to behave in a particular way: to act dishonestly, aggressively, lustfully or negligently. When a court is sentencing a man for a fraud it treats as relevant a previous conviction for theft, but not his driving offences, even if they are serious and frequent. And when a man is being sentenced for a violent or sexual offence, however respectable his 'character' it is the evidence of a violent or lustful disposition which is likely to tip the balance in favour of a precautionary sentence (see chapter 5).

Choice Theory

Yet character is not what most judges and magistrates think they are sentencing; and academic character theory is opposed by what appears to be commonsense 'choice theory', notably in the form offered by Moore (1990). Excuses excuse 'because and only because at the moment of [an action] one did not have sufficient capacity or opportunity to make the choice to do otherwise'. ('Opportunity' need not distract us for long: an example of such an excuse is necessity: 'he could not have been expected to do otherwise'). What choice theorists usually have in mind is temporary or lasting *incapacity* to choose not to do the wrong thing. Examples are the terror of duress, an insane belief that one is being attacked, the pessimism of extreme depression, the stupidity of mental impairment. According to choice theory the proper object of moral blame and secular punishment is a person's decision to do wrong when he could without much difficulty have done right (or nothing). Retributivists have a natural preference for choice theory (Moore, as we saw in chapter 1, is a retributivist who appeals to intuition). Blaming character seems to imply that one can help one's dispositions. Aristotle thought one could: we know what dispositions we ought to have, and can cultivate them and suppress those we ought not to have. Even if this is psychologically unrealistic, treating people as responsible for their characters is 'effective and functional' (Kupperman, 1991). But that is a utilitarian view. Whether we really regard people as responsible for their characters or not, it is useful to behave towards them as if they are.

Character Theory

Not that retributivists are bound to reject character theory. Fletcher himself reasons like a retributivist:

> An inference from the wrongful act to the actor's character is essential to a retributive theory of punishment. A fuller statement of the argument would go like this: (1) punishing wrongful conduct is just only if punishment is measured by the desert of the offender, (2) the desert of the offender is gauged by his character – i.e. the kind of person he is, (3) and therefore a judgement about character is essential to the just distribution of punishment . . .

This seems to lead to the view that retributive sentencers should take into account the full list of the defendant's acts and omissions, not just the single act or omission for which he has just been tried, in order to assess his character. Fletcher feels forced to argue that

> . . . the limitation of the inquiry to a single wrongful act follows not from the theory of desert but from the principle of legality. We accept the artificiality of inferring character from a single deed as the price of maintaining the suspect's privacy . . .

This is true, however, only when the excuse is one which excuses completely, and thus leads to an acquittal. Partial excuses – such as provocation – do leave judges and magistrates free to inquire into the defendant's previous record when they come to their choice of sentence. When the Criminal Justice Act 1991 tried to limit this freedom the judicial reaction was so sharp that, as we shall see in the next chapter, the Act was hastily amended. Fletcher seems to have strayed into a very difficult position, and his appeal to the suspect's right to privacy is really an appeal to procedural fairness rather than logic.

Obeying a Disposition

It would be more plausible to claim that what we are justified in blaming (and therefore punishing) is the combination of a forbidden act (or omission) *and* a presumption that it is consistent with the offender's character (or more precisely with at least one of his dispositions). This would not oblige us to say that it is character – or a disposition – which deserves blame: we would be saying that it is *acting in accordance with* a disposition. We may, for example, *dislike* a person who admits to sadistic desires – or, if we are more discriminating, dislike that part of his character – yet reserve *blame* for actions which are prompted by those desires. This may not fit our moral reactions to some kinds of offenders. Some people give way to antisocial dispositions with so little effort to control them that we call them 'psychopaths' – or, in more modern parlance, 'sufferers from personality disorders' – and treat their actions as wholly or to some extent excusable (see chapter 10). Indeed, although Fletcher cited insanity as an example of a condition which *precludes* an inference about any disposition, in fact most psychiatric excuses attribute behaviour to disorders which *are* dispositions, and therefore part of 'character'. We excuse them wholly or partially because we do not think that disordered people can 'help being like that' and acting accordingly. But this is talking choice theory: we are saying that, as Moore would put it, they do not have the capacity to choose to act otherwise. It is an awkward fact, of course, that even psychotic and psychopathic offenders often seem to choose to behave correctly in circumstances in which one would not expect them to if they lacked this capacity. They sometimes respond like automata, but not always. The most that choice theorists can say is that they sometimes lack the capacity, and that when they offend we should give them the benefit of any doubt about this excuse. Finally, it is not too hard for choice theorists to think of actions which are 'out of character' and yet usually regarded as blameworthy. What the news media call 'mindless vandalism' is often the result of an impulse which does not reflect a destructive disposition.

Capacity for Choice

Choice theory, however, also has to face difficult examples. Crimes of negligence are not the result of choices – rather of a failure to choose to act with care – and choice theorists such as Moore concede that they cannot fit them in. Careless[2] drivers do not choose to have accidents. Herbert Hart (1968) manages to blame negligent offenders only by saying that if they had the capacity and a fair opportunity not to do what they did they are culpable for not exercising the capacity. That is not choice theory. On the other hand it is not character theory either. It could be called 'capacity-for-choice theory'. It could accommodate Fletcher's point about excuses by saying that when someone infringes a code of conduct the question whether he had a disposition to act thus (or to be negligent) is relevant to culpability but not decisive. We also need to know whether he had the capacity to control his disposition; and if we are satisfied that he had that capacity but did not exercise it we can fairly hold him to blame. We are not obliged to use the concept of choice, at least until we try to distinguish degrees of culpability. At that stage it seems relevant to ask whether the offender's failure to exercise his capacity to conform with the law was the result of a conscious decision, an unreflecting impulse, or mere overhasty inadvertence. Each seems less culpable than its predecessor; but culpability is not completely negatived unless capacity was zero. Sometimes it will not be easy to assess whether an offender had the capacity to conform, especially if there are no known occasions on which his capacity has been tested. In discussions Barbara Wootton and Glanville Williams used to dismiss as silly the question whether an offender who yielded to a temptation did in fact have a capacity to resist it. Either he did resist it, in which case he could, or he didn't, in which case he couldn't. Yet this oversimplifies. If one knows enough about offenders' histories one can distinguish those who seem never or hardly ever to resist from those who sometimes but not always do; and it makes sense of a rough and ready sort to say that those who sometimes resist have the capacity to do so, unlike those who never resist. It is true that even if there have been plenty of occasions on which a person has shown himself capable of self-control (or adequate care), he may be able to claim that in the incident for which he has been called to account he had been temporarily deprived of that capacity, whether by provocation, mental disorder or some other circumstance. But that does not discredit the notion of capacity. It is the attribution of a capacity – whether for self-control, due care or whatever else is relevant – which makes us (and the law) expect the offender to explain why he did not use that capacity, if he wishes to escape or reduce blame.

Criminal Responsibility

Note, in passing, that it is possible to discuss these theories without using the phrase 'criminal responsibility', in spite of the number of books that have been written about it. Most of them have been attempts to provide a unifying definition of it, for example by identifying 'rationality' as its essence (Fingarette, 1972). They are the result of reifying responsibility, as if it were a skill like mathematical ability or an attribute like trustworthiness.[3] Judges talked of it in this way, and so did the draftsmen who defined 'diminished responsibility' in the Homicide Act 1957. It is not necessary, however, to think or talk in this way. Being criminally (or morally) responsible need mean no more than 'having no excuse that is accepted by the relevant code of law (or of morals)'.[4] Responsibility is mistaken for an attribute in the same way as black – an absence of any colour – is mistaken for a colour. Like the scientific concept of a vacuum it not only can but has to be defined in negative terms. If one cannot offer the excuse of accident, automatism, insanity, idiocy, senility, mistake, necessity, duress, superior orders, believed justification or irresistible motivation, one was 'responsible' for one's act or omission. Having been partially responsible is having been in a situation or state in which it would have been difficult but not unthinkable to act otherwise: provocation is the classic example (see chapter 11). There is no need to complicate discussions of choice, capacity and disposition by inventing a fourth notion.

But that is by the way. Of the three theories, retributivists seem likely to prefer choice, with its implications of free will. Determinists ought to prefer capacity for choice. Utilitarians are not necessarily determinists, but if their only – or main – aim is to reduce the likelihood of future offending by the offender in question their interest should focus not on his culpability but on his dispositions and the prospects of correcting or restraining them. They will not allow personality disorder to excuse a man from precautionary detention, or inadvertence or impulsiveness to mitigate a penalty if a sharp reminder seems necessary as an *aide-mémoire*.

Harm

Should a sentence reflect the harm which has actually been done by an offence, or the harm which was intended or likely? Until recently 'the spirit of the laws' seemed to be heading in the direction of the latter. If, as is the case with most offences, intentionality matters, *what* is intended is crucial. The Criminal Attempts Act 1981 said that maximum sentences for attempts at crimes were to be the same as the maxima for crimes achieved,[5] which pleased both retributivists and utilitarians. In 1996, however, a politically correct Home Secretary promised those who had suffered from crimes that the Victims' Charter meant that sentencers would take into account their losses, damages, injuries and fears of future victimisation (Home Office, 1996). This seemed to mean that if, by bad fortune, the harm actually done was more than usual the severity of the sentence would be more than usual. By the same token, presumably, if the victim's luck or the offender's incompetence means that little or no harm is done, the sentencer should be lenient. As Ashworth (1993) has said, 'English law has no clear approach to this question of principle'. It is more fully discussed in chapter 8.

These short introductory chapters are not meant to sell or condemn any of the theories they have outlined: merely to summarise them and their main problems, without preaching any intellectual obligation to buy. The remaining chapters will examine the reasoning which prompts – or more often is implied by – the approaches of legislators and criminal courts to aggravation, mitigation and mercy. This Part is intended simply to make it easier to diagnose the different kinds of reasoning.

NOTES

1. See, for example, Hill (1992).

2. To be distinguished, of course, from 'reckless' drivers who choose to take risks.

3.   Perhaps because a person can be vaguely called 'responsible' in the same way as he can be called 'trustworthy'. It is even possible to call a person or thing 'responsible for' an effect, in a purely causal sense.

4.   My impression from discussions with Hart is that this was his view, but I cannot find any passage in which he develops the point. It follows from it that whether a person might be held to be criminally or morally responsible would depend on whether he had an excuse which is recognised by the people who are judging him (unless one allows him to be his own judge).

5.   With exceptions which will be explained in chapter 8.

PART II
AGGRAVATION

Chapter 4
Statutory and Miscellaneous Aggravations

Some aggravations are recognised by statute, some by practice directions of the Court of Appeal, and some by case-law.

General

The Criminal Justice Act 1991, s. 3 requires courts to take into account 'all such information about the circumstances of the offence (including aggravating and mitigating factors) as is available'. Section 7 applies this requirement to community sentences. It refers only to 'the circumstances of the offence'; but when the court is considering whether a special sentence is needed to protect the public from serious harm from the offender (see the next chapter) it may also take into account any information about the offender which is before it (for example in a pre-sentence or psychiatric report). Section 28 is even more liberal where mitigation is concerned: 'nothing in this Part of this Act shall prevent a court from mitigating an offence by taking into account any such matters as in the opinion of the court are relevant in mitigation of sentence'; but there is no similar provision for aggravation. Ashworth (1992) argues that these sections allow factors which are not related to the seriousness of the offence to mitigate but not to aggravate. We shall see, however, when we come to 'prevalence', how far the courts are prepared to stretch the meaning of 'the circumstances of the offence'.

Previous Criminal Record

The most obvious exception is the offender's previous criminal record. The ordinary sentencer regards earlier convictions and failures to respond to sentences as good reasons for sentencing more severely than he would otherwise. The ordinary criminal, an unsophisticated retributivist, resents what he regards as being punished twice for his earlier misdoings. The Court of Appeal used to take a similar view (for instance in *Queen* (1981), and the 1991 Act in its original version laid down that an offence was not to be regarded as more serious by reason of a previous conviction or failure to respond to previous sentences. The Government was soon persuaded, however, to amend this rigid rule so as to allow – but not oblige – sentencers to regard both of these as aggravations (s. 29 of the 1991 Act as amended by the Criminal Justice Act 1993). More recently the Court of Appeal has even allowed a police warning to aggravate: it upheld the trial judge's view that *Ibrahim* (1998), who had been warned by police not to continue selling obscene video-cassettes, merited a more severe sentence for doing so. On the other hand the Court has interpreted 'failure to respond to previous sentences' in a fairly restrictive way. A failure to respond to a single sentence after only one court appearance is not sufficient: there must be at least two appearances and two sentences (*Ager* (1992)).

It certainly makes prima facie sense of a utilitarian kind to try a more severe measure when a milder one has failed; but retributive purists who want severity to be as proportional as possible to culpability (see chapter 1) find it hard to see how culpability can be increased by previous offences, however similar. One rather artificial suggestion is that having a clean record should be regarded as a mitigation. It can be made plausible by treating it as a 'Fletcherian' excuse (see chapter 3) and arguing that the commission of a single offence does not justify the inference that the offender is 'the sort of person who does that sort of thing'. If so, suggests Ashworth (1992), with each successive conviction there is a 'progressive loss of mitigation'. One could argue, however, that it takes only one previous similar conviction to rebut any presumption that the offender is not 'that sort of person', and that something more plausible is needed to explain the feeling that each successive conviction justifies greater severity. It seems less artificial to say simply that the number of previous convictions is a measure of the offender's lack of respect for the law. Either way, he is being sentenced for character as well as deed. In this context utility makes more sense than desert.

Taking Other Offences into Consideration

In this context one should not overlook the practice of asking the sentencer to 'take into consideration' ('t.i.c.') offences with which the offender has not been charged. It is established by custom, not statute, and depends upon the cooperation of prosecution and defence. The prosecution is saved from the necessity of proving what can be a large number of similar offences by the defendant. The defendant has an incentive to incriminate himself because by doing so he protects himself against being charged with the t.i.c. offences on a later occasion, and he can be fairly sure that the increase in the severity of his sentence will be less than if he were formally convicted of them. No amount of offences t.i.c. allows the sentence to exceed the maximum for the offence of which he has been convicted. Many petty offenders voluntarily aggravate their sentences in this way. The sentencer can refuse to t.i.c. an offence, however, and is likely to do so if it is more serious than the offence(s) of which the defendant is convicted, or of a quite different nature.

Statutory Principles

Until the early 1980s offences were either 'imprisonable' or 'non-imprisonable' (i.e. punishable at most with fines). If an offence was imprisonable it was left to the court's discretion whether it should choose imprisonment or some more lenient measure. Now, as a result of an increase in the prison population, legislation has, in effect, stipulated that an imprisonable offence must be an aggravated one if imprisonment is to be used. The current statutory provision is section 1 of the Criminal Justice Act 1991, which specifies certain aggravations as needed if a custodial sentence is to be justified. It was preceded by section 1 of the Criminal Justice Act 1982 and section 123 of the Criminal Justice Act 1988, which restricted only the custodial sentencing of young adults and juveniles. Now section 1(2) of the 1991 Act provides that, irrespective of age, a custodial sentence is ruled out unless the court is of the opinion

(a)   that the offence, or the combination of the offence and one or more offences associated with it,[1] was so serious that only such a sentence can be justified for the offence; or
(b)   where the offence is a violent or sexual offence, that only such a sentence would be adequate to protect the public from serious harm from him.

The second of these conditions will be discussed in the next chapter, since dangerousness is an aggravation of a special sort. For the moment we are concerned with 'seriousness'. Although it justifies a custodial sentence it does not make it mandatory if it is mitigated (*Cox* (1993)) But what sorts of offences are 'serious'? In *Bradbourn* (1985) Lawton LJ said that in this context a serious offence was

the kind of offence which . . . would make right-thinking members of the public, knowing all the facts, feel that justice had not been done by the passing of any sentence other than a custodial one.

His much-quoted *dictum* in effect leaves it to the courts to decide what a right-thinking person would feel. It is the advice of a man with his back to a wall that is not of his own choosing. The draftsmen of criminal legislation are notorious for using adjectives such as serious (or 'grievous' or 'grave') which invite courts to make distinctions without offering any criteria to help them. 'Serious' is also used, both in the 1991 Act and in the Mental Health Act 1983, to mean something different: to distinguish the sorts of harm which justify lengthy precautionary detention from the sorts of harm which do not, again without criteria: see the next chapter. Appendix A lists offences which statutes or the Court of Appeal have classified as meeting one or more of the different criteria.

Committal to the Crown Court

Committal to the Crown Court, whether for trial or for sentence, means that the defendant is at risk of a more severe custodial sentence than is within the magistrates' powers. Section 38 of the Magistrates'

Courts Act 1980 (as amended by section 25 of the 1991 Act) allows a magistrates' court to commit a defendant aged 18 or older for sentence if it is of the opinion that his offence or the combination of it and other offences associated with it was so serious that the punishment should be greater than the court has power to impose.[2] The Lord Chief Justice's *Practice Note* of 1990 (3 All ER 979) guided magistrates' courts in deciding whether to commit a triable-either-way offence to the Crown Court for trial, and most of the considerations listed in it are obviously such as to aggravate the sentence to an extent that justifies imprisonment:

Burglary

1. Dwelling house. (1) Entry in the daytime when the occupier (or another) is present; (2) entry at night of a house which is normally occupied, whether or not the occupier (or another) is present; (3) the offence is alleged to be one of a series of similar offences; (4) when soiling, ransacking, damage or vandalism occurs; (5) the offence has professional hallmarks; (6) the unrecovered property is of high value.
2. Non-dwellings. (1) Entry of a pharmacy or doctor's surgery; (2) fear is caused or violence is done to anyone lawfully on the premises (e.g. nightwatchman, security guard); (3) the offence has professional hallmarks; (4) vandalism on a substantial scale; (5) the unrecovered property is of high value.

Theft and Fraud

(1) breach of trust by a person of substantial authority, or in whom a high degree of trust is placed; (2) theft or fraud which has been committed or disguised in a sophisticated manner; (3) theft or fraud committed by an organised gang; (4) the victim is particularly vulnerable to theft or fraud, e.g. the elderly or infirm; (5) the unrecovered property is of high value.

Handling

(1) dishonest handling of stolen property by a receiver who has commissioned the theft; (2) the offence has professional hallmarks; (3) the property is of high value.

Social Security Frauds

(1) Organised fraud on a large scale; (2) the frauds are substantial and are carried out over a long period of time.

Violence (ss. 20 and 47 of the Offences against the Person Act 1861)

(1) The use of a weapon of a kind likely to cause serious injury; (2) a weapon is used and serious injury is caused; (3) more than minor injury is caused by kicking, headbutting, or similar forms of assault; (4) serious violence is caused to those whose work has to be done in contact with the public, e.g. police officers, bus drivers, taxi drivers, publicans and shopkeepers; (5) violence to vulnerable people, e.g. the elderly and infirm. The same considerations apply to cases of domestic violence.

Public Order Act 1986 Offences

1.   Cases of *violent disorder* should generally be committed for trial.
2.   *Affray* (1) Organised violence or use of weapons; (2) significant injury or substantial damage; (3) the offence has clear racial motivation; (4) an attack on police officers, ambulance men, firemen and the like.

Violence to and Neglect of Children

(1) substantial injury; (2) repeated violence or serious neglect, even if the harm is slight; (3) sadistic violence, e.g. deliberate burning or scalding.

Indecent Assault

(1) substantial disparity in age between victim and defendant, and the assault is more than trivial; (2) violence or threats of violence; (3) relationship of trust or responsibility between defendant and victim; (4) several similar offences, and the assaults are more than trivial; (5) the victim is particularly vulnerable; (6) serious nature of the assault.

Unlawful Sexual Intercourse

(1) Wide disparity of age; (2) breach of position of trust; (3) the victim is particularly vulnerable . . .

Drugs

1.   Class A. (a) *Supply; possession with intent to supply*: these cases should be committed for trial. (b) *Possession*: should be committed for trial unless the amount is small and consistent only with personal use.
2.   Class B. (a) *Supply; possession with intent to supply*: should be committed for trial unless there is only small scale supply for no payment. (b) *Possession*: should be committed for trial when the quantity is substantial.

Reckless Driving

(1) alcohol or drugs contributing to recklessness; (2) grossly excessive speed; (3) racing; (4) prolonged course of reckless driving; (5) other related offences.

Criminal Damage

(1) Deliberate fire-raising; (2) committed by a group; (3) damage of a high value; (4) the offence has clear racial motivation . . .

A few of the considerations listed raise evidential or other problems which make trial by a higher court preferable, but plainly most are simply seen as aggravating factors. Some of them will be discussed in the course of this chapter, others later.

When deciding whether to commit for *sentence* magistrates are now expected to take into account 'all relevant aspects of [the defendant's] character and antecedents [i.e. criminal record]'. Where the gravity of the offence is such that even with allowance for guilty plea and mitigation (see chapter 7) it is obvious that the punishment should be greater than they can impose, they should commit without a pre-sentence report or the hearing of mitigation, but should allow the defence and the prosecution to make submissions on the subject (*Warley* (1998)).

Eventually the Court of Appeal tried another tack. It acknowledged, in *Howells and others* (1998), that

> . . . it cannot be said that the 'right-thinking members of the public' test is very helpful, since the sentencing court has no means of ascertaining the views of right-thinking members of the public and invariably attributes to such right-thinking members its own views.

No doubt; but Lawton LJ had at least seen the difficulty. All that the Court has done in *Howells and others* is to set out five types of mitigation or aggravation which, unlike most of those in the 1990 *Practice Note*, are not concerned with the 'seriousness' of the *offence*, but are related to the previous or subsequent behaviour of the *offender*. They will therefore be cited in their proper place in this and later chapters; but they do not tell us what sorts of offences are 'serious'. The best I have been able to do is to list in Appendix A types of law breaking which the Court of Appeal seems to have accepted since 1991 as sufficiently serious in themselves, without any special aggravating features, to justify imprisonment.

Community Service and Custodial Sentences

The 1991 Act requires 'the restrictions on liberty' involved in a community service order to be 'commensurate with the seriousness of the offence'. Community service orders are not often the subject of appeals, but when they are the Court of Appeal draws an important distinction between cases in which a custodial sentence would have been a justifiable alternative, and cases in which it would not. In the latter type of case the number of hours should be short: for example 75 hours for the thefts by *Nawaz* (1991). If a custodial sentence was a justifiable alternative the Court tends not to interfere with orders for as many as 180 or even 200 hours (the statutory maximum is 240).

Statutory Distinctions

A few statutes define specific offences as aggravated forms of a wider category. Aggravated burglary is burglary committed by a person who 'at the time has with him any firearm or imitation firearm, any weapon of offence, or any explosive' (s. 10, Theft Act 1968). It is worth noting that notwithstanding the drafting of the section it must be clear that the burglar not merely had one of these things with him but intended to use it (*Stones* (1989)). On the other hand a burglary in which fear or injury is caused to an occupant without the use of a weapon is not 'aggravated' in the statutory sense, although it must be tried by the Crown Court like aggravated burglary (Schedule 1 of the Magistrates' Courts Act 1980). For 'aggravated burglary' a judge has the choice between a determinate sentence of any length and 'life', whereas for an ordinary burglary of a dwelling the maximum is 14 years. In practice 'life' is rarely used, and then only if the offender fulfils certain criteria (see chapter 5).

'Aggravated vehicle taking' consists of taking a vehicle unlawfully if it is then driven dangerously or so that a person is accidentally injured, or so that property is damaged, of if the vehicle itself is damaged before being recovered (s. 12A, Theft Act 1968). The defendant need not have been the driver. The maximum penalty if it is tried on indictment is two years' imprisonment (five years if a death results); but if it is tried summarily the usual maximum of six months applies. Disqualification from driving is obligatory.

Criminal damage – including arson – is aggravated if committed with the intention of endangering the life of another, or recklessly as regards that danger (s. 1, Criminal Damage Act 1971). It can result in a life sentence (but again subject to the criteria described in the next chapter), whereas the maximum for simple criminal damage or arson is 10 years' imprisonment (or six months' imprisonment in a summary court).

Trespassers cannot be prosecuted; but the Criminal Justice and Public Order Act 1994 (s. 68) created the offence of 'aggravated trespass'. Aimed at aggressive demonstrators, such as hunt saboteurs, it is defined as trespassing on land in open air and doing anything intended to intimidate, obstruct or disrupt lawful activities there. The maximum penalty is three months' imprisonment.

The Road Traffic Act 1988 distinguishes careless driving, driving under the influence of drink or drugs, dangerous driving and causing death by dangerous driving, with varying penalties. Disqualification, obligatory for most of these offences, is discretionary for merely careless driving, which is also not imprisonable. More will be said about these offences in chapter 8 under the heading of 'the relevance of harm'.

These are everyday examples. Many other statutes, however, which deal with specific offences provide higher maximum penalties if they are committed in certain ways or in certain circumstances. For example the maximum penalty for sexual intercourse with a girl under 16 years of age is only two years, but if she is under 13 it is 'life' (again subject to special criteria, discussed in chapter 5).

Sacrilege

The unstated principle which seems to underlie some of these distinctions (e.g. in the case of criminal damage) is that the more morally reprehensible the behaviour the more severe should be the maximum penalty. Sometimes the criterion is obviously the seriousness of the likely harm (see chapter 8). Sometimes, however, the criterion is more subtle. Perjury (punishable with seven years' imprisonment) is distinguished from tendering false written statements in criminal proceedings (punishable with only two years' imprisonment), although the only material difference seems to be that the latter does not involve the ritual of swearing or affirming. Perjury must be regarded as a sacrilegious form of lying. Burglary used to be aggravated, and called 'sacrilege', if it consisted of breaking and entering a church and stealing a chattel from it. The maximum penalty in the nineteenth century was death, and in the twentieth century 'life' (under the Larceny Act 1916). This form of burglary is no longer distinguished from others; yet even today there is a whiff of sacrilege in sentencers' minds when human corpses are stolen, in whole or part. *Lowey* (1982), who had stolen skulls from a mausoleum for occult purposes, was lucky to have his prison sentence of three years reduced to two years by the Court of Appeal, which said that 'the element of affront' should be taken into account in such cases. In 1998 *Kelly*, a sculptor with a blameless record, received a short custodial sentence for stealing parts of human bodies, not from a church or graveyard but from the Royal College of Surgeons. If he had merely stolen books he would almost certainly have been dealt with non-custodially.

Offending while on Bail

One other statutory rule of a general nature must be mentioned. If an offence is committed by someone who is on bail: 'the court *shall treat* the fact as an aggravating factor' (s. 29, Criminal Justice Act 1991, my italics). This provision was a reaction to the prevalence of reoffending by offenders whom the magistrates' courts had felt obliged by the Bail Act 1976 to set free while awaiting trial. No doubt it was hoped that it would serve as a deterrent. If so, the justification is hoped for utility, and legislators must be allowed hope. A retributive justification – that offending on bail is a breach of trust – is too artificial: but breach of trust will be discussed later. The words which I have italicised – '*shall treat*' – are worth noting. It is unusual for a penal statute to use the imperative: more usual is 'may'. The mandatory wording suggests that the legislators were not at all confident that if courts were given discretion they would use it as they were supposed to. There are other examples of this. The Road Traffic Acts made endorsement of licences and disqualifications obligatory in certain circumstances because magistrates' courts were too easily persuaded to deal leniently with careless or drunken drivers. More recently the Crime (Sentences) Act 1997, with its minimum sentences for recidivist burglars and drug dealers and the obligation to pass 'life' sentences in certain other circumstances (see the next chapter), was a reaction to what the Home Secretary saw as the leniency of judges, and the need for a deterrent which was not merely probable but certain.

Guideline Cases

Courts are also guided by a number of cases in which the Court of Appeal has not merely upheld or varied a sentence but has indicated what factors sentencers should regard as aggravating (or mitigating) offences of the type in question. Some of these cases are expressly called 'guideline cases', but a few are not, although they seem to offer general advice on specific topics. The important cases will be found in Appendix B. The extent to which sentencers are expected to follow the Court of Appeal's lead will be discussed in the final chapter. There will soon be additions to its guidelines as a result of the Crime and Disorder Act 1998, and the relevant section will also be discussed in the final chapter. The rest of this chapter is concerned with more specific issues.

Premeditation

'Other things being equal' said the Lord Chief Justice in *Howells and others* (1998) 'an offence which is deliberate and premeditated will usually be more serious than one which is spontaneous and un-premeditated, or which involves an excessive response to provocation'. In the Crown Court premeditation is one of the factors most likely to tip the balance in favour of a custodial sentence, especially when the offence is a violent one (Flood-Page and Mackie, 1998). A special kind of premeditation is conspiracy, which the Court of Appeal clearly regarded as aggravating the offence itself in *Ward and others* (1996) Four young anti-Semitic men had prepared to deface Jewish graves with paint when they were intercepted by police. 'The agreement to deface' said the Court 'was an act more wicked than the actual application of paint'.

Unnecessary Violence

Frequently mentioned is violence of a gratuitous or excessive nature: that is 'violence over and above the violence necessarily involved in the act itself' (the guideline case of *Roberts and Roberts* (1982)). The *Practice Note* of 1990 specified sadism as a feature of violence to a child which requires magistrates' courts to commit the case to the Crown Court for trial. It is odd that sadism is not mentioned in the context of violence to adults – for example to wives.

Prevalence

Even if an offence is not regarded as serious the fact that it is prevalent in an area will often turn the scale in favour of prosecution (The Crown Prosecution Service's 1994 Code). When it comes to sentencing it might be supposed that it is now ruled out as an aggravation by the 1991 Act's insistence that only the circumstances of the particular offence can aggravate. The Court of Appeal, how-ever, has always allowed local prevalence to do so. As early as 1909 in *Warner* it referred with approval to:

> a rule laid down years ago by Sir Ralph Littler of punishing with exceptional severity housebreaking in Middlesex, inasmuch as the small householders there, from the unavoidable insufficiency of police, can only be protected from London housebreakers by deterrent sentences, and experience had proved that the rule was efficacious.

Prevalence need not be local, however. In *Silverman* (1983) the Court clearly approved sentences with the principal aim of deterring others. 'In cases of this kind, the sentence is not so much directed at the defendant but to others of a like kind who commit frauds of this type [with stolen cheques], which are still so prevalent'. And in *Cunningham* (1993) the Court said that the prevalence of an offence does not justify sentencing an individual offender with special severity in order to make an example of him or her, but is 'a legitimate factor in determining the length of the custodial sentence to be passed'. This can only mean that prevalence justifies *consistently* long sentences for a whole class of offences. The Court's justification for this principle was the alarm which robberies or rapes cause in a locality: 'the sentence commensurate with the seriousness of the offence may need to be higher there than elsewhere'. This can hardly mean that otherwise similar rapes or robberies are more serious in London than in Lincoln: it must mean that prevalence is, in the words of the 1991 Act, an aggravating *circumstance of the offence*. Cunningham's robbery, in plain words, was aggravated by the fact that a lot of other robbers were active in Crawley. This shows how far the meaning of 'circumstance' can be stretched.

It is also an example of an aggravation which is accepted without proof. Most aggravations are either part of what is charged or at least proved by the evidence. When the sentencer, however, says that the offence is prevalent in a locality he is not, apparently, expected to quote statistics for example to show that robbery was commoner in Crawley than elsewhere. Similarly when the defendant in *Williams* (1995) was sentenced to four years for intimidating a witness it seems to have been accepted by all concerned that this was 'particularly prevalent' in Liverpool. It is not easy to think of another sort of aggravation which is accepted so unquestioningly.

Exemplary Sentencing

What has to be distinguished from consistent severity of that kind is 'exemplary' sentencing which singles out occasional examples for unusual severity. In 1954 a series of racially motivated attacks in the Notting Hill Gate area of London came to an end not long after the ringleaders received abnormally long prison sentences; and many judges have claimed that this demonstrated the efficacy of exemplary sentencing. My closer look at the facts cast doubt on this (Walker, 1985), and Baxter and Nuttall's (1975) study of the *Storey* incident in 1975 reinforced these doubts. Storey's quite exceptional sentence was 20 years for a brutal mugging in Birmingham, and it was well publicised in both local and national newspapers. Yet week-by-week statistics of subsequent muggings in Birmingham, Liverpool and Manchester showed no decrease in muggings. This does not prove that exemplary sentences never discourage any type of crime. Muggers may not study the news as closely as, say, embezzlers or drug traffickers. It is the absence of any sound evidence – as so often when deterrence is invoked – that is disquieting.

In the sixties Lord Chief Justice Parker tried at his judges' conferences to discourage the term and the practice, but the term continued to be used occasionally to justify severity. Examples are *Elvin* (1976) for arson; *Ivey* (1981) for grievous bodily harm in a fight; *Salter* (1982), a doctor who misused his power to prescribe drugs. Sometimes the Court was upholding consistent severity, sometimes exceptional severity. The ambiguity was indefensible. The 1991 Act, with its insistence on commensurateness, might be thought to rule out exceptional severity for unaggravated offences; and it was noticeable that when increasing the sentences of *McMaster and Case* (1998) for a group assault the Court of Appeal seemed to be using 'exemplary' to mean 'consistently severe'.

Victims

'Vulnerable victim' appears frequently as an aggravating circumstance not only in the *Practice Note* of 1990 but also in the Magistrates' Association's *Sentencing Guidelines, 1997*. The old age or youth of a victim is likely to attract severity, and as we have seen may even place the offence in a more serious category if the offence is sexual. 'Vulnerability' can be psychological. It was the main reason why the Court of Appeal upheld severe prison sentences in the cases of *Ball and Bateman* (1997) who had been selling heroin to clients of a drug rehabilitation centre. Violence to an elderly or disabled victim has a similarly aggravating effect. Violence to able-bodied adults seems closer to 'fair play'.

Increased severity is also justified when the victim of violence is a police officer (*McKenlay* (1979)). In his case the Court of Appeal may have been worried by the current problem of violent picketing, although it did not say so. There are other cases, however, in which the principle seems to have been applied: examples are *Coleman* (1975); *Bell* (1973); *Cockram* (1996). Since police are physically fit and trained to deal with violence the justification can hardly be vulnerability or unfairness. It must be that people who choose risky occupations in the public interest need to be protected by particularly deterrent sentences.

Abuse of Trust

The *Practice Note* of 1990 also mentions abuse of trust, and it is one of the factors most likely to tip the balance in favour of a custodial sentence (Flood-Page and Mackie, 1998). It is a breach of trust to commit a robbery while on parole from a sentence for robbery, and the offence is aggravated accordingly (*Ward* (1996)), although it is not an aggravation if the offender is under a suspended sentence (*Harrison* (1993)). The distinction seems to be that while parole is an act of trust, a suspended sentence is merely a threat. However that may be, corruption and embezzlement provide many examples of breach of trust; and misuse of an expense account is regarded as similar (*Woodley* (1979)). A policeman is in a position of trust when interrogating people, so that *Lewis* (1976), who beat up a man for withholding information, was unsuccessful in his appeal against a two-year sentence. Sexual offences against children by teachers or other people who have been given charge of them are also severely punished (an example is *Seaman* (1982). Even a qualified nurse who indecently assaulted a student nurse aged 20 was held to have abused trust (*Drysdale* (1993)). Treachery, too, must be both deterred and punished, said the Court of Appeal to *Smith* (1996), whose consecutive sentences for selling technical information to Russia totalled 25 years. They took into account his low security rating and the relative harmlessness of the information, but subtracted only five years. Guideline cases on breach of trust are *Barrick* (1985), a case of thefts by a firm's accountant, and *Clark* (1997).

Almost any sort of dishonesty in breach of trust is regarded as serious enough to justify a custodial sentence. There have been exceptions when only small sums of money have been involved, and the Magistrates' Association's *Sentencing Guidelines, 1997* suggest two unusual mitigations – 'previous inconsistent attitude by employer' and 'unsupported junior'.

Neither statute nor the Court of Appeal has provided a general definition of abuse of trust. If the Sexual Offences (Amendment) Bill reaches the statute-book in something like its original version it will create a new offence of 'sexual intercourse or activity while in a position of trust'. With certain exceptions a person over the age of 18 will be guilty of that offence when he engages in sexual intercourse or activity with a person under that age if he 'looks after' persons in an institution of a listed kind, and the other person is in that institution. 'Looking after' is defined as 'regularly caring for training, supervising or being in sole charge of'.

Exactly what is and what is not a position of trust needs a little consideration. It has to be distinguished from abuse of authority, as the Court of Appeal acknowledged in *Malloy's* case (1997). He was a chef who was assisted by a washing-up boy of 15 whom he buggered. The trial judge called this 'abuse of authority', and re-garded it as an aggravation. The Court of Appeal disagreed: 'the boy was in no sense in the care of the appellant in the way that might occur between teacher and pupil . . .' – a decision which should be compared with that in *Drysdale*, cited above. A father is in a position of trust in relation to his children (*Brian Arthur C (1998)* who had raped his underage daughter). Abuse of trust has not, however, been defined for sentencing purposes. In the simplest situation A hands B his wallet for safekeeping while he bathes in the sea, trusting B to return it. Similarly if B applies for and accepts a post which clearly involves dealing with other people's money he has been entrusted with responsibility for it. The same seems true if the responsibility is for children's welfare, or sensitive information. By applying for a post B has given an implied undertaking not to take improper advantage of it. But suppose that B, not being employed to teach or care for children, is suddenly obliged to take temporary care of some children because a teacher or carer has been taken ill, and agrees somewhat unwillingly to do so, then molests one of them. He has certainly done wrong, but has he abused trust? Did Elaine *Edney* (1994) abuse trust when she stole £37,000 from the aged mother for whom she had cared alone for years? (The Court of Appeal thought not, and suspended her sentence.) Does a general practitioner abuse a position of trust if he responds to the sexual advances of an adult patient? What were

Phelps and Stickitt (1993) abusing when, as chartered accountants, they told their trusting clients how to cheat the Inland Revenue? The Court of Appeal thought that they were abusing their professional position.

Abuse of Hospitality

Abuse of trust is not quite the same as abuse of hospitality. The usual example of the latter is the petty thief who takes advantage of someone who has befriended him or her. The concept, however, has been stretched. *Kitosi* (1997) was a refugee from Burundi, living on British income support, who had attempted to rape a 23-year-old woman a few months after his arrival. The judge who sentenced him to six years' imprisonment, and recommended deportation, was clearly influenced by what she regarded as an abuse of this country's hospitality. The same reason was given by another judge for a five-year sentence passed in 1998 on *Kepa*, a Kosovan refugee, again for rape. Yet rapists from Scotland are not sentenced more severely than Englishmen. It seems unlikely that the Court of Appeal would have upheld this as a reason for special severity if the refugees had appealed. It could hardly have reasoned that they had been 'trusted' any more than Englishmen to be law-abiding. Being foreign is not nowadays supposed to be an aggravation. Yet visitors to England whose stay is meant to be short may find that they are dealt with slightly more severely. Foreign shoplifters are often not given time to pay fines, for the purely practical reason that the usual procedures for enforcing payment would be rendered ineffective by their departure. By way of contrast, if the sentencer is hesitating between a fine and a brief prison term he may decide against custody because of the problems which this would create for a tourist. Nevertheless, the fact that *Mbelu* (1981) was merely in transit at Gatwick between Nigeria and Los Angeles did not save him from an 18-month prison sentence for smuggling a substantial amount of cannabis, because of the seriousness of the offence.

Absence of Remorse

Occasionally a defendant is unlucky enough to be the subject of a report which comments on his lack of remorse. The presence of remorse (real or apparent) is dealt with in chapter 7. Judges in a utilitarian mood are apt to regard its absence as an indication that the offender is likely to reoffend. When a psychiatrist's report said that *Meikle* (1994) showed no remorse for his sexual offences against children and was therefore classed as 'a danger to the public', the Court of Appeal agreed. Retributivists have to think twice when asked why absence of remorse should aggravate. They can argue that it is an indication of character; but most are not happy about punishing for character. Nozick might say that it shows that only a particularly severe penalty will bring home to the offender the wrongfulness of what he did. Only intuitionists see no need to explain. The Magistrates' Association's *Sentencing Guidelines, 1997* list remorse as a possible mitigation where most types of offence are concerned, but are silent about the absence of it.

Professionalism

The 1990 *Practice Note* treats thefts, frauds and dishonest handling as aggravated if they show signs of professionalism. The Court of Appeal has upheld long prison sentences imposed because the offender was regarded as a 'professional'. In *Brewster* (1980) it referred to 'professional criminals, who have long records, great skill as criminals, and who from time to time make very valuable hauls'. In that case the express justification for the seven-year sentence was the incapacitation of the offender – a justification which would nowadays be held to be inconsistent with section 2(2)(b) of the Criminal Justice Act 1991, since the offence was neither sexual nor violent: see chapter 5. The underlying justification nowadays for treating professionalism as an aggravation is probably the utilitarian assumption that its rewards are so attractive that greater deterrents are needed to compensate for the offender's skill in avoiding identification or conviction.

Motives

Motives matter; but it is seldom possible to tell from reported cases how much effect they have on the sentence. Which of the seven deadly sins – all of them common motives – arouses the strongest disapproval? Not avarice these days, although greed is still regarded as worse than need. (*Clark's* embezzlements, for example, were

aggravated by the fact that he used the moneys for personal gratifica-
tion (1998)). Envy and gluttony do not lead to the Old Bailey. Pride
may lead to libel suits, but hardly ever to criminal charges (unless it
takes the form of a violent defence of one's honour). Sloth may
culminate in criminal negligence. It is lust, however, which ranks
highest amongst aggravating motives; but in the special case of
bigamy it is regarded with more indulgence than a mercenary motive.
Perverted desires are treated either as the worst forms of lust or – if
harmless – as merely ridiculous, an example being fetishism. Anger
is often looked upon with sympathy, especially when provocation can
be pleaded (see chapter 11), but racial hatreds now rank so high that
the Crime and Disorder Act 1998 (ss. 22–25, 82) now *requires*
specially severe penalties when they lead to violence: the only
example of a statutory aggravation based on motive. (Attempts during
the passage of the Bill to extend these clauses to religious and
homophobic hatreds were rejected.) Crimes committed as part of a
political campaign were especially condemned in the case of *Cruik-
shank and O'Donnell* (1995), two IRA supporters who had planted
incendiary devices in several shops in Leeds. Their sentences were
reduced because they had not intended to cause deaths, merely risked
doing so, but the Court added that:

> . . . it must be clearly understood by activists for whatever cause
> that to seek to destabilise the community or exert pressure must be
> met with severe deterrent sentences.

Interestingly, having no discernible motive is often regarded as an
aggravation. Vandalism and personal violence is particularly condemned when it can be called 'mindless'.

Military Discipline

Members of the armed services may find themselves subject to more
severe penalties than civilians. A court-martial dismissed Staff Sergeant *Love* (1997) from the Army for sending indecent or obscene
material through the post. The Court of Appeal thought that the
appropriate penalty would have been a mere fine, but upheld the more
severe sentence on the assumption that the court-martial knew best
what was needed for the maintenance of discipline and efficiency.

This decision seems to carry the important implication that the Court of Appeal is unlikely to interfere with a court-martial's sentence on the sole ground that it is too severe: yet in the case of Colour Sergeant *McEnhill* (1999) it did quash a sentence of imprisonment for indecent assault because of the effect which dismissal would have had on his family.

Defendant's Tactics

It is not an aggravation that a defendant has attacked the honesty and integrity of the police involved in his case (*Bernard* (1996)), although the trial judge had so treated it. Apparently the police are fair game, whereas some other accusers are not. The nation was scandalised in 1997 when a rapist dismissed his counsel and subjected two of his victims to unnecessarily lengthy and intimate questioning, obviously for pleasure or revenge. This probably contributed to his very long 16-year sentence. A singular point is made in the Magistrates' Association's *Sentencing Guidelines, 1997*. Efforts to avoid detection or arrest are to be regarded as aggravations where driving offences are concerned, but are not mentioned in other contexts. Even more striking is the advice to treat casting suspicion on others as an aggravation when theft in breach of trust is concerned. It is true that such tactics may be commonest in such contexts, but the Magistrates' Association can hardly mean that it is only these types of offence which are aggravated by it.

Procedural Principles

An awkward situation arises when an offender has served all or part of the sentence passed by a lower court which the Court of Appeal considers too lenient. *Earlam and Earlam* (1997) had completed the hours of community service for wounding with intent by the time the Attorney-General's reference reached the Court of Appeal. It agreed that the sentence should have been a custodial one, but:

> with some hesitation concluded that it would not now advance the public interest to order these offenders to serve a custodial sentence. We have alluded to the elements which guide the imposition of such a sentence: the need for punishment, the need for deterrence, and the need to mark public disapproval of such conduct . . . but paying attention to the unique facts of this particular case . . . with

some hesitation we conclude that we should not now impose any different sentence.

The Court was certainly in a difficult position. It could hardly substitute a custodial sentence for community service which had already been completed (custody and community service cannot be imposed for the same offence). By the same token it could not even use a suspended sentence. To argue, however, that 'the public interest' did not call for a custodial sentence is to invite the question 'Why not?'. And to add that the position was 'unique' is to offer false reassurance, since it is quite likely to arise again unless Attorney-General's references are invariably dealt with speedily (as in most cases they now are). It would have been more honest to acknowledge this, and the fact that it was the law that did not allow matters to be put right.

When taking aggravations into account sentencers should make clear what they are, but should not feel obliged to indicate how much of the resulting sentence is attributable to this or that feature (*Craney and Corbett* (1996)). Nor did the Court of Appeal think that it should 'lay down, by way of guidelines, a series of bands of sentencing in different classes of case . . . The circumstances of cases vary enormously . . .' (ibid.). It was talking about racially motivated violence. Yet in at least one other type of case, concerning the periods for which company directors should be disqualified, it has approved 'bands' suggested by the Official Receiver (see chapter 6).

NOTES

1. 'The combination of the offence and other offences associated with it', refers to offences of which the offender is convicted in the same proceedings or for which he is sentenced in the same proceedings (including offences which he asks the court to 'take into consideration' in sentencing him: s. 31). This does not, however, allow the sentencer to take into account other similar offences alleged by the prosecution but disputed by the defendant (as the judge did in *Clark* (1996)).

2. Committal of a violent or sexual offender for a sentence designed to protect the public is dealt with in chapter 5, n. 3.

Chapter 5
Precautionary Detention

Dangerousness is the most important of aggravations because it can so greatly increase the length of custodial sentences, and can supplement non-custodial penalties with onerous restrictions. For this reason, and because it is a controversial subject, it deserves chapters to itself.

It is controversial because it involves a conflict between the utilitarian and the retributive justifications for sentencing. There are single-minded retributivists who argue that detention beyond what is deserved for an offence is never justified. An example is the Swedish Working Party for Criminal Policy (1978):

> The ethical problem is that incapacitation as a reason for penal intervention means that a person is punished not for what he has done but for what it is believed he may do in the future . . . This . . . can be compared to the sentencing of an innocent person.

The implication is that no restraint should be imposed even on someone who has declared a firm and credible intention of committing very serious harm. The logic is far from sound. The person being restrained is not exactly 'innocent' (even in the rare cases in which he has merely threatened serious harm). He has demonstrated or declared what harm he is capable of inflicting. People who have not yet done or threatened serious harm to others benefit not from the presumption of innocence but from the presumption of harmlessness, and we have to run the risk of being harmed by one of them because imposing restraints on everyone would be unthinkable. But when someone has shown, by word or deed, that he is capable of serious harm, the utilitarian believes that we have the right to do so. He does not, however, mistake the right for a duty: he recognises that there will be cases in which society has been given the right to impose precautions but may sensibly decide that they are not necessary.

The more serious flaw, however, in the Swedish Working Group's reasoning was the assumption that the only proper aim of sentencing is retributive punishment. No penal codes exclude utilitarian aims such as deterrence or correction; and if those aims are proper why not prevention? It is true that preventive custodial sentences tend to be longer than those intended merely to deter or correct; but that is a reason for using them carefully, not for outlawing them.

The need for extreme care is emphasised by more moderate anti-protectionists. They point out that precautionary detention is usually reserved for offenders who have done serious personal harm to others; but that it is only a minority of them who repeat their crimes. Consequently any extension of custody which is intended solely for the protection of others is bound to involve more mistakes than would result from a policy which eschewed precautionary extensions. The arithmetic is reversed only when the offenders' criminal records (or other behaviour) already demonstrate their tendency to repeat their offences. The counting of 'mistakes', however, is a rhetorical trick, since it implies that one can use the same scales to weigh unnecessarily prolonged detentions against releases which have tragic consequences. Low probabilities should certainly be taken into account, but again are not a reason for outlawing prolonged detentions altogether.

The anti-protectionist's last resort is to attack the word 'dangerousness', and what it stands for, as a label which should never be applied to people. It is not people, he argues, but situations that are dangerous. There are two answers. In the first place it is possible, indeed more precise, to discuss the problems of precautionary sentencing without using the word at all, as the rest of this chapter will demonstrate. Secondly it is an optimistic fallacy to assume that all nasty crimes are situation-dependent. Not only are there violent and sexual offenders who are more likely than most people in similar situations to give way to their impulses. There are offenders who do not merely react to situations but look for them and even manage to create them.

Dangerousness in Practice

'Dangerousness' is not a word which actually appears in any English penal statute or in the Crown Prosecution Service's Code (1994); but a factor which tends to turn the scales in favour of prosecution is

> grounds for believing that the offence is likely to be continued or repeated, for example by a history of recurring conduct.

Nor does the word figure in statutes concerned with sentencing; but in the statutes dealing with custodial sentences or compulsory admissions to mental hospitals there are plenty of references to the need to protect the public from 'serious harm'.[1]

Before 1991 there had been special prison sentences for recidivists – 'preventive detention' from 1908 until 1967, and after that the 'extended sentence'. Their effect was to allow the judge to pass a longer sentence than the offence itself would have justified, and to allow a longer than normal period of compulsory supervision after release. Any sort of offence was eligible, so long as it was imprisonable. The other conditions which had to be satisfied, however, were complex, and included a minimum number of previous convictions and custodial sentences for indictable offences, with the result that most of the offenders eligible for the precautionary sentence were thieves and burglars, not men of violence or sexual offenders. Partly for this reason, partly because judges were reluctant to be more severe than the tariff for the offence, preventive detention and extended sentences were little used.

The introduction of parole in 1967 meant that any substantial prison sentence created the possibility that an offender's release would be delayed for precautionary reasons. The 1991 Criminal Justice Act limited this possibility to sentences of four years or more, but allowed the Parole Board to delay release from the half-way stage to the three-quarter stage, the only permissible consideration being whether 'the safety of the public will be placed unacceptably at risk'. The

Home Secretary's directions tell the Parole Board that a risk of a sexual or violent offence is more serious than a risk of other types. A crude but not entirely misleading index of the Board's attitude to comparative risks is the percentages of prisoners whom they regard as safe to release at first review (i.e. as soon as they are eligible):[2]

Sexual offenders: 24%
Property offenders: 38%
Violent offenders: 45%
Drug offenders: 64%

It is not surprising that sexual offenders fare worst; but it is interesting that property offenders fare worse than violent offenders and much worse than drug offenders. It is possible to think of reasonable explanations. For example, drug offences do direct harm only to willing victims. Property offenders are likely to have the most previous convictions, and thus to be the most likely to reoffend. The Home Secretary's directions do not say that property offences are never a threat to public safety. But these explanations are speculative.

Longer-than-commensurate (LTC) Sentences

The 1991 Act also replaced the extended sentence with one designed only for certain kinds of offence – serious violence or sexual molestation. Custodial sentences must normally be 'commensurate' with the seriousness of the offence, but can be longer (subject to any statutory maximum) if the offence is a violent or sexual one and the court thinks it 'necessary to protect the public from serious harm from the offender' (s. 2(2)(b)).[3] For this purpose a sexual offence is one of those listed in section 31 (see Appendix A); but a violent offence is defined in general terms as one 'which leads, or is intended or likely to lead, to a person's death or to physical injury to a person'. For the removal of doubt the draftsman added that this includes arson, but unfortunately left other doubtful cases to be decided by the courts. As for the 'serious harm' from which the public is to be protected, section 31 makes it expressly clear that this means death or serious personal injury, *whether physical or psychological*. On a strict interpretation section 2(2)(b) is mandatory when these conditions are satisfied, but

if the court can decide that the offender is unlikely to repeat the harm
– however serious it was – it can escape the obligation.

Attempts and Threats

The result has been some decisions which the legislators can hardly
have intended. *Robinson* (1993), convicted of attempted rape, appealed against an LTC sentence on the ground that attempts at sexual
offences were not mentioned in section 31; and it was only after heavy
consideration that the Court of Appeal rejected his argument. Robbers
who have threatened their victims with knives which they claimed
that they did not intend to use have had LTC sentences replaced with
commensurate ones. A remarkable example was *Murray* (1993), who
had pulled a shopkeeper across his counter and held a large kitchen
knife to his head – behaviour judged not to be a violent offence.
Another example was *Bibby* (1994). Even express threats to murder
do not necessarily qualify for LTC sentences. Such threats can be
uttered without any real intention in the heat of a quarrel. *Richart*
(1995), however, was mentally disordered, enjoyed using handguns,
and was described by a psychiatrist as a danger to others. The trial
judge thought that the danger justified an LTC sentence; but the Court
of Appeal ruled that because the threats were delivered by telephone
and post, and had not led to physical injury, and because there was
no evidence that they were intended to do so, they were not violent
within the meaning of section 31. In *Ragg* (1996) the Court confirmed
that even a threat to kill is not necessarily a 'violent offence'. but
conceded *obiter* that it could be if it led to death without any further
action – for example if it caused a fatal heart attack. Yet in *Mortimer*
(1997) three different judges upheld what must have been an LTC
sentence of seven years for a violent man's threats to kill, although
the effect had not been fatal. And when *Wilson* (1998) threatened to
kill his wife, telling several people of his intentions, and hiding his
butcher's knives in a convenient place, this was held to qualify for an
LTC sentence (possibly the scales were tipped by psychiatric reports
which confirmed his dangerousness). In this case the Court of Appeal
judges were clearly aware of the decision in *Richart* but felt able to
distinguish *Wilson's* case because he seemed likely to carry out his
threats. Yet both offenders had been the subject of psychiatric reports
which stressed their dangerousness.

The Length of LTC Sentences

The Court of Appeal has been restrictive in other ways. The length of an LTC sentence must not, it holds, 'be out of all proportion to the nature of the offending' (*Mansell* (1994)). This seems to refer to the nature of the proved offence, which is scarcely logical, since the purpose of the sentence is to prevent future harm of a serious kind. Again, the court often reduces the length of LTC sentences by small allowances for mitigating considerations, even when these do not reduce the seriousness of the harm done or the likelihood of the offender's doing serious harm in the future (e.g. *Bingham* (1993)). In *Bowler* (1993) the court compromised weakly by conceding that mitigating considerations would not have the same weight as in the case of commensurate sentences.

The *Criminal Statistics (England and Wales)* do not distinguish LTC from ordinary prison sentences, but Flood-Page and Mackie's survey in the mid 1990s found that for violence they averaged 7.2 years and for sexual offences 5.1 years (compared with 2.3 years and 3.0 years when the sentences were not LTC). Only 3 per cent, however, of sentences for violence and 6 per cent of sentences for sexual offences were LTC, so that the samples were small. The first reported appeal, in 1993, was against a six-year sentence, and was unsuccessful (the appellant, *Utip* (1993), who had a record of violence, had picked a fight with a stranger and slashed his face). Some sentences, however, are so short as to make no sense. The Court of Appeal itself has approved LTC sentences as short as three and a half years (in *Apelt* (1994), who had indecently assaulted young girls in a park), with the result that he was entitled to automatic release after 21 months. It is true that most LTC sentences exceed four years, so that the Parole Board could prevent or recommend release at any stage between the half-way and the three-quarter date; but when the length is five, six or seven years its discretion is limited to months. Such cases illustrate the extent to which the intentions of utilitarian legislation are diluted by the retributive orientation of the judiciary.

In 1994 longer sentences, of 14 and 15 years, were passed (on *Watford* (1994) for kidnapping a youth in order to enforce a debt against his father; and on *Fleming* (1994) for a violent attempt at rape, but both were reduced to 12). By late 1996, when some 40 LTC sentences had been imposed, judges had become bolder: a 27-year

LTC sentence was passed in the case of *Bramble* (1997) for his robberies, and was reduced by a mere seven years in the Court of Appeal. Clearly the totality principle (see chapter 7) does not apply to LTC sentences.

The Harmfulness of the Current Offence

Perhaps the most important way in which the Court of Appeal has restricted LTC sentences has been its rejection of them in cases in which the current offence is not itself very harmful, but the offender's history included harmful offences of a similar kind, which the offender seemed quite likely to repeat. These are usually sexual cases. *Creasey* (1993) had indecently assaulted a boy of 13 on three occasions, and had a record of sexual assaults on a much younger boy and sexual intercourse with a girl under 13, an offence for which the maximum penalty is 'life'. The judge who passed a five-year LTC sentence was reproved by the Court of Appeal for confusing high risk with serious harm. The current offence may not have seemed serious, but the earlier ones could hardly be dismissed so lightly. A similar case was *Nichols* (1996), whose current offence was a minor indecent assault on a 12-year-old boy, but whose record included buggery of children: his LTC sentence was also replaced by a short one. There is no support in section 2(2)(b) for this focus on the harmfulness of the current offence rather than of possible future offences. It seems indefensibly inconsistent with the Court's policy as regards restriction orders for mentally disordered offenders, as we shall shortly see.

Life Sentences

The official use of indeterminate detention is at least as old as the thirteenth century, when Boniface VIII approved it not as a punishment but 'for the completion of repentance', and the statute Westminster II allowed it for the crime of kidnapping. Elizabeth I used it for heterodox clergy. The naval galleys, or later transportation for life were the usual fates of felons who were spared execution by the royal mercy, but in the nineteenth century 'life' imprisonment was substituted for death for many offences which had been capital. In 1957 a mandatory life sentence replaced the mandatory death sentence for non-capital murder, and in 1965 this was extended to all types of murder.

For some other crimes it is merely the maximum permissible penalty: attempted murder, manslaughter, arson, criminal damage intended to endanger life, aggravated burglary, robbery, buggery, incest or sexual intercourse with a girl under the age of 13, kidnapping and – at least in theory – unlawful abortion, infanticide, possessing a Class A drug with intent to supply it to others, and – an obvious anachronism – forgery of registers of births, deaths or marriages. In most cases the legislators intended 'life' as just deserts and a deterrent, but it is nowadays used only as a precautionary sentence, except in the case of murder, for which it is still mandatory because successive Home Secretaries have insisted that it is needed to emphasise the unique gravity of the crime.[4]

As a precaution an indeterminate sentence has one clear advantage over an LTC sentence. The latter in effect sets a date by which the offender must[5] be released, however apprehensive those who know him are about the harm which he may do. A discretionary life sentence merely specifies a minimum period for which he must be detained for the purpose of deterrence and desert (s. 34 of the Criminal Justice Act 1991). The assumption that the periods needed for deterrence and desert coincide is odd but old. After he has served this period he is not to be released until the Parole Board consider that he does not represent a serious risk to others.

In spite of this advantage the Court of Appeal has not encouraged courts to use life. Over a quarter of a century ago Parker LCJ laid down its policy in *Picker* (1970). He was a 17-year-old lad who had lost his temper with an elderly man and beaten him to death with a piece of wood. The jury acquitted him of murder, but convicted him of manslaughter. The judge passed a life sentence, probably with the merciful intention that he would not be detained for more than a few years. Parker LCJ, approved this intention, but not the life sentence, which he reduced to four years. This was surprising, because in debate in the House of Lords he had emphasised that 'life' could be used in just this lenient way. His reasoning now, however, was that it was acceptable only:

in a case where the nature of the offence and the make-up of the offender are of such a nature that the public require protection for a considerable time unless there is a change in his condition, maybe a mental condition at present unknown . . . But where no such condition exists a judge should not pass the difficult matter of sentencing and the length of detention to others.

His assumption seems to have been that in the case of the mentally normal nobody but a judge could be trusted with the decision to decide when release would be safe. This was remarkable when one considers that for generations the Home Office had been releasing mentally normal lifers, and that three years before *Picker* the Parole Board had been created to advise the Home Secretary on releases from long sentences. However that may be, the Court of Appeal has usually substituted a determinate sentence for life unless there is psychiatric evidence that the offender is mentally disordered or at least unstable, so that it cannot be predicted when it will be safe to release him (*Blackburn* (1979)). Later it conceded that psychiatric evidence was not essential, if the nature of the offence and the offender's history demonstrated instability (see, for example, *De Havilland* (1983)). In Hatch (1996) it decided that repeated paedophilic behaviour which would not respond to treatment satisfied the criterion. Eventually the court yielded to realism and acknowledged that there are offenders who, though not 'unstable', are simply so dangerous and likely to remain so that only an indeterminate sentence is appropriate (e.g. *Allen* (1987), who was a persistently vengeful ex-lover). In *Whittaker* (1997) the Court made it quite plain that a life sentence could be justified if there were 'grounds for believing that the offender might be a serious danger to the public for a period which could not be reliably estimated at the date of sentence'. Even so, the Court is still happier if 'the grounds' include psychiatric evidence, and discretionary life sentences for the mentally normal continue to be rare.

This led the Home Secretary to complain in the 1996 White Paper *Protecting the Public* that discretionary life sentences were not being used as often as they should be. In 1994 there were 217 cases in which they could have been passed for serious violent or sexual crimes by men who had previous convictions for such crimes; but only 10 of them were sentenced to life. The Home Secretary's Crime (Sentences) Bill therefore proposed mandatory life sentences for second or subsequent convictions of one of a list of serious violent or sexual offences, unless the offender is under the age of 18.[6]

The judiciary objected vociferously to this encroachment on their discretion, and the eventual legislation exempted them from the

obligation if there are 'exceptional circumstances relating to either of
the offences or to the offender' which justify not imposing a life
sentence (or its juvenile equivalent). In *Kelly* (1999), which reads like
a guideline, the Court of Appeal said that to be exceptional a
circumstance need not be unique or unprecedented or very rare, but it
could not be one that is regularly or routinely or normally encoun-
tered. The offender's youth at the time of the first offence, the long
interval between the two serious offences, their dissimilarity, and his
good conduct in the interval, could scarcely be called 'exceptional'.
It had been argued (not very plausibly) that Kelly presented no
continuing threat or danger to the public; but that did not alter the
Court's opinion. Whether mental disorder would justify the substitu-
tion of a hospital order (see chapter 10) has still to be decided.
Meanwhile it is noticeable that in the few cases in which judges have
been obliged to impose 'life' for non-fatal violence, they have
specified rather short minimum periods to be served before release
should be considered, in Kelly's case only three years. This does not,
however, seem contrary to the intention of the statute, which was that
release dates should be determined solely by the consideration of
public safety.

It is worth noting that the 1997 Act's list of 'serious offences' does
not include abortion, infanticide, possessing a Class A drug with
intent to supply it, or forgery of registers of births, deaths or
marriages. In practice the statutory power to impose 'life' for these
offences has not been used for many years, and seems to have been
more or less extinguished by the Court of Appeal's decision in
Robinson (1997). He had a long record of violence and attempts at
sexual offences and psychiatrists' reports met the criteria for 'life'.
His offence, however, was possession of an imitation firearm with
intent to commit burglary: he pleaded guilty but denied that he had
rape in mind this time. The trial judge understandably passed a life
sentence; but because the firearm was not a real one the Court of
Appeal held that the offence was not a violent one within the meaning
of the 1991 Act, and thus ruled out a longer-than-commensurate
sentence. Section 2(4) of the 1991 Act appears to say – in a rather
obscure way[7] – that a life sentence is longer than commensurate, so
that it can be imposed only for an offence which is a sexual or violent
offence within the definitions in that Act; and using an imitation
firearm is not. Nor, presumably, are abortion (at least when the mother

consents), possessing a Class A drug with intent to supply, or forging registers of births, deaths or marriages.

Aggravating 'life'

In theory a life sentence allows release at any stage, even after a few months. When the Murder (Abolition of Death Penalty) Bill. was being debated in the House of Lords, Lord Parker successfully moved an amendment to allow judges to recommend the minimum period which the murderer should serve, intending that in deserving cases short periods should be recommended. In practice this has not happened. The Court of Appeal laid down in *Flemming* (1973) that for murder they should not recommend less than 12 years. In murder cases recommendations cannot be the subject of appeal because they are not part of the sentence (*Bowden* (1983)). On the other hand judges who are passing discretionary life sentences for violent or sexual offences are expected to recommend minimum periods unless in their view the gravity of the offence calls for literal detention for life (s. 34, Criminal Justice Act 1991; and see the *Practice Direction* of 1993 in [1993] 1 WLR 223). Such recommendations are regarded as part of the sentence, and therefore appealable. At the end of that period the lifer is to be released unless the need to protect the public makes this inadvisable. In murder cases, but not others, the Home Secretary can adopt a longer or shorter period than that recommended by the judge,[8] a power which makes it all the harder to defend the absence of a right of appeal.

Mentally Disordered Offenders

The ways in which mental disorder (including personality disorder) is allowed to affect sentencing will be described in chapter 10, including the hospital order which substitutes compulsory admission to a psychiatric institution for any penalty. One section, however, of the Mental Health Act 1983 (s. 41) is designed to prevent release in cases in which the protection of the public is a consideration. The Crown Court can add a 'restriction order' to a hospital order if it thinks this necessary to protect the public from serious harm. The effect is that the offender-patient must not be discharged from hospital, transferred to another hospital or given temporary leave unless either the Home Secretary or a Mental Health Review Tribunal has agreed. What amount to guideline cases for the use of these orders are *Gardiner* (1967) and *Birch* (1989) which make a number of points. The first two are from *Gardiner* the rest from *Birch*:

(a)   although the statute allows the court to set a time-limit to the restriction this should be done 'only where the doctors are able to assert confidently that recovery will take place within a fixed period';

(b)   '. . .in the case of crimes of violence, and of the more serious sexual offences, particularly if the prisoner has a record of such offences, or if there is a history of mental disorder involving violent behaviour . . . there must be compelling reasons to explain why a restriction order should *not* be made' (my italics);

(c)   but '. . . there is nothing in the Act which requires a causal connection between the offender's mental state and the "index" offence';

(d)   a restriction order should never be used as a punishment, or merely to mark the gravity of the offence;

(e)   a restriction order can be made even when the psychiatrists are unanimous that it is not necessary;

(f)   the harm to be prevented must be serious but 'need not be limited to personal injury. Nor need it relate to the public in general, for it would suffice if a category of persons, or even a single person, were adjudged to be at risk';

(g)   'a minor offence by a man who proves to be mentally disordered and dangerous may properly leave him subject to a restriction'.

(h)   '. . the word "serious" qualifies harm rather than "risk". Thus the court is required to assess not the seriousness of the risk that the defendant will re-offend, but the risk that *if* he does so the public will suffer serious harm' [my italics].

The last of these points is particularly important because it is the clearest exposition of the Court of Appeal's attitude to the vexed question of probability, which is discussed later in this chapter. Read strictly it appears to say that the court does not have to worry about the probability of the offender's re-offending, only about the likely consequences *if* he does. Nothing so precise has been said by the Court about LTC sentences. The wording of the statute is similar; but the Court seems to think in terms of probability.

Points (f) and (g), however, demonstrate differences between the attitude of the Court of Appeal to offences by the mentally disordered and offences by others. Longer-than-commensurate and life sentences are to be used only for violent or sexual offences, whereas restriction orders may apparently be used to prevent other sorts of harm, defined only as 'serious'. In theory they could include serious financial harm (such as the malversation of pension funds). What is more, the 'index' offence for which the mentally disordered offender is receiving a restriction order does not itself have to be serious, it can be 'minor': occasional examples are theft, criminal damage and public order offences (Street, 1998). This is tough but realistic. An offence which has not inflicted serious harm can reveal an offender who may well do serious harm if not restrained. If so, however, why is the same logic not applied to offenders who are apparently not disordered? Is this an example of unthinking discrimination against the disordered?

Some judges add restriction orders almost automatically when an offender qualifies for a hospital order (Flood-Page and Mackie, 1998). Others distrust them because they allow offender-patients to be discharged by the decisions of local Mental Health Review Tribunals, whereas a long or indeterminate prison sentence means that release is controlled by the national Parole Board, with its greater experience. In *Howell* (1985) a judge who for this reason used a life sentence instead of a restriction order to deal with a schizophrenic rapist was rebuked by the Court of Appeal. In *Fleming* (1993), however, the Court upheld a life sentence even when a secure hospital bed had been offered, but only because Fleming, a homicidal man with diminished responsibility, had already been released from a restriction order by an over-optimistic Mental Health Review Tribunal, as a result of which he was now being dealt with for another homicide. Since Fleming was quickly transferred to Broadmoor he suffered no injustice.

Probability

It is clear from dicta in cases such as *Picker* (1970) and *Blackburn* (1979) that the judicial stereotype of mental disorder emphasises the unpredictability of its course. The future behaviour of non-disordered offenders is assumed to be more rational and more consistent with their present behaviour. Yet this scarcely justifies dismissing as insufficiently violent men such as *Bibby* (the knife-wielding robber

(1994)) or *Richart* (who threatened to kill (1995)). This emphasises the central difficulty of sentencing for dangerousness. The definition of the sorts of apprehended harms which are to justify prolonged detention calls for care – more care than it has received from draftsmen. But the crucial question is 'How probable must it be that the harm will be done?'. A crime that shows what the defendant is capable of doing may be harmful enough to create the right to *consider* such drastic interference with his liberty; but that consideration must take some account of the likelihood or unlikelihood of his doing it again. In *R v L* (1994) a stepfather had many times indecently assaulted his stepdaughters of 10 and 11 years of age, but the Court of Appeal reduced his LTC sentence of eight years to three years because it was told – and accepted – that he represented no danger to children who were not in his household.

This case is of the kind to which we cannot hope to apply actuarial reasoning. There are no statistics to tell us how often paedophiles who have – so far as is known – restricted their molestations to children in their own households have later molested children not in their households, or have managed to become members of other households containing children. We know that this has happened, but not its relative frequency. This is the state of our knowledge of most sexual offending, which so often takes place without being reported to the police, that figures from follow-ups can lead only to underestimates. This is less true of non-sexual violence. Several sound follow-ups of large samples tell us that the probability of a repetition increases with each successive conviction. It is low at first – around one in five – but high after four or more convictions for violence[9] – around four in five. As for indictable offences in general there is the much more precise Offender Group Reconviction Scale[10] which uses age, gender, offence-type and previous record to estimate fairly accurately the probability of an individual's reconviction within two years.

As critics of the scale point out, however, this kind of probability is not a property or attribute of the individual. All it says is that so far as variables *x, y, z* can tell us, the group of people he most resembles is the group of which such and such a percentage were reconvicted of indictable offences within (so many) years of being sentenced. There may be some feature not taken account of by the prediction formula (for example because it is an infrequent feature, such as a progressively disabling disease) which makes it highly unlikely that this person will be reconvicted (just as some infrequent feature, such as membership of the Mafia, might make it much likelier than the formula suggests). In practice, while the scale offers useful estimates of the likelihood of a reconviction for offences of dishonesty because such reconvictions are frequent, convictions for violent and sexual offences are far too infrequent to be the subjects of accurate prediction tables. It is not only a statistical fact that the rarer the type of offence the greater must be the rate of false predictions: there are practical difficulties as well:

(a)   an experiment would be necessary which would allow individuals who have shown themselves capable of serious violence or sexual molestation to remain free (perhaps even unsupervised) in order to see which of them repeats his type of offence and which does not;

(b)   long follow-ups would be required, and the longer the follow-up the greater the likelihood that the offender will be put out of action by death, emigration, illness, imprisonment for some non-violent or non-sexual offence or some other irrelevant factor;

(c)   his chances of committing a violent or sexual offence, as the case may be, without being detected or reported to the police are by no means negligible, especially if his tendency is to molest people who do not know him.

It follows that any witness who offers a court a percentage probability that a violent or sexual offender will repeat his offence should be distrusted. In any case, where danger is concerned the use of numerical probabilities encourages pseudo-scientific statements of the kind *danger = harm × probability*, which can yield nonsensical results: for example that a compulsive indecent exposer is more dangerous than a rapist with one rape to his credit.

The alternative is what is called 'clinical prediction', based not on assigning individuals to groups of supposedly similar individuals but on careful investigation of the individuals' own careers, attention to their own accounts of their motivation and study of the circumstances in which they offended. Clinical prediction does not offer probabilities expressed in spurious percentages. What it can do is make one of the following four statements about the defendant:

(a)   that his offence shows that he is *capable* of, say, sexual molestation, but that nothing he has said or done at other times suggests that he is likely to repeat it; or

(b)   that he is capable of it, and that what he has done at other times, or said in interviews, suggests that *given a similar situation* he is likely to do the same; or

(c)   that (b) seems to be true, but also that he seems to find himself *in similar situations more often than would be expected to happen by mere chance*; or

(d)   that (b) and (c) are true, and that his *modus operandi* or other evidence indicates that he *seeks or makes opportunities* for his offences.

The reports which 'clinicians' – whether they are psychiatrists, psychologists or probation officers – render to sentencers should point to one of these four possible conclusions. Obviously the four categories are meant to indicate different levels of probability. But they do not justify estimates expressed in percentages. On the assumption that the harm in question is of a kind which calls for precautionary detention, statements of type (c) and (d) justify prolonging it. Statements of type (a) do not; and statements of type (b) may or may not, depending on the likelihood that the offender will find himself under the same conditions (for example because of his occupation, leisure pursuits or lifestyle). Occasionally, of course, there will be circumstances, such as physical disablement, which rule out the possibility of a repetition of a violent or sexual offence. This is the logic of the sentencer's situation.

Whose Risk?

Sentencers who are conscious of the risk involved in allowing an offender to be free sometimes reason as if the risk is wholly theirs. *Simcox's* first wife divorced him for violence. He strangled his second wife. His death sentence was commuted because Parliament was debating the future of capital punishment. After serving 10 years of his life sentence he was released on licence, and soon married again. It was not long before his third wife became afraid of him and went to live with her mother. In 1963 he was found prowling round their house with a firearm, and brought to court. The judge was reluctant to revoke his licence because he had spent so many years in prison, but his probation officer was apprehensive and said that to leave him at large would be 'a calculated risk'. The judge retorted that 'the risk would be taken by me and the calculations made by the probation service'. The wife was not asked whether she was prepared to take the risk. The Home Office could have recalled Simcox to prison for breaching the conditions of his licence, but did not feel justified in overriding the judge. Eleven days later Simcox wounded his wife and her brother, killed her sister, and shot himself in the stomach. He was again sentenced to death, and his appeal on the ground of diminished responsibility was dismissed. The sentence was commuted to 'life' because it was regarded as inhumane to hang a man doubled up in a wheelchair. He died in prison some years later.[11]

Compassionate Risk-taking

At least another chapter would be needed to deal with the problems involved in deciding whether it is safe to release a prisoner or patient. They are outside the scope of this book; but two points can be made briefly. One is that there is a tendency on the part of the Parole Board and Mental Health Review Tribunals (but not, on the whole, the Home Office) to take a compassionate risk when deciding whether to release, on the assumption that skilled supervision will compensate for the risk. The unlikelihood that supervision will be adequate will be made clear in the next chapter.

Conditions of Detention

One other point, however, needs to be made. In almost every long sentence there comes a stage when it can no longer be argued that further detention is justified by desert or deterrence, and when it can be justified only by the belief that it is needed to protect others from some sort of harm. At that stage the offender is being disadvantaged solely in order to safeguard other people's quality of life. This is not inherently objectionable, but it seems to create an obligation to enhance the quality of his or her life in detention as much as is consistent with security. A formal acknowledgement of this obligation by those responsible for prisons and hospitals would establish an important humanitarian principle.

NOTES

1.   In this context the word 'serious' sets a higher standard than in section 1 of the Criminal Justice Act 1991, which merely draws a

distinction between offences of a kind which justify custodial sentences and those which do not (see chapter 4).

2.   The source is the Parole Board's *Report for 1996/1997*. Sentences of seven or more years are excluded because in their case the Parole Board merely advises and does not take the decision.

3.   Since custodial sentences in summary courts are subject (with exceptions) to a maximum of six months, section 25 of the 1991 Act allows a summary court to commit a convicted offender to the Crown Court with a view to a LTC sentence if he appears to meet the statutory criteria.

4.   Successive committees, however, have strongly recommended that it should be discretionary (as it is for attempted murder); and this symbolic anomaly can hardly survive criticism much longer.

5.   Except in those rare cases in which the prisoner is clearly so mentally disordered and dangerous to himself or to others that compulsory admission to hospital can be arranged.

6.   If the offender is under the age of 18 the court is allowed but not compelled to impose the juvenile equivalent of life: see chapter 9.

7.   Section 2(4) reads: 'A custodial sentence for an indeterminate period shall be regarded for the purposes of subsection (2) and (3) above as a custodial sentence for a term longer than any actual term'.

8.   In murder cases, according to one Home Secretary's statement, his aim is sometimes to maintain public confidence in the system, which comes close to saying 'the public decides'.

9.   See the table in Walker (1985), para 22.41.

10.   See Walker and Padfield (1996, Appendix C).

11.   My sources are the unpublished transcript of the sentencing proceedings and a personal communication.

Chapter 6
Non-Custodial Precautions

Anti-protectionists do not raise objections to non-custodial precautions, such as disqualifications from driving or teaching children. Non-custodial precautions are obviously less objectionable, being directed at activities of the specific kind which led to the harm done, whereas custody interferes with a wide range of activities, few of which are relevant. It is unfortunate that non-custodial precautions are much less effective.

The commonest of them is disqualification from driving. For some offences the Road Traffic Offenders Act 1988 leaves it to the court to decide whether to order this; but bitter experience has shown that magistrates, most of them motorists themselves, may be too lenient, so that for many sorts of improper driving disqualification is now mandatory. Even so, the mandatory periods are short.

'Special Reasons' and 'Mitigating Grounds'

Mandatory disqualification from driving is interesting because it is the only penalty for which legislators as well as the Court of Appeal have tried to limit mitigation. The Road Traffic Act 1972 (s. 93) allows a court to refrain from an obligatory disqualification (or indeed endorsement) for one of three 'special reasons':

(a)   if the offence is merely one of aiding, abetting, counselling or procuring the offence, and not of committing or attempting it;

(b)   if the court makes a hospital or guardianship order without convicting a mentally disordered offender (a stipulation which seems to ignore the precautionary nature of disqualification);

(c)   if the court decides that there are 'special reasons' or 'mitigating grounds' for refraining from disqualification (mitigating grounds may also allow disqualification for a shorter period than the statutory minimum).

A 'special reason' must fulfil all of four criteria (*Wickins* (1958)), confirming earlier rulings, such as Lord Goddard's in *Whittall* v *Kirby* (1947):

(a)   it must be a 'mitigating or extenuating circumstance';

(b)   'it must not amount in law to a defence to the charge';

(c)   it 'must be directly connected with the commission of the offence' (thus ruling out hardship resulting from the disqualification);

(d)   it must be a matter 'which the court ought properly to take into consideration when imposing punishment'.

These should probably be regarded as guidelines. Note the use of the word 'punishment'. Originally, of course, the aim of disqualification was the protection of other road-users from harm, and the punishment consisted of a fine or imprisonment. This no longer seems to be so. References to 'punishment' and 'mitigation' in these and more recent cases confirm that the Court of Appeal sees disqualification – at least for the short periods which are mandatory – as something other than a precaution: perhaps as just deserts, certainly as a deterrent. Legislators too have drifted into this approach. Only a retributivist would make an exception of a mentally disordered person because he had not been convicted. And section 39 of the Crime (Sentences) Act 1997 envisages[1] disqualification as a penalty for offences which have nothing to do with driving. It is a point to which I shall return.

Lord Goddard's four criteria seem to allow a wide variety of special reasons. From the long list in Wilkinson (1995) some examples are:

(a)   driving for a very short distance and in circumstances in which the driver was unlikely to encounter any other road-users;

(b)   being misled as to the constituents of a drink;
(c)   having to drive in an emergency when there was no practicable alternative.

More instructive, however, are clear statements of what are *not* acceptable as special reasons:

(a)   being of good character, with a good driving record: *Whittall* v *Kirby* (1947);
(b)   the hardship that will be experienced by the offender, his family or employer (*ibid.*);
(c)   the fact that the offender is a doctor or in some other occupation in which service to the public requires him to drive (*Holroyd* v *Berry* (1973));
(d)   the fact that the offence itself was not serious (*Nicholson* v *Brown* (1974)).

Unless the prosecution admits the facts offered as special reasons the defence must establish them by evidence on a balance of probabilities, and not merely as a reasonable possibility (*Pugsley* v *Hunter* (1973)). 'Mitigating grounds' are relevant only when the court is considering whether to refrain from a 'totting-up' disqualification, or whether to disqualify for less than the mandatory minimum period. Section 35 of the Road Traffic Offenders Act 1988 says that the court must have regard to all the circumstances which are not excluded, but then excludes:

(a)   any circumstance alleged to make the offence or any of the offences for which penalty points were incurred not a serious one;
(b)   hardship, other than exceptional hardship: this includes hardship to people other than the driver. Wilkinson (1995) suggests that exceptional hardship must mean hardship experienced as a result of special circumstances, as distinct from the hardship experienced by anyone prohibited from driving;
(c)   any circumstances which, within the three years immediately preceding the conviction, have been taken into account as mitigating grounds in connection with disqualification from driving. (The justice of this will be discussed in chapter 8, under 'The effect of the sentence on others'.)

Although even a magistrates' court can disqualify a driver for life the Court of Appeal is as reluctant to approve this as it is to approve life sentences of imprisonment. *Nevison's* (1995) life disqualification was upheld only because the Court was told that his dependency on alcohol would be lifelong. *McCluskie's* (1992) was not, in spite of a much worse driving record. The Court said that at 'a more mature age' (he was 44) he might be able to drive responsibly without excess alcohol. It was not clear on what evidence this hope was based.

Other Disqualifications

This formidable mixture of statute and case-law demonstrates the lengths to which legislators and the Court of Appeal have gone in order to counter the influence which a professional defence can have on magistrates and even judges. It can be contrasted with the comparative freedom which courts have when disqualifying someone from directing a company, under section 2 of the Company Directors Disqualification Act 1986. Apart from setting a maximum period of 15 years the Act provides no rules.[2] In *Sevenoaks Stationery (Retail) Ltd* (1991) a court adopted the Official Receiver's proposal that there should be three 'brackets': 10 to 15 years for the most serious types of case, six to ten years for fairly serious cases, and two to five years for 'not very serious' cases, and the Court of Appeal has referred respectfully to this in later cases. Yet it has also held that a disqualification of this kind should not be used if it would prevent the company director from making enough money to pay a compensation order (*Holmes* (1992)), which seems to override the precautionary function of disqualification.

Young's case (1990) demonstrated that the Court of Appeal some-times reasons retributively in such cases. The trial judge had clearly considered Young hardly to blame for doing what as an undischarged bankrupt he should not have done, and let him off with a conditional discharge, but at the same time imposed a two-year disqualification. On appeal the disqualification was quashed, as inconsistent with the absence of culpability implied by a conditional discharge.

The Court of Appeal often uses the word 'punishment', however, when it seems to have in mind deterrence rather than retribution. In *Griffiths* (1997) it argued that:

. . . other factors come into play in the wider interests of protecting the public, namely a deterrent element . . . In spite of the fact that the courts have said that disqualification is not a punishment, in truth the exercise that is being engaged in is little different from any sentencing exercise. The period of disqualification has to reflect the gravity of the offence and certain deterrent elements . . . It would not send out a wrong message to fix the period of disqualification by starting with an assessment of the gravity of the conduct, and then allowing for the mitigating factors, in much the same way as a sentencing court would do.

The main points made are that disqualification can properly be used to deter potential offenders, and that like any other sort of penalty it can be mitigated; but nothing is said as to what can and what cannot mitigate. Still less guidance is on offer where other precautionary orders are concerned, even those which are mandatory. Examples can be found in the

Protection of Animals Act 1911
Food and Drugs Act 1955
Licensing Act 1964
Gaming Act 1968
Firearms Act 1968
Medicines Act 1968
Juries Act 1974
Dangerous Wild Animals Act 1976
Licensed Premises (Exclusion of Certain Persons) Act 1980
Representation of the People Act 1983
Public Order Act 1986
Education Reform Act 1988
Children Act 1989
Public Bodies Corrupt Practices Act 1989
Football Spectators Act 1989.

Most of these statutes rely on courts' discretion to apply the disqualification; but some make it automatic. (For example a custodial sentence of three years or more prohibits the possession of firearms and ammunition.) In other cases it is left to Chief Constables or specialist authorities such as the General Medical Council, with the possibility of appeals to a court.

A few of the restrictions in these Acts are easily enforceable. An example is a ban on entering specified public houses. Most, however, are easy to evade. The most carelessly drafted was probably the section in the Football Spectators Act 1989 (s. 15) which allowed a court to required a football hooligan to report to a police station at the time of certain matches. Failure to do so can lead to a custodial sentence; but until he fails he cannot be prevented from going to a match. He cannot even be arrested when about to board a plane which will make it impossible for him to report to the police station at the time of the match. By the end of 1997 only 10 such orders had been made. Courts were either overlooking their power or recognising its ineffectiveness. The Crime and Disorder Act 1998 (s. 84) merely increased the penalties for non-compliance; but by the end of 1998 the Home Office was considering legislation which seemed likely to be more effective.

List 99

Far from futile is the power of the Secretary of State for Education and Employment, under the Education Acts, to bar the employment of a person as a teacher in schools or further education institutions, or as a worker with children or young persons. There is a register of those who have been barred, with the discreet but sinister title 'List 99'. Barring is automatic in the case of anyone who pleads guilty or is found guilty of a serious sexual offence which involves a child under 16. For a number of other specified types of offence – sexual, drug-related, violent and dishonest – it is discretionary. It is also discretionary for misconduct which is not a criminal offence – for example a sexual or 'otherwise inappropriate' relationship with a pupil.[3] There is no appeal to an independent authority, but the Secretary of State can sometimes be persuaded that the bar was unjustified or is no longer necessary for the protection of pupils. Otherwise inclusion in List 99 is permanent (unlike most other disqualifications). When one considers that it usually deprives a teacher of the only sort of job for which he is professionally qualified, and when one compares the system with the disqualifications ordered by criminal courts, the extent of the Minister's unfettered discretion is remarkable. By way of contrast the Department of Health merely operates what it calls 'a consultancy service' from which local authorities and voluntary organisations can – but are not obliged to – seek information about applicants for posts involving child care. The service notes convictions of people who were at the time employed in child care, and encourages employers to report the circumstances of relevant resignations and dismissals; but employers are not required to inform or consult the service, and are not debarred from appointing anyone about whom the service provides discouraging information.

A more rigorous system will be created if the Protection of Children Bill is enacted without drastic amendments. Child care organisations will be obliged (and other organisations allowed) to report to the Department of Health individuals whom they have dismissed, transferred or suspended for 'misconduct' or 'incompetence' which harmed or risked harming a child, whether or not law enforcement agencies have been involved. (Resignation or retirement in such circumstances will not protect the individual from being reported). The Secretary of State will include him in the new list if he agrees that it was reasonable to consider him 'guilty of misconduct or incompetence', and if he therefore considers him 'unsuitable to work with children'. Child care organisations will be obliged to consult the list when filling 'child care positions', and will not be allowed to appoint listed persons. Other organisations proposing to fill a child care position, and nursing agencies, will be allowed to consult the list, and (apparently) to use their discretion as regards the appointment of listed persons. There will now be a tribunal to deal with appeals. The Bill provides for the eventual extension of the system to protect the mentally impaired, subject to Parliament's concurrence.

General

Von Hirsch and Wasik (1997) have made four points about disqualifications, and with some force. First, they should never be imposed as punishments, only as precautions. By 'punishments' they mean retributive penalties. They do not discuss the Court of Appeal's argument that disqualifications can protect the public not only by incapacitating but also by functioning as general deterrents. This has a bearing on proportionality. Since disqualifications must not be retributive they should be proportional, in von Hirsch's and Wasik's view, not to the gravity or culpability of the committed offence but to the gravity of what the offender might do in the future if not disqualified. If the

Court of Appeal's argument, however, is accepted it would justify also taking into account the harm that might result if potential imitators were not deterred.

Secondly they propose, persuasively, that precautionary disqualifications should be used only if the offender's conviction gives real grounds for apprehension that he will (i) abuse a fiduciary position (for example as a company director); (ii) take advantage of especially vulnerable people or (iii) engage incompetently in an activity that is hazardous to others (driving a motor vehicle being the obvious example). Most of the disqualifications listed above seem intended for use in this discriminating way, but in von Hirsch's and Wasik's view are used too routinely. They find one or two even more objectionable on the ground that they reduce offenders to 'second-class citizens': for example when automatically depriving prisoners of a vote during their sentence.

Interestingly, however, they argue for one exception to their own principles. They acknowledge that it is advisable to disqualify a person from holding some types of appointment because of a conviction which suggests not that he will abuse the appointment, or risk harming others, but simply that he will so diminish his standing and authority that he will not be able to carry out his duties properly. Their example is a judge convicted of a domestic assault, but a similar argument could be applied to persons in positions of leadership, whether military, political or religious.

They are unhappy, however, about any sort of automatic disqualification which excludes a proper assessment of the risk involved in each individual case. One might well agree in principle; but if the principle were applied to driving disqualifications summary courts would have difficulty in dealing with the volume of business. Worse, they would return to the idiosyncratic local decisions of the past, which led, as we have seen, to the strict rules laid down by statute and case-law.

Criminal Record Certificates

Not all non-custodial precautions rely on the offender to comply. The List 99 system for protecting pupils has already been described. From time to time Governments have considered proposals for making it possible to ban individuals convicted of offences against children from entering into types of employment which involve the care of children (for example the proposal of the Advisory Council on the Penal System (1970)); but so far without adopting them. Instead a much more elaborate and comprehensive precautionary scheme has now been embodied in the Police Act 1997 (but is unlikely to be brought into operation before the end of 1999). It will create three kinds of certificate: criminal conviction certificates, criminal record certificates and enhanced criminal record certificates. The first kind will deal only with convictions which have not become 'spent' (i.e. deniable) under the Rehabilitation of Offenders Act 1974 (see chapter 8 under 'Stigma'). It will be obtainable by anyone, and any employer who thinks it worth the trouble will be allowed to demand it. The second kind will list spent as well as unspent convictions, and cautions, and will be obtainable by a prospective employer only if his application is countersigned by a registered body which represents employers who are allowed by the Rehabilitation of Offenders Act 1974 to ask about unspent convictions because of the nature of their work. The third kind, 'enhanced criminal record certificates' will deal with spent and unspent convictions, cautions and (be it noted) any other information which the police think it proper to mention. This kind too will be obtainable only with the countersignature of a registered body, in this case acting on behalf of employers who care for, train, or supervise juveniles, or who are involved in the gaming industry. There will no doubt be employers who will not bother to ask for certificates, or who are not represented by the necessary registered body. There will also be 'civil liberty' problems of the kind discussed by Uglow (1998): for example the disclosure of offences which are stigmatising but irrelevant to the job for which a person is applying.

Registers of Sexual Offenders

It is sexual offenders, however, who have been singled out in the nineties for the most drastic non-custodial precautions. The Sexual Offenders Act 1997 requires them to notify local police of their names and addresses, and any changes of either. It applies only to scheduled types of sexual offence (but against adults as well as children), and only to offenders who were convicted or cautioned on or after 1 September 1997,[4] or were at that date awaiting sentence, in prison, subject to compulsory supervision, serving a community sentence, detained in hospital or under Mental Health Act guardianship for a scheduled offence. The requirement to keep the police informed of name and address lasts for different periods, modelled on the Reha-bilitation of Offenders Act 1974; but after a custodial sentence of 30 months or more, or a hospital order with restrictions, the period is indeterminate. Schools and other organisations which care for children will be able to ask police whether anyone on the register is living or working in their area; but police will be allowed discretion in answering questions. In *Thorpe and another* (1998) the Court of Appeal endorsed the Home Office's advice to police on disclosing information:[5]

> There was no formal procedure with which the police should be obliged to comply. The police should be allowed to act in a sensible and pragmatic way . . .

The Court acknowledged, however, that information should be dis-closed only when there was a pressing need for it. The social consequences of being identified – especially by neighbours – as a sexual offender can be very unpleasant. At least one judge has mitigated a prison sentence (for indecently assaulting a 13-year-old girl) to take account of this (*Daily Telegraph*, 29 September 1997). The sentence was already very short (nine months) and the reduction was trivial (to six months), but the effect was that the man would be on the register for only seven years instead of 10.

Sex Offender Orders

Teeth were added to registration by the Crime and Disorder Act 1998 (s. 2), which allows Chief Constables to persuade magistrates' courts that a sexual offender has 'acted . . . in such a way as to give reasonable cause to believe that an order . . . is necessary to protect the public from serious harm from him'. The offender need not necessarily be on the register: his conviction,[6] caution[7] or sentence may have taken place well before 1 September 1997. The action leading to the order, however, must have occurred since his last conviction or caution for a sexual offence. The prohibitions in the order should be those necessary to protect the public from serious harm from the defendant. No doubt the Home Secretary had in mind behaviour such as frequenting places where children congregate. Orders will have effect for at least five years, but can be varied on application by either party. Disobedience will risk a fine or imprisonment (with a maximum of five years on indictment). A sexual offender order is very like a disqualification: it threatens but does not impede.

Retroactivity

What is most unusual about these orders is the definition of a sexual offender. Not only does it include anyone convicted of or cautioned for one of the types of sexual offence listed in the 1991 Act (or found not guilty of one by reason of insanity): it includes people 'punished' abroad for such offences. More interesting still, it includes people convicted, cautioned or punished abroad *before the 1998 Act came into operation*. If a sex offender order is regarded as part of the penalty this breaches the principle that offenders should not be penalised in a way that would not have been allowable when they committed their offences. The Sexual Offenders Act 1997 also breached it when it required registration not only by offenders convicted or cautioned on or after 1 September 1997 but also by those awaiting sentence, serving custodial or community sentences, under supervision or subject to hospital orders as a result of sexual offences committed well before that date. I cannot recollect any similar breaches of the principle in post-war penal legislation. It is arguable that compulsory registration is not a penalty; but the imposition of restrictions by means of an order is not very different from a disqualification. It is true that some disqualifications can be imposed without a conviction or a caution. Drivers can have their licences withdrawn for guiltless medical reasons. Yet when the reason *is* guilt retroactivity is – or should be – objectionable to retributivists, although not, of course, to utilitarians.

Anti-social Behaviour Orders

Another precautionary device in the 1998 Act (s. 1), not limited to sexual offences, is the 'anti-social behaviour order'. The Chief Constable or the council for the local government area can apply for this to a magistrates' court. It prohibits a person or persons from specified behaviour in order to protect people in the area from 'harassment, alarm or distress'. The Home Office's circular 38/1998 explains that such orders are 'intended to be used to put an end to persistent and serious anti-social behaviour . . . not minor disputes between neighbours'. Orders will be in force for at least two years, and cannot be 'discharged' earlier without the consent of the parties. Breaches without reasonable excuse risk fines or custodial sentences, up to a maximum of five years on indictment.

Efficacy

Non-custodial precautions are obviously less likely than detention to achieve their purpose. Excessive reliance on compulsory supervision when seriously harmful offenders are released has already been mentioned (in chapter 5 under 'Compassionate risk-taking'). The 1998 Act (s. 58) allows judges who are passing custodial sentences of four years or more to add to the 'custodial period' an 'extension period' of supervision (and possible recall to custody). If the offence was sexual the extension period can be as long as ten years: if violent, five years. Even the most experienced probation officer, however, cannot reduce the risk of reoffending more than slightly. In practice being supervised means attending the local probation office at regular intervals for an interview with a probation officer or – in a minority of cases – participation in a group discussions intended to improve anger-management or attitudes to sex offences. The office's records are supposed to include descriptions of the offender's offences and what leads up to them, but the records are often inadequate (see Shaw, 1991 and the Home Office Probation Inspectorate's 1998 report). In 1998 Hedderman and Vennard studied 107 murders, rapes and other serious offences committed over a few months by men and women while under the supervision of probation officers. Deficiencies in supervision had been identified in 42 of the cases. In recent years a series of Home Office inspections and circulars has demonstrated increasing concern about standards of supervision. It is only realistic to acknowledge that there are some serious offences which even the most conscientious probation department cannot be expected to prevent, especially when made responsible, willy-nilly, for an 'opportunity-maker' (see chapter 5). A supervisor can reduce risk by frequent contact with a supervisee, but he cannot be at his elbow. A supervisor's only effective power is to recommend recall to prison or hospital when he has cause for concern, and his recommendation must be convincing. Yet supervision is often assumed by decision-makers to be little short of surveillance.

As for disqualifications, they are no more than prohibitions backed up by threats which impress only the law-abiding. Unless one is well known to the local police, or has hostile and watchful neighbours, the risk of detection when driving while disqualified is low, and the probability of a custodial sentence lower still (lower than for obtaining a driving licence by deception!). The same is true of most other disqualifications and prohibitions. Nearly all, too, are subject to appeal, and long-term driving disqualifications are not infrequently cut short in this way.

Prevention

Genuine non-custodial prevention is another matter, but opportunities for it are rare and special. Motor vehicles can be permanently confiscated, but only when used for the commission of an offence carrying two years' imprisonment or more (s. 43 of the Powers of Criminal Courts Act 1973). Some sexual offenders can be persuaded (but not compelled) to accept long-lasting injections of libido-reducing drugs. Other drugs can be used to calm – not cure – mental disorders which predispose to violence. Tagging has yet to be developed in such a way as to make adequate surveillance of sexual offenders practicable. Failing such expedients it is not surprising that courts feel forced to resort to detention when the likelihood of grave harm seems substantial. The result, however, is often a determinate sentence so short that it merely postpones the risk.

NOTES

1.   'Envisages' because it allows this use of disqualification only by courts which have been notified by the Home Secretary that they can exercise this power (s. 39(3)).

2.   It is worth noting that section 6 of the Act allows a Chancery court to impose a similar disqualification, but subject to a lower maximum period of 5 years, when a company director has not been

convicted of any offence but the court is satisfied that he is unfit to manage a limited liability company. It is possible to justify the difference between the maxima of section 2 and section 6 by arguing that section 6 is designed for cases of incompetence, not criminality. Yet incompetence is even less likely to diminish over time.

3. The quotation is from the Department's Circular 11 of 1995, which describes the system in detail.

4. It will of course be several decades before the registers can be expected to include all or nearly all the names of living sexual offenders. There are thousands at liberty who completed their sentences or periods of compulsory supervision before 1 September 1997, and who will have to die to make the registers comprehensive.

5. In Home Office Circular 39/1997.

6. Or an acquittal by reason of insanity, or a punishment abroad for a sexual offence.

7. Or a reprimand or warning for a sexual offence while he was a juvenile (see chapter 9).

PART III
MITIGATION

Chapter 7
Statutory and Miscellaneous Pleas

Mitigation, like aggravation, is usually, though not always, based on retributive reasoning, which concludes either that the offender's culpability was not as great as the nature of the offence suggested or that, while he was fully culpable he will suffer more than most offenders would from the normal penalty – that is, suffer more than is intended. Occasionally, as we shall also see, the sentencer has in mind a third sort of consideration: that the offender has behaved in a meritorious way which, though it affects neither his culpability nor his sensitivity to the penalty, should count in his favour. Sometimes, however, a sentencer reasons non-retributively. He may wish to lubricate the wheels of justice by rewarding the defendant's cooperation. He may have hopes that the offender's personality or circumstances are such that a rehabilitative or nominal measure will be enough to render him law-abiding. He may have in mind the harm that custody will inflict on the offender's dependants – but that, and mental disorder, youth and gender, are the subjects of later chapters.

STATUTORY CONSIDERATIONS

Sentencers are encouraged by statute (s. 3 of the Criminal Justice Act 1991) to take into account a wider range of considerations when mitigating than when aggravating penalties. It is only 'information about the circumstances of the offence' which can aggravate; but 'nothing in this part of this Act[1] shall prevent a court from mitigating an offence by taking into account *any such matters as in the opinion of the court are relevant* in mitigation of sentence' (s. 28: my italics). Before forming an opinion as to the propriety and length of a custodial sentence a court is required to obtain and consider a pre-sentence report on the offender, unless, when the offence is of the serious kind that is triable only on indictment, it decides that a pre-sentence report is unnecessary (s. 3)

Pleading Guilty

There are only two factors, however, which the statutes *oblige* sentencers to consider as possible mitigations. When the defendant pleads guilty the court '*shall* take into account the stage of the proceedings at which he indicated his intention of doing so, and the circumstances in which this indication was given' (s. 48, Criminal Justice and Public Order Act 1994, which recognised a long-standing practice of the Crown Court). When the Crime (Sentences) Act 1997 introduced a minimum custodial sentence of seven years for a third conviction of trafficking in a Class A drug it limited the allowance for a guilty plea to one-fifth of the minimum sentence; but in no other circumstances do the statutes themselves guide sentencers. The Court of Appeal has suggested one-third of the sentence (for example in *Buffrey* (1993)); and the Magistrates' Association's *Sentencing Guidelines 1997* make the same suggestion for a 'timely' plea. A third sounds a generous fraction; but when only half of the sentence is served in custody it reduces the half by a mere sixth. The plea does not appear to tip the balance against a custodial sentence, only to reduce it (Flood-Page and Mackie, 1998). It can also reduce a fine or the hours of community service.

The circumstances in which the guilty plea is tendered may suggest that it was voluntary and praiseworthy (for example intended to save the victim of a sexual offence from having to testify), or merely that it was more or less forced by the weight of the evidence, in which case no allowance might be granted (as in *Hastings* (1996)). The stage at which the defendant takes the decision is important because an early indication saves courts more time and trouble than a late one. It is worth noting, however, that in Moxon's (1988) sample of cases, taken before the 1994 Act, late decisions seemed to earn larger allowances than early ones. The explanation may be that *changes* of plea in court made more impression on judges. Moxon estimated the average allowance as about 20 per cent, but as much as 50 per cent was deducted in a case in which the offender gave himself up voluntarily to the police before detection. As has been said, the justification for such allowances may be mere expediency – encouragement to save trouble – or moral credit if the offender convinces the court that he acted from remorse or consideration for his victim; but since offenders are supposed to know that a timely plea will be rewarded sentencers can be forgiven for being cynical. These allowances are among the practices which have been criticised as 'oiling the conveyor belt'; but without oil it would grind to a halt.

A guilty plea can on occasion be a safeguard. *Latham* (1996) had pleaded guilty to manslaughter with a knife, having been 'properly advised' that the tariff was about seven years' imprisonment. The Attorney-General referred the sentence to the Court of Appeal, arguing that the tariff itself was too low (the first occasion on which he challenged the tariff). The Court of Appeal agreed that it should be increased to between 10 and 12 years, but said that it would be wrong to increase *Latham's* sentence in view of the understanding on which he had pleaded guilty.

The Totality Principle

Another principle now recognised by statute is 'the totality principle', although it was enunciated in one of the Court of Appeal's earliest cases. If an offender is receiving more than one custodial sentence or fine 'nothing in this Part [of the Criminal Justice Act 1991] shall prevent a court . . . from applying any rule of law as to the totality of sentences' (s. 28). This endorses the Court of Appeal's view that even when each of the sentences were in themselves correct they might add up to a penalty which was excessive. An example was *Hunter* (1979), whose total of eight years for a series of indecent assaults was reduced to six. The justification of the principle cannot be that it oils the conveyor belt, still less that it is likely to reduce the crime rate. Arguably it is a subtle piece of retributive arithmetic: that eight years' imprisonment is excessive because it is more than four times as severe as two years. It may even be a rare example of a limit to severity which is based on humanity rather than desert or utility (see chapter 1). It applies even when an offender is being sentenced while an earlier suspended sentence is being activated, as the Court of Appeal made clear in *Taylor* (1997). It also applies to multiple fines (*Birchall* (1989)). Whether it applies to community service is undetermined.

Concurrent Sentencing

The totality principle often prompts a court to make two custodial sentences concurrent when they could properly be consecutive. An example is *Morgan* (1971). He had received sentences of seven, four and three years, all consecutive, but because he was only 19 the Court of Appeal made them concurrent. Although the statutes are silent on the subject, it is regarded as proper to make sentences consecutive if they are for unconnected offences, but concurrent if the offences are committed 'in the same transaction' (*Faulkner* (1972)): a doctrine which Lord Chief Justice Lane called 'binding' in *French* (1982)). Thus sentences for driving with excess blood-alcohol and while disqualified should be concurrent (*Jones* (1980)). Yet *Wheatley* (1983), for example, received consecutive sentences for the same driving offences as *Jones*, and this was upheld because he had so many similar convictions.

'Transaction' seems to cover even a series of similar – for example sexual – offences against the same victim (as in *Lewis* (1972)) but not apparently a series with different victims (see *Birch* (1971)). The distinction calls for subtle reasoning. It is easier to see why a sentence for assaulting an arresting police officer should be consecutive to the sentence for the offence for which the arrest was being made (as in *Hill* (1985)), or why the same rule applies to burglary accompanied by violence against someone who interrupts the burglary (as in *Bunch* (1971)). The distinction seems to be between an additional offence which the offender could not avoid committing if he was to commit the principal offence, and one which was supererogatory. This does not, however, explain the distinction between series of offences with the same and different victims. In practice this is sometimes disregarded. *Rogers* (1998) received consecutive sentences although the victim of his series of burglaries was the same 87-year-old woman.

Equally intriguing is the question whether determinate and indeterminate sentences should ever be consecutive. It was raised by *Jones'* case (1961). He was serving a 14-year sentence when a court added a consecutive life sentence. The Court of Appeal took the unusual step of consulting the Attorney-General as *amicus curiae*, and was told only that it had no practical effect but was undesirable, which they accepted. A few months later *Foy* (1962), who had committed robbery with violence and other crimes, appealed against the 14-year sentences which had been made consecutive to his life sentence. Although he abandoned the appeal against sentence the Court commented that it was

> not a valid sentence. Life imprisonment means imprisonment for life. No doubt many people come out . . . while they are still alive, but . . . it is only on licence, and the sentence [of imprisonment] remains on him till he dies. Accordingly, if the court passes a sentence . . . consecutive to life, the sentence is no sentence at all in that it cannot operate until the prisoner dies.

So the sentences should have been concurrent. The Court's reasoning seems artificial, especially now that most life sentences are accompanied by specified minimum periods to be served (see chapter 5). There would be no illogicality in deciding that a lifer who had served the specified period and could be released without risk to the public should nevertheless serve at least part of a sentence for another crime, again in the interests of retribution or deterrence. Only the totality principle might make this seem a little heartless. This may be why the Court of Appeal interfered with *Nugent's* (1984) sentences. He had been given life for each of four rapes, and concurrently several consecutive determinate sentences, totalling 25 years for arson and robberies. The court reduced some of the determinate sentences and made others concurrent, so as to add up to 15 years, with the intention that, allowing for remission, they would not interfere with the Home Secretary's discretion to release him on a lifer's licence after 10 years. No doubt for similar reasons in *Brown* (1998) the Court thought it 'a little odd' to make a three-year sentence consecutive to a 10-year LTC one and made it concurrent.

A consecutive sentence can have the effect of converting a short-term prisoner into a long-term one (i.e. one serving four or more years), so that – if the Parole Board think fit – his release may be delayed until he has served two-thirds instead of half of the aggregate sentence. A judge should consider whether to reduce the consecutive sentence to allow for this, said the House of Lords in *Francois* (1998).

Suspended Sentences and Exceptional Circumstances

When legislators decide to deprive sentencers of discretion – as they have done, for example, over the disqualification of drunken drivers – they usually offer a compromise. When disqualification or endorsement of licence is mandatory, exceptions can be made for 'special reasons' or on 'mitigating grounds' (see chapter 6). From 1968 until 1991 a prison sentence of two years or less could be suspended at courts' discretion, to be activated – again at discretion – if during the 'operational period' (usually two years) the offender was reconvicted of an imprisonable offence. The 1991 Act (s. 5) limited this power to 'exceptional circumstances', with marked effect.

Percentages of men's sentences suspended (percentages for women in brackets)

	In the Crown Court	In magistrates' courts
1990	33.6 (54.4)	49.2 (66.2)
1993	6.1 (19.0)	9.2 (19.7)
1994	4.7 (16.1)	5.7 (15.9)
1995	4.7 (18.8)	3.8 (10.7)
1996	5.0 (18.7)	3.0 (8.9)

By 1994 judges had found and kept steadily to a new low level. Magistrates' courts took longer to find their new level, but in the end it was lower, perhaps because magistrates are so discouraged from using prison sentences that they tend to reserve them for cases in which there are no 'exceptional circumstances'. A similar loophole for exceptional circumstances is offered by the Crime (Sentences) Act 1997 when it prescribes life imprisonment or minimum terms in certain circumstances (see chapter 5); but it is too early to start counting examples. There is an interesting difference, however, between the Criminal Justice Acts and the Road Traffic Acts. The latter, as we saw in chapter 6, expressly rule out some circumstances as 'mitigating grounds':

(a) any circumstances alleged to make the driving offence not serious;

(b) hardship, unless 'exceptional';

(c) any circumstances which, in the three years preceding the conviction have already been taken into account as mitigating grounds in connection with a disqualification – an odd provision which will be discussed in chapter 8.

In contrast the Criminal Justice Acts leave it to sentencers and the Court of Appeal to decide what circumstances are exceptional. In *Okinikan* (1993), however, the Court of Appeal could only say what were *not* exceptional circumstances:

> This Court cannot lay down a definition of 'exceptional circumstances'. They will depend on the facts of each individual case. However, taken on their own, or in combination, good character, youth, and an early plea [*sc.* of 'guilty'] are not exceptional circumstances which justify a suspended sentence. They are a common feature of many cases. They may amount to mitigation sufficient to persuade the Court that a custodial sentence should not be passed, or to reduce its length . . .

Note that considerations which are too common to justify suspension of a prison sentence can nevertheless justify substituting a non-custodial one. The Court was realistically treating suspension as more lenient than a fine or a community penalty.

As *Okinikan* also suggests, the Court's interpretation of 'exceptional', however vague, was strict. In *Lowery* (1993) it said that the phrase allowed the sentencer 'to take into account all the relevant circumstances surrounding the offence, the offender and the background circumstances', but that the circumstances must be '*very* exceptional' (my italics). Lowery's breach of trust outweighed the plea that he had ruined his career. A few months later, however, the Court's criterion had become less strict. *French* (1993) is the case which the Court itself regarded as exemplifying the relaxation. Mrs French had conspired to defraud an insurance company by claiming that a car had been stolen. Her six-month sentence was suspended on appeal because of her long-standing depression and the likely effect of even a short prison sentence upon it. In fact depression is not as uncommon as this decision implies, and it is hardly to be regarded as *very* exceptional. But the Act merely stipulated 'exceptional' and, since *French*, depression and other psychiatric diagnoses have been frequent reasons for suspending a sentence on appeal, and no doubt in lower courts too. A judge went too far, however, when he suspended Beatrice Costaine's sentence for soliciting a man to murder a creditor, because a psychiatrist testified to her 'fragile and labile personality'. In *Costaine* (1997) a reference by the Attorney-General persuaded the Court of Appeal to substitute a four-year sentence. These cases illustrate the extent to which judicial discretion can fluctuate in the interpretation of what legislators intended. We shall see in chapter 11 that even revenge, if called 'delayed provocation' can lead to suspension, and so can an offence as serious as conspiring to assist an escape from prison with a firearm: *Armstrong* (1997) had earned it by 'grassing' at great personal risk. Another strikingly exceptional circumstance was reported in *Andrew* (1997), where the defendant was a research student who had supplied friends with Ecstasy. A prison sentence seemed inevitable, but was suspended because he was engaged in what was said to be valuable work on a drug being designed to relieve angina. If the judge was assuming that he would have been hard to replace the reasoning was very utilitarian.

Reasons for suspension are seldom as exceptional as this, however, and are more often typical of pleas in mitigation of the kinds to be discussed in this and later chapters. The commonest reasons are the physical or mental state of the offender, his responsibility for a dependent relative and previous good character (Flood-Page and Mackie, 1998). What the reasons must not be is a mere multiplicity of mitigations, at least if *Murti* (1996) is a case to be followed. She had been persuaded by two other women to obtain about £10,000 dishonestly from the Department of Social Services. Her counsel offered no less than seven reasons why her sentence should be suspended. She had been a reluctant accomplice. She had given evidence against her fellow-accomplices. She was in a post-natal depression. Her husband had left her. She had two small children to care for. Her employer was going to re-engage her. While in prison she had slashed her wrists. The Court of Appeal said that the judge was right not to suspend her sentence – but it substituted probation.

The survey by Flood-Page and Mackie (1998) noticed an odd fact: that a fraud was twice as likely as any other type of offence to result in a suspended sentence. They did not suggest an explanation, but it is possible that fraudsters are more likely to be of 'good character', or to be impoverished people who have cheated the social security system, although there are also less charitable explanations.

A complication of the original legislation (in the Criminal Justice Act 1967) is that a sentence of more than two years cannot be suspended. In at least one case, however, a quite usual sentence of four years was reduced to two by the Court of Appeal in order to enable them to suspend it (*Robert W* (1996)). The defendant had repeatedly committed indecent assaults on a much younger sister when he was aged between 14 and 16. Had he been sentenced at the time the maximum term would have been 12 months' detention; but his offences did not come to light until he was 23. The Court of Appeal heard that his home had been a very disordered one, in which the children had witnessed much sexual behaviour, and that they had all eventually been taken into care. Robert W had ceased to act in this way, and had indeed behaved very well. The Court ruled that his sentence should have been two years, suspended. (It is worth noting that if he *had* been unlucky enough to be tried and sentenced while he was a young adult the court would have had no power to suspend his sentence, for a curious reason which will be discussed in chapter 9.)

NON-STATUTORY CONSIDERATIONS

There are many more kinds of mitigating plea which are not specified in a statute. Most of them in effect ask the court to recognise that the offender was less culpable than the offence might suggest.

Motivation

Motives for law breaking are usually of the aggravating kind, but occasionally they mitigate. Fear excites sympathy (except perhaps in courts-martial) and, when self-defence or duress (see below) is successfully pleaded, can excuse completely or mitigate heavily. 'Love and blind devotion' saved *Carol Scotchford-Hughes* (1998) from a prison sentence when she helped her lover to sell rhinoceros horn illegally. Love, too, reduced D's sentence (from 12 to three months) for contempt of court when he breached an injunction by writing love-letters to his estranged girlfriend. The Court of Appeal reasoned that violence, not the 'tortured emotions of young lovers' was what the injunction was meant to control (*Cambridgeshire County Council* v *D* (1998)). Even an understandable grievance can mitigate. A middle-aged mother who had embezzled £65,000 received only a short custodial sentence because she had what the judge considered an understandable financial grievance, being paid half the usual salary for directors of university sports (*Daily Telegraph*, 24 December 1997). Seven bus-drivers, who believed that their employer was making excessive deductions from their pay, devised a complex way of embezzling passengers' fares. When they were convicted the judge sympathised with their grievance and decided that a community penalty was sufficient. (It is worth noting that the Crown Prosecution Service was subsequently criticised for not investigating the alleged grievance more closely (*Times*, 30 September 1997)). Absence of the usual mercenary motive may mitigate: supplying cannabis free to friends deserves a less severe sentence than selling it (*Bennett* (1998)).

Abnormal motivation is dealt with ambivalently by courts. A compulsion to pilfer – called 'kleptomania' in the era of 'manias' – will mitigate, but not a compulsion to molest people sexually. A single act prompted by overwhelming sexual desire is not usually presented to courts as pathological if the object is a person between certain age-limits; but paedophilia and gerontophilia are psychiatric diagnoses. Sadism may be pathological, but as a plea in mitigation it is a non-starter. Revenge, on the other hand, is not regarded as abnormal by courts, and may even mitigate, especially when it can be called 'delayed provocation' (see chapter 11). Racial hatred is too common to be 'medicalised', even if it is sometimes associated with paranoia; and as we saw in chapter 4 it aggravates violence.

Temptation

Temptation, especially if the victim voluntarily contributed to it, often persuades courts to be lenient. An example was *Wilbourne* (1982), whose 15-year-old promiscuous daughter twice seduced him into incest: his 12-month sentence was suspended. For an example of financial temptation see *Oakes* (1974), a salesman who was in pecuniary straits and kept payments which should have been passed to his employers. His prison sentence was reduced *and* suspended.

Impulsiveness

The Magistrates' Association's *Sentencing Guidelines, 1997* mention 'impulse' as a possible mitigation for a small number of offences. It is not surprising that they include acts of violence or criminal damage, but a little odd that they also include the fraudulent use of vehicle licences. The special kinds of impulse involved in provocation and revenge are discussed in chapters 11 and 12.

Entrapment

A special kind of temptation is entrapment. If evidence against a defendant has been obtained by a trick it is sometimes ruled inadmissible, although English courts, supported by the House of Lords in *Sang* (1980), are reluctant to do this. As a ground for mitigation, however, entrapment is quite likely to be given some weight. *Tonnessen* (1998) was a heroin addict who was persuaded by two undercover journalists to obtain the drug for them, and then named in *News of the World*. Her 12-month sentence was halved by the Court of Appeal because it did not adequately reflect the element of entrapment. In passing the Court commented that entrapment was a mitigating consideration whether committed by police or journalists, but a less powerful one when committed by police, since the detection of crime was their job. When *Shaw* (1993) was persuaded by an undercover agent of the police to supply heroin, this six-year sentence was reduced by only one-sixth. The distinction is hard to justify. Entrapment mitigates because of the claim (or assumption) that without it the defendant would not have committed the particular offence of which he has just been convicted. It hardly seems to matter in what capacity the trapper acted.

Ignorance

Even when a strict interpretation does not allow ignorance of the law as a defence it can mitigate. *Watson* (1973) who had illegally tried to recruit for the Rhodesian army received a conditional discharge because (as the police confirmed) he did not know that this was prohibited. Even sophisticated ignorance can mitigate. *Stammers* (1998) who thought he could legally use bridleways to drive his Land

Rover home after drinking, was disqualified by magistrates, but persuaded a judge on appeal that his ignorance was a 'special reason' for not disqualifying him. It is sometimes pleaded that the offender comes from a country in which his action would not have been criminal, or would have been regarded as trivial; but this does not usually move the Court of Appeal. *Adebayo* (1998) had tried to get a driver's licence by arranging for an impostor to take his test. In spite of a pre-sentence report saying that he was ignorant of the consequences and 'the culture of this country' his six-month prison sentence was upheld.

Incompetence

Whether successful and unsuccessful attempts should be equally penalised will be discussed in chapter 8. Sometimes, however, an attempt is so incompetent that it elicits leniency. *Hosker* (1982) was an alcoholic with a substantial debt. Hoping to defraud his insurance company he tried to persuade two men in a pub to burgle his house. When they refused he set alight the carpet in his front room and went drunk to bed. Half an hour later he awoke to find the house ablaze, and had to be rescued by the fire brigade. He confessed to arson and explained his motive. His four-year sentence was reduced to three by the Court of Appeal because his attempt 'was not a calculated, cleverly planned attempt to defraud an insurance company. It was one which, in all the circumstances, was doomed to failure, and the appellant, indeed, was lucky that he himself was not the man who suffered, perhaps with his life . . .'.

Necessity and Duress

Even the eleventh century Laws of Cnut acknowledged the relevance of necessity. Breaches of codes are usually regarded as morally justified when intended to avert a greater evil (or, less often, achieve a greater good) than would have resulted from obedience. The statutory definitions of some offences concede this. Abortion is declared by section 5 of the Abortion Act 1967 not to be unlawful if done with certain aims. Otherwise, what is known to lawyers as 'necessity' used not to be accepted as a defence, although the concept of 'duress' has been enlarged so as to include something very like it.

Originally 'duress' was a defence based on threats of harm intended to induce the commission of an offence. 'The essence of [this] defence is that the will of the subject of the threats is no longer entirely under his own control because of the fear engendered by those threats' (*Ortiz* (1986)). The jury is expected to reject the defence if it is sure that 'a sober person of reasonable firmness, sharing the characteristics of the defendant would not have yielded to the threat' (*Paul* (1982)). Relevant characteristics include age, sex and in certain circumstances physical health or disability, but not, surprisingly, abnormal suggestibility or low intelligence, so that the conviction of *Bowen* (1997) was upheld by the Court of Appeal. It is odd that he did not appeal against his sentence of 18 months' imprisonment, since a failed defence of duress may still persuade the sentencer to be lenient. An example was *Taonis* (1974), who smuggled cannabis into this country after being tortured and threatened with the torture of his mistress. Since he had had time to tell this to the police before the smuggling duress was not accepted as a defence, but the Court of Appeal reduced his prison sentence from four to two years. Recently several road traffic cases have persuaded courts to recognise 'duress of circumstances' as a defence (for example when *Willer* (1986) drove recklessly to escape a gang of youths. This was 'duress of circumstances' because he, not the threateners, chose his way of escape (*Cole* (1994)).

A complication is the old exception. Duress is not a defence to a charge of murder (*Howe* (1987)) or attempted murder (*Gott* (1991)), even when the threat was death:

> The ordinary man of reasonable fortitude is . . . supposed to be capable of heroism if he is asked to take an innocent life rather than sacrifice his own (Lord Hailsham in *Howe*).

Heroism of this sort is not usually expected of the ordinary man. And sometimes the threat is not to him but to his nearest and dearest. The injustice is exacerbated by the fact that the sentence for murder cannot be mitigated. At present all that the sentencing judge can do is recommend early release to the Home Secretary and, if he does not, the omission is not appealable. From time to time it has been suggested that duress should invariably be a mitigating plea rather than a defence, or that in murder cases it should be a special plea, of diminished responsibility or something similar; but neither proposal has been seriously considered. The Law Commission thought that duress should be a defence without any exceptions.

Absence of Dishonesty

Less easy to classify is the case of *Dickens* (1993), an unfortunate down-and-out, who had found that a £20 note he had been given in change was a forgery. As he believed he had no chance of returning it to the pub where he had been given it, he tried to use it in a sweet shop. His 12-month sentence was reduced to six months because the Court had to accept that he had not acquired it with a view to using it dishonestly. If one believes his account it is tempting to call his situation 'duress of circumstances'.

Intoxication

Before the nineteenth century drunkenness was no excuse, did not mitigate and might even aggravate (*Coke*, 1644). In the nineteenth and twentieth centuries case-law has made step-by-step concessions, allowing voluntary intoxication to support defences such as lack of specific intent, or mistakes in special circumstances. It is so easy to claim intoxication, however, that each concession has been the subject of judicial disagreement, and the law is still very restrictive. Intoxication can be an offence in itself or an aggravation, especially where driving is concerned. Merely careless driving is non-imprisonable, even when it causes a death – unless the driver has been drinking, in which case the maximum sentence is 10 years' imprisonment. When intoxication is offered as a plea in mitigation the Court of Appeal originally treated it as a mitigating consideration, for instance in 1909 reducing *Haden's* 12 months' hard labour to three months (for stealing a pair of boots). Nowadays it usually rejects this plea. An example is *Bradley* (1980), an 18-year-old with a clean record who had violently resisted arrest. Upholding his six-month sentence, Lord Chief Justice Lane said, 'The day is long past when someone can come along and say "I know I have committed these offences, but I was full of drink"'. In fact the day was not quite past, for a couple of years later two other judges reduced a six-year sentence to four years for *Spence* (1982), a 41-year-old man who had violently raped a strange woman in the street. The only mitigations seem to have been that he had a clean record (but so had *Bradley*) and that he was 'under the influence of alcohol at the time'. Such cases are more frequent than the Criminal Appeal Reports suggest. In 1998, for example, a local newspaper reported the sentencing of *Susan Crane*, who had severely bitten a nurse while being treated in a casualty department. The Recorder considered a prison sentence but instead discharged her conditionally because she had been drunk. 'If you had been sober you would never have dreamed of doing as you did', he said. Both *Spence* and *Crane* benefited from Fletcherian reasoning: that when sober they were 'not like that'.

Involuntary intoxication can of course excuse completely, unless it was reckless. *Tandy's* case (1989) bears on the interpretation of involuntariness. She was an alcoholic who strangled her young daughter. Her plea of diminished responsibility was unsuccessful, but *obiter dicta* of the Court of Appeal implied (a) that an alcoholic's craving could make intoxication involuntary, and (b) that medical evidence might indicate that an alcoholic's brain was sufficiently damaged to sustain a plea of diminished responsibility (see chapter 10), although neither seemed to be true of *Tandy* herself. It seems possible that the Court would take a similar line on the subject of other addictions. Sentencers are not usually moved by the plea that addicts' thefts were motivated by an overwhelming desire for drink or drugs; but Bingham LCJ did concede in *Howells and others* (1998) that

> where offending has been fuelled by addiction to drink or drugs, the court will be inclined to look more favourably on an offender who has already demonstrated (by taking practical steps to that end) a genuine, self-motivated determination to address his addiction.

Change of Lifestyle

That is a rather special example of the frequent plea that the offender intends to change his way of life, although it rarely has much influence on the Court of Appeal. It was one of the three mitigating considerations[2] offered by counsel (the others were unimpressive) which had persuaded the trial judge to choose community service rather than imprisonment for wounding with intent to cause grievous bodily harm in the case of *Earlam and Earlam* (1997: cited in chapter

4 under 'Procedural points'). It persuaded the Court of Appeal in
Killen (1982). He had 'an absolutely appalling record' of burglaries,
for the latest of which he had been sentenced to 12 months'
imprisonment. His pre-sentence report, praised by the Court of Appeal

> . . . did not mince words but made it plain . . . that if this young
> man is to have a chance this is the time for him to have it, the point
> being . . . that a major change has taken place in this young man's
> circumstances, in that he has formed a relationship with a girl . . .
> who is described as 'a sensible, level-headed girl who is convinced
> that their relationship holds the key to Thomas' future good
> behaviour' . . . We have to say that we are concerned that since
> their relationship was formed there has been the commission of this
> particular offence which is the subject matter of an appeal, which
> in itself has worked against our forming the view that he should be
> given a chance, but even so we think it right that he should be given
> the opportunity to mend his ways . . .

The chance took the form of community service. Such optimistic
utilitarianism was commoner in the fifties than in the eighties or
nineties, but is occasionally the reason for deferring sentence for a few
months, in the hope of receiving a reassuring report.

Good Character

'Some measure of leniency' said Bingham LCJ in *Howells and others*
(1998) 'will ordinarily be extended to offenders of previous good
character, the more so if there is evidence of positive good character
(such as a solid employment record or faithful discharge of family
duties) as opposed to a mere absence of previous convictions'. An
example was *Clark* (1999), whose six-month sentence for a six-year
series of frauds was reduced to a week because of her voluntary
service to the local community and her bringing up of four motherless
nephews and nieces. Good character, as we have seen, is still
accepted, at least by some sentencers, as an 'exceptional' reason for
suspending a prison sentence, although it is unlikely that the Court of
Appeal would approve. Even a substantial record can sometimes be
offset by a subsequent period of (more or less) law-abiding conduct,
as in the case of *Bennett* (1981), a burglar who for the previous 10

years had incurred only a suspended sentence. It was assumed that the suspension meant that the offence could not have been a serious one.

Meritorious Conduct

Sentencers are sometimes influenced by a principle which seems to be retributive in spirit: that deserts can be reduced by meritorious conduct. This is most likely when the conduct is an attempt to undo, reduce or compensate for the harm of the offence, especially if the attempt is made before detection. An offer of compensation when the offender faces prosecution is less likely to influence the court. More remarkable are cases in which the court is influenced by meritorious conduct which has nothing to do with the offence or the trial. Men have had prison terms reduced or suspended because they have fought well in a war (*Cook* (1976), cit. Thomas, 1979), saved a child from drowning (*Keightley* (1972)) or started a youth club (*Ducasse* (1974), cit. Thomas, 1979). These cases are interesting because they seem to combine two assumptions: (a) that offenders are being sentenced not for culpability but for moral worth; and (b) that moral worth can be calculated by a moral form of bookkeeping, in which spectacular actions count for more than unobtrusive decency. The Court of Appeal revealed its ambivalence about this kind of bookkeeping in *Reid* (1982). After his burglary but before his trial Reid had saved two children from a burning house at some personal risk, but had not mentioned this to his solicitors or counsel, and was sentenced to three months' detention. Told this, the Court of Appeal said:

> While this Court would not usually interfere with a sentence because the defendant had committed [*sic*] an act of bravery, we think that if the Recorder had known about this incident it may well be that he would have formed a different view of the appellant; he might have come to the conclusion that the appellant was a much better and more valuable member of society than his criminal activities had led him to suppose.

The Court substituted a conditional discharge. Its reasoning has two oddities. It is doing what it said that the Recorder should have done but it would not do. And it is denying that it would do what it had in fact done, for example in the case of *Keightley*, who had saved a child from drowning.

Penal Bookkeeping

Another sort of bookkeeping is occasionally observable. *Benstead* (1979) had served nearly two-thirds of a six-month prison sentence when the Court of Appeal was persuaded to substitute a one-day sentence. It acknowledged that, beyond ordering his immediate release, it could do nothing to put matters right, but directed that a note of what had happened should be placed on his record documents so that if he were later convicted of some other offence it could be taken into account in his sentence. In plain words, his next sentence should be less than he deserved because his present one had been more than he deserved. More often the Court simply substitutes a sentence of such length that it so happens that the prisoner is due for release that day. Neither solution has so far figured in a guideline.

Assisting Law-enforcement

Moral bookkeeping is not what is in judges' minds when they reward offenders for giving the police or prison staff useful information. In *Sinfield* (1981) it was quite clearly the utilitarian hope of encouraging other offenders to do likewise. So Sinfield, convicted of eight counts of robbery and with 53 similar offences taken into account, who had had his sentence reduced to eight years by the trial judge, persuaded the Court of Appeal to reduce it still further to five. It seems that assisting law-enforcement can outweigh aggravations such as breach of trust. *Johnson* (1998), who robbed a bank while on day release from prison, was sentenced to only five years' imprisonment because he had cooperated with police, whereas his accomplice, who was on licence from a sentence for robbery, received a 15-year sentence. On the other hand the Court has made it plain that there is no 'tariff of discounts' for assisting the police: each case should be decided on its merits (*Rose and Sapiano* (1980)). Nor can police promise a discount as an inducement. The most they can properly offer is to stress the offender's helpfulness when they are asked for their testimony at the sentencing stage. Nor can there be any discount for a prisoner who helps the police long after he has begun to serve his prison sentence (*X* (1994)). Guidelines for the presentation of police evidence of helpfulness were provided in the case of *X* (1999). When an accomplice gives truthful and useful evidence against a principal he is entitled to 'some discount', which should reflect the seriousness of the offence, the importance of the evidence and the effect of giving evidence on the future circumstances of the witness (*sc.* what risks he is running: *Wood* (1996)).

Occupation

As for type of occupation, we saw in chapter 4 that an offender's occupation as a policeman, teacher, accountant, may aggravate his offence because it is regarded as a breach of trust. In the light of courts' respect for meritorious deeds one might expect to find that some occupations mitigate offending because of the self-sacrifice or risks which they demand. I have found no reported cases or statistics, however, which confirm this. A policeman who uses unnecessary force, for example, may hope for a sympathetic jury, but not, apparently, a sympathetic judge. As for 'professional men' they should 'expect to be punished as severely as others, and in some cases more severely' (*Barrick* (1985)).

Remorse

Remorse is routinely mentioned in the Magistrates' Association's *Sentencing Guidelines 1997* as a possible mitigation where almost any sort of offence is concerned, even handling stolen goods or refusing a specimen of urine. Remorse may tip the balance against a custodial sentence, said Bingham LCJ in *Howells and others* (1998):

> The court will have regard to an offender's admission of responsibility for the offence, particularly if reflected in a plea of guilty tendered at the earliest opportunity and accompanied by hard evidence of genuine remorse, as shown (for example) by an expression of regret to the victim and an offer of compensation . . .

Cynics might be sceptical about these examples of 'hard evidence', unless the offender has expressed regret and offered compensation before being questioned by the police. However that may be, remorse is a frequent plea when the offence is personal violence or causing death by dangerous driving. The trial judge accepted it when sentencing *Mortiboys* (1997) for attempted murder. Although the only evidence of remorse was Mortiboys' plea of guilty the Court of Appeal thought his 10-year sentence too harsh and reduced it to eight. A guilty plea also convinced the Court of *Toombs'* (1997) remorse for causing death by dangerous driving. Even a defendant who pleads not guilty can sometimes convince a court of his remorse, as *Norman* did in 1994. He had pleaded self-defence after killing an aggressive neighbour in a struggle, but was convicted of provoked manslaughter. His remorse was one of the Court's reasons for reducing his sentence. Remorse manifested during a prison sentence is a consideration for the Parole Board rather than the Court of Appeal (*Waddingham* (1983)).

Genuine remorse, like its absence (see chapter 4) is something which a utilitarian sentencer has no difficulty in taking into account, on the assumption that it helps to predict whether the offender will behave similarly in the future. Retributivists have more difficulty in explaining why remorse should reduce desert, unless they concede that it is character which deserves, or take one of the other lines suggested in chapter 4. Remorse is more credible after impulsive violence or unintended harm than after a lucrative or sexual offence; and a guilty plea is far from strong evidence of it, being a tactic which is known to be likely to earn a reduction of sentence. It is worth noting, however, that some violent offenders are so horrified by what they have done that they suffer from genuine amnesia, whereas sexual offenders hardly ever do so, probably because of the pleasure involved.

Relationship to Victim

The offender's previous relationship to his victim can mitigate. Rape, for example, tends to be sentenced less severely when there has been a previous sexual relationship (examples are *Brown* (1993) and *Hamilton* (1993)). The principle probably applies only when the offence is an act of a kind to which the victim previously consented: it is unlikely to apply to thefts, for instance.

Individualisation

Late in the 1970s David Thomas (1979) wrote that:

a sentence which would be considered inappropriate as an application of tariff principles may be considered entirely correct if seen as an individualised measure based on the courts' assessment of the needs of the offender as an individual . . .

Individualisation is thus distinct from culpability-based mitigation. The most striking examples used to be cases in which offenders with long histories of custodial sentences for dishonesty were unexpectedly put on probation, usually as a result of an encouraging pre-sentence report. An instance was *McNamee* (1979). Individualisation does not seem to be entirely ruled out by sections 1 and 2 of the 1991 Act, but the Attorney-General's power to refer to the Court of Appeal cases of what he considers excessive leniency has somewhat discouraged it. An interesting example is *Wheeler* (1998). The trial judge had put him on probation for arson. Varying this to four and a half years' imprisonment the Court said

> There is a psychiatric report upon this man, but it is important to notice that it is not a case where there is any mental trouble or any recommendation for medical treatment. That, it is suggested by the Attorney, is one of the only circumstances [*sic*] in which it might be permissible for the Court to pass anything other than an immediate prison sentence, if it was in fact a case of mental trouble. That again we would accept.

This demonstrates a more restrictive attitude to individualisation.

Double Jeopardy

Although 'double jeopardy' traditionally means the retrial of a defendant who has already been acquitted of the same charge, the Court of Appeal nowadays applies the term to cases referred by the Attorney-General because the sentences seem unduly lenient, and if it increases a sentence it almost always remembers to declare that it has allowed for the defendant's state of suspense. Anxiety in other situations – for example, while awaiting a long-delayed trial, or the result of pre-sentence enquiries – is sometimes pleaded, but I have not found a reported case in which a court expressly made allowance for it.

Double jeopardy of a sort is what saved the *Earlams* from a custodial sentence. As we saw under 'Change of lifestyle' their pleas in mitigation had so impressed the trial judge that he sentenced them to community service instead of custody. The Attorney-General considered that a non-custodial sentence was much too lenient, and referred the case to the Court of Appeal, which agreed. By that time, however, they had completed their community service, and were the subjects of very satisfactory reports from probation officers. The Court decided 'with some reluctance . . . that it would not now advance the public interest to order these offenders to serve a custodial sentence . . . We should not now impose a different sentence'. 'The public interest', as we shall see in later chapters, is a vague concept, invoked constantly by the Crown Prosecution Service, and occasionally by courts. Here the Court must have meant that having undergone what was meant as retributive punishment (but as such was inadequate) the brothers would be too severely punished if imprisoned, and that no utilitarian purpose would be served by imprisonment.

Incorrigibility

It might seem unlikely that incorrigibility could ever be a reason for mitigation, unless perhaps in a case of personality disorder; but in *Thomas* (1983) the Court of Appeal reduced the period of a driving disqualification from two years to one, in spite of the statute which stipulated a minimum of two years. It reasoned that he seemed incapable of obeying the disqualification for so long a period, which would thus increase the likelihood of his committing further offences. There was no suggestion that he suffered from a personality disorder. The Court's reasoning was certainly not retributive, but it is difficult to call it utilitarian, since the only likely benefit was the postponement of his next appearance in court. Traffic offences seem to be the subject of very special pleading, and it is unlikely that the Court of Appeal would approach any other type of offence in the same way.

Using up Mitigation

An unusual case was *Frankson's* (1996). His seven-year sentence for drug-dealing was reduced by two years because his co-defendant had benefited from what the Court regarded as excessive mitigation. She had pleaded pregnancy and her responsibility for three young children; but the Court's view was that she had 'well and truly used up the credit for those responsibilities in her history of criminal offences'. The comment is interesting because it implies that a consideration which is valid on one court appearance may cease to be on a subsequent one. It is reminiscent of the odd provision in section 35 of the Road Traffic Offenders Act 1988 that a driver whose licence is due to be endorsed or suspended cannot plead as a 'mitigating ground' something which he has pleaded in mitigation on an earlier occasion in the last three years. It is as if mitigating considerations were an account which could become overdrawn, but in which the overdraft would disappear with time. One may be sceptical about the *bona fides* of a repeated plea, but if still true and valid it must surely remain a proper consideration. Frankson's girlfriend presumably still had three children, not to mention the new pregnancy.

Consistency

Retributivists, as we saw in chapter 1, feel bound to aim at consistency in sentencing. If there is no sound reason for differentiating the penalties imposed on two or more offenders, it is assumed that they should suffer equally. The Court of Appeal's view has changed over the years. In *Reeves* (1964) it felt obliged to reduce what seemed a proper sentence because his accomplices, who had wisely pleaded guilty in a magistrates' court, had received what the Court regarded as excessively lenient sentences. Yet in *Broadbridge* (1983) it refused to reduce his prison sentence in spite of the fact that his accomplices' sentences had been suspended by another court. The judge's duty, it said, was to deal fitly with the case before him. Occasionally, it is true, the court has been influenced by what can be called 'subjective injustice' – the likelihood that the offender will feel that in comparison with others he is being penalised too harshly. In *Bishop* (cit. Thomas, 1979) it reasoned that if he received the appropriate penalty he might well 'feel that he has suffered an injustice when compared with his comrades in the crime'. This was not a guideline, for in *Large* (1981) the Court dismissed subjective injustice in a purple passage:

> . . . those who prey on the public by attempting to steal with the aid of sawn-off shotguns cannot expect their disappointment about

sentences to weigh heavily in the balance against the duty of this
court to protect the public – let him who has been properly and
severely punished rejoice in the good fortune of his companions . . .

Yet two years later the Court reduced the sentence of *Fawcett* (1983)
to correspond with his accomplice's over-lenient sentence in order not
to outrage his sense of justice. In *Beard* (1993) the converse was
upheld: it was wrong to penalise him as severely as the rest of his
gang when his culpability was less. I shall return to the subject of
consistency in the final chapter.

The Credibility of Mitigation

Unlike aggravations, mitigating considerations are often based on facts
which have not been established in the trial or by a plea of guilty; and
the facts may not be facts. Earlier in this chapter a case was described
in which the Crown Prosecution Service was criticised for not
challenging three bus-drivers' allegations of a grievance about pay.
Prosecuting counsel have a duty, says the Bar's 1990 *Code of Conduct*,
'to draw the attention of the defence to any assertion of material fact
which the prosecution believes to be untrue'. In *Guppy and Marsh*
(1995) the Court of Appeal drew an important distinction between
facts which are strictly relevant to conviction and 'extraneous matters':

> . . . in relation to extraneous matters of mitigation raised by a
> defendant or appellant, a civil burden of proof rests on the
> defendant or appellant, though of course in the general run of cases
> the sentencing judge will readily accept the accuracy of defending
> counsel's statements in this context.

In other words the court is free to form an opinion about the
credibility of a mitigating plea on what is called 'a balance of
probability'. When *Gross* (1982) was convicted for the nth time of
illegally offering his cab for hire at Heathrow Airport he claimed to
have offered to convey the passenger without charge, but offered no
evidence in support of this claim. The magistrates said that that they
did not believe it, and fined him £100. He appealed to the Divisional
Court, which upheld the magistrates' decision. If defence counsel is
going to offer information by way of mitigation which is inconsistent

with other information in the court's possession, or is otherwise likely to be disbelieved, he must decide whether to adduce evidence in support of it. If he decides to call evidence he may do so before, during or after his address. The court is not bound to warn him of its disbelief, 'but it might have been better' if it had done so.

On the other hand if the facts are not 'extraneous' but intrinsic to the offence the rules are more complex. If the offender has pleaded 'not guilty' the intrinsic facts can usually be established by the evidence on which he was convicted. If he pleads 'guilty' but adduces a version of the facts which differs from the prosecution's the latter may or may not be in a position to rebut it. *Tolera* (1998) pleaded guilty to possessing heroin with intent to supply it, but claimed that he was a mere courier under orders, a claim which the judge did not accept. In such cases, if the sentencer is sceptical, there should (failing any other resolution) be a hearing of evidence (of the kind called a *Newton* hearing), and the prosecution bears the burden of contesting the defendant's claim, with a criminal standard of proof. When, however, the mitigating plea is wholly implausible, or is based on matters outside the prosecution's knowledge – as was *Broderick's* (1994) claim that she was under duress when trying to smuggle cannabis past Customs – there is no obligation to hold a *Newton* hearing.

General

Long as the list of mitigating considerations has been – and there are more to come – it cannot be exhaustive. Magistrates and judges are lenient for reasons which never reach the Court of Appeal, and may not even be explicit. Defendants never appeal against leniency, and Attorney-Generals do so only when it seems extreme. What can safely be said is that the reasoning which leads to the mitigation of a sentence is usually retributive, based on factors which seem to reduce culpability, or – as we shall see in the next chapter – which make it likely that the offender or his dependants will suffer excessively from the normal penalty. Sometimes the sentencer has utility in mind – the effect on the offender's future conduct. Occasionally the objective is merely the encouragement of offenders to plead guilty or to give evidence against others. Now and again a guideline preaches what sounds like Bentham's 'frugality – the principle that punishment should not exceed what will achieve utility. In 1980 judicial concern about the overcrowding of prisons persuaded Lord Chief Justice Lane to use *Bibi's* case (1980) as the basis for a guideline. Begum Bibi herself had played a very minor role in the importation of cannabis, and the Court cut short her three-year prison sentence for mitigating reasons which were special to her circumstances (see the next chapter). The Lord Chief Justice, however, used her sentence to encourage courts to use shorter terms for 'minor cases of sexual indecency' and 'petty frauds'. Since *Bibi's* offence belonged to neither category one wonders why he chose it, or indeed why he felt obliged to hang his homily on a particular case. However that may be, what he said was:

> This case opens up wider horizons because it is no secret that our prisons at the moment are dangerously overcrowded . . . sentencing courts must be particularly careful to examine each case to ensure, if an immediate custodial sentence is necessary, that the sentence is as short as possible, consistent only with the duty to protect the interests of the public and to punish and deter the criminal. Many offenders can be dealt with equally justly and effectively by a sentence of six or nine months' imprisonment as by one of 18 months or three years. We have in mind not only the obvious case of the first offender for whom any prison sentence, however short, may be an adequate punishment and deterrent, but other types of case as well.

Bentham would not have used 'punishment' in this retributive sense, nor would he have omitted to mention the deterrence of potential imitators; but otherwise he would have agreed with a policy of minimum necessary severity.

NOTES

1.   It seems odd that this declaration is expressly limited to 'this Part of this Act'. Did legislators really have in mind some sentencing provision elsewhere which ought to prevent a court from taking into account any matters which in its opinion are relevant in mitigation of sentence?

2.   What saved them in the Court of Appeal was the quite different consideration described under 'Double jeopardy'.

Chapter 8
Harm

HARM TO VICTIMS

In some cases it is the gravity of the harm, irrespective of culpability, which the sentencer has in mind. Sometimes the harm is merely probable, as when a motor vehicle is driven dangerously or by a drunken driver. When actual harm has been done the evidence necessary for conviction usually gives the sentencer some idea of its seriousness. Sometimes the victim has submitted a documented claim for compensation. In some foreign jurisdictions the procedure allows victims to present a statement of what they have suffered, and even to propose what the sentence should be. Following the publication of the Victims' Charter in 1990 the Home Office (1996) promised that police would ask victims about their fears of further victimisation and details of their loss, damage or injury, and that magistrates and judges would take this information into account when making their decisions.[1] This raises a crucial question. Should a sentence reflect the *likely* effect of the offence or its *actual* effect? In many cases – especially driving offences – the extent of the harm done is a matter of luck. Statutes and case-law sometimes point in one direction, sometimes in the other, as we shall see.

The maximum sentences allowed by statutes for various offences crudely reflect the harm likely to result, and while maxima are seldom used they influence the norm. Sexual intercourse with a girl under the age of 13 is more severely punishable (with 'life') than intercourse with a girl of 13, 14 or 15 (with two years) because it is presumed that the former has been more severely damaged by the experience. The maxima for offences involving drugs take account of the relative harmfulness of those in Class A, Class B and Class C. And so on; but more interesting is the way in which the Offences against the Person Act 1861 dealt (and still deals) with personal violence. It distinguishes 'actual' and 'grievous' bodily harm, but does not define the difference (nor did the Court of Appeal help much when it said that 'grievous' meant 'really serious', in *Saunders* (1985)). At first sight it hardly matters, since the maximum penalty is the same – five years' imprisonment – perhaps for the very reason that the seriousness of the injury is usually a matter of luck. It does matter, however, if it is provable that the injury was intended to be grievous, in which case the crime is punishable with 'life' (ss. 18, 47 and 20 of the Act).

The Politics of Death

It is death, however – or more precisely the politics of death – which results in the oddest distinctions. A minor offence which has fatal results for someone else can be prosecuted as manslaughter if the act was such that 'all sober and reasonable people would inevitably recognise [that it] must subject the other person to, at least, the risk of some harm . . . albeit not serious harm' (*Church* (1966)) and is punishable accordingly. The criterion is *likely and foreseeable* harm. Yet if the act by sheer good luck inflicts little or no harm it is not criminal, unless of course it contravenes a specific statute, as careless or dangerous driving does.

It is driving offences which have the oddest range of penalties. Merely careless driving is non-imprisonable, and until the Court of Appeal's decision in *Simmonds* (1999) sentencers were not supposed to take a resulting death into account (see for example *Morland* (1998)). If, however, the careless driver had taken unprescribed drugs or more than the permissible amount of alcohol, the death allows a maximum sentence of 10 years' imprisonment, the same as for causing death by dangerous driving (both maxima were increased from five years in 1993). Two or more deaths should attract more severity than one, said the Court of Appeal in *Shepherd and Wernet*

(1994), admitting that this was illogical, but defending it as being in accord with 'public perception'. Finally if the dangerous driving causes no injury, or even severe non-fatal injury, the maximum sentence is two years' imprisonment. This basic illogicality was criticised by the James Committee in 1975 and the Criminal Law Revision Committee in 1976, but defended – as we shall see – by the North Committee in 1988, and retained when reckless driving was redefined as 'dangerous driving' in the Road Traffic Act 1988 (the new maximum of 10 years was not, however, recommended by the North Committee).

The issue is one of principle, and so important that the North Committee's arguments in favour of its decision are worth quoting. They agreed with most of the legal organisations they consulted that the distinction is morally illogical, but managed to produce a long list of reasons for preserving it:

(a)   it is generally accepted in the law that consequences can affect the nature of an offence, as may be illustrated by the different offences of murder and attempted murder, and murder where there is no intent to kill but where there is intent to cause grievous bodily harm which has resulted in death;

(b)   the public sense of justice requires that the very bad driver who has killed should be guilty of a more serious offence;

(c)   the seriousness of the penalty is desirable in order to have a deterrent effect;

(d)   juries are reluctant to convict of manslaughter in most causing death cases. Death should be singled out for special treatment because it is the most serious consequence of a criminal act, and doing so would exemplify the concern of the law for the sanctity of life;

(e)   though logic might suggest that consequences should be irrelevant, public opinion is strongly in favour of the retention of such an offence;

(f)   the case for the retention of an offence of causing death by dangerous driving is strong if there is no longer a complete overlap with the offence of manslaughter or culpable homicide;

(g)   outside the motoring sphere, reckless acts may amount either to no offence at all or, if death happens to result, to manslaughter or culpable homicide; so consequences should be no less relevant in the road traffic context;

(h)   if someone drives so badly as to be reckless, the consequences are not fortuitous, for the driver has created a real risk of
death or injury;

(i)   if there continues to be some overlap between causing death
by dangerous driving and manslaughter, it would be strange to be
able to take consequences into account in the latter but not the
former.

A list of this length is obviously the work of a committee. The
clinching arguments, in the Committee's view, however, were that:

to abolish the offence in the absence of compelling reasons for
doing so would mean that some cases of very bad driving were not
dealt with with appropriate seriousness . . .

and

though logic might pull us towards arguments in favour of abolition, neither English nor Scots law relies entirely on intent as the
basis for offences.

It is interesting to note how little the Committee relied on retributive
reasoning. More than one of their arguments appeal to the public's sense
of justice; but utilitarians can do that without implying that the public is
right. The other arguments are mostly in terms of expediency, but
surprisingly one of the clinchers seems to be the rather weak argument
that the offence is not inconsistent with the state of English or Scots law.
Argument (h) is another rather odd argument from a committee which is
recommending the replacement of 'reckless driving' with 'dangerous
driving'. One can drive dangerously without appreciating or intending
the risk, and without being aware that one is doing anything wrong.
Accepted at face value, however, it makes one wonder why they did not
take a step in the direction of logic by recommending that the offence be
'causing death *or injury* by dangerous driving'.

Categorising Harms

There have been efforts to categorise harms. The first scientific
attempt was by Wolfgang and Sellin (1963), who invited samples

from various groups of people in the USA to rank short descriptions of different criminal acts, which varied details, including the harm done. A quite different approach was adopted by von Hirsch and Jareborg (1991). They suggested classifying criminal harms according to their effect on the victim's 'quality of life'. Death apart, the 'grave' category would be harm which allowed survival, but 'with maintenance of no more than elementary human capacities to function'. The 'serious' category would allow 'maintenance of a minimal level of comfort and dignity'; and so on. Categorising minor physical injuries does not seem to be a problem for the Magistrates' Association, whose *Sentencing Guidelines 1997* suggest the amounts of compensation for such injuries as 'loss of a front tooth (£1,000)';[2] and civil courts award equally precise damages for graver physical injuries. Compensation, however, takes account of harm actually done, whereas, as we have seen, it is arguable that sentences should have more regard to the harm intended or the harm likely to result from the offence.

The harm done by violence is easier to assess than psychological damage. This is particularly so when children are the victims of sexual molestation. The internationally respected forensic psychiatrist Trevor Gibbens used to warn against the assumption that they invariably suffer lasting trauma. He suggested that when the offence itself had not caused pain or fear it was often the horrified reactions of parents and other adults which traumatised.[3] Nowadays it is usually assumed that any victim of a sexual offence, but particularly a child, will suffer from it for years. The Court of Appeal, however, has ruled that sentencers must not base sentences on the assumption that the harm suffered by victims has been serious: there must be evidence of it. If the prosecution adduce such evidence the defence must be given sufficient notice to allow it to be challenged (*Hobstaff* (1993) and *Peter O'S* (1993), both concerned with child victims of sexual offences). Once again it is open to question whether sentences should be determined by the actual harm or the harm that the offence was likely to cause.

The victim's forgiveness sometimes affects the court's estimate of the harmfulness of the offence. In *Hutchinson* (1993) the Court of Appeal inferred that a woman who had been raped by her ex-partner, but had indicated forgiveness, could not have suffered much harm, and they reduced the sentence accordingly. This is one of these cases in which they apparently cast around for an argument which would support what they wanted to do, possibly because the rapist was a former lover. It would have been safer to argue that whatever the nature of the harm the victim was in the best position to judge whether the rape had been to some extent *excusable*.

Harm Attempted

The tension between sentencing for actual and for likely harm is paralleled when we turn to attempted harm. The 'right-thinking man' is less likely to react punitively to a criminal attempt which fails than to one which succeeds.[4] The utilitarian sentencer can sometimes argue that an unsuccessful attempter – unless failure was due to sheer luck – is less likely to succeed in any future enterprise of the same kind, and therefore need not be dealt with so severely. The retributivist, however, is usually more severe. He may be lenient with half-hearted attempts, or attempts which are abandoned before achievement (as the Court of Appeal was with *Rackley's* effort to rape (1994)). But if what prevents achievement is mere bad luck or incompetence, the retributivist usually reasons that what counts is the intention, and that if a person acts in order to carry out a criminal intention he is equally culpable whether he succeeds or fails. Until the Law Commission overhauled the law on attempts in the late 1970s, however, the Court of Appeal took a less austere view. *Robson* (1974) met a girl by chance and tried to persuade her to go into the woods with him, intending, as he admitted, an indecent assault; but on seeing a police car in the distance he ran away. The Recorder gave him five years, the maximum for indecent assault, but the Court of Appeal reduced this to three years, because the attempt had been unsuccessful and the girl was unharmed. It added that it was unusual to 'visit [an attempt] with punishment to the maximum extent that the law permits in respect of a completed offence'. (It seems likely that the Recorder had suspected Robson of intending rape rather than mere indecent assault.)

Instinctive leniency in the case of attempts can be rationalised. Duff (1996) offers a neat proposal. Like Nozick (see chapter 1) he now[5] regards punishment as an effort to communicate with the offender – 'a formal way of saying "Look what you did". By punishing an attempt more leniently we are saying "Look what you tried to do, but thank God failed to"'. Ingenious as this is, the problems of real life need to be considered. Duff seems to assume that the receiver of the message knows (or has just been told) what the penalty would have been had he succeeded, and *will be affected by the discount as we would want* (unless, like Nozick, Duff thinks it sufficient to *try* to 'connect'). But suppose that the message is successfully communicated to an offender who doesn't agree that God should be thanked, and still wishes that the attempt had succeeded? Should he be penalised more severely in order to communicate disapproval of his attitude, or is it sufficient that we have made him appreciate *our* relief? Nozick would probably say that it is, so long as we have tried to 'connect' the offender with our values. Duff does not discuss the dilemma.

The Law Commission and the Criminal Attempts Act 1981 took a tougher moral line. Hitherto most attempts to commit crimes had been mere common-law misdemeanours; but the Act provided that they should be subject to the same maximum penalties as the completed crimes. Unlike the American Law Institute's Model Penal Code, however, it did not go all the way. It merely allowed and did not oblige sentencers to punish attempts as severely as completed crimes. And it left irrational exceptions. For attempted incest the maximum penalty is two years' imprisonment instead of seven, and for an attempt at unlawful sexual intercourse with a girl under the age of 13 the maximum is seven years instead of 'life' (s. 37 and sch. 2 of the Sexual Offences Act 1956). The explanation of this inconsistency is partly historical. The Law Commission's report on which the Act was based had been written while the Criminal Law Revision Committee was reviewing the Sexual Offences Acts, and the Commission therefore abstained from recommending the obvious amendment. What is not obvious is why the legislators responsible for the Sexual Offences Act regarded failed or frustrated attempts at unlawful intercourse as so much less serious than completed acts. Perhaps they simply assumed that they would be less harmful.

The other oddity is attempted murder: the 1981 Act *permitted* 'life' but did not make it mandatory. Attempted murder is the only kind of attempt which the *Criminal Statistics (England and Wales)* tabulates separately from the completed offence. A few defendants found guilty of it are dealt with by hospital orders or psychiatric probation orders (see chapter 10); but most are sentenced to imprisonment or young offender institutions. A comparison between the sentences for men in

1976–79 (before the year of the Criminal Attempts Bill) and those passed in 1994–6 is interesting.

Custodial sentences for attempted murder by men

length of sentence	1976–79 men %	1994–96 men %
life	13	11
over 10 years	8	26
10 years or less	79	63
7 years or less	61	34
5 years or less	35	16
4 years or less	24	10
3 years or less	16	5
Numbers (= 100%)	88	127

The men whose sentences exceeded 10 years would probably have been sentenced to life if the Court of Appeal had not expressly discouraged this in cases in which there was no indication of mental instability or disorder (see chapter 5). A few of those whose sentences were shorter had no doubt been able to plead that they were provoked, and might thus have escaped mandatory life sentences if their victims had died. No doubt, too, there were other cases in which, if the crime had been murder but the judge had not been constrained to impose 'life', he would have chosen a determinate sentence of less than 10 years because of other mitigations. Yet, all in all, the comparison suggests that at least some judges are nowadays sentencing attempts at murder more severely than before the 1981 Act.

A fact worth passing interest is that sentences for soliciting to murder (which in detected cases is almost always a premeditated hiring of an agent) are usually more lenient than for attempted murder. The reason may be that the hirer is usually a woman, or that – in the cases which come to trial at least – the transaction has been aborted before any physical harm has been done, whereas most attempts at murder inflict bodily injury. In a rare case in which the murder was actually carried out the instigator, *Jean Daddow* (1996), received a long sentence of 18 years.

For utilitarians these tensions between penalising for harm actually done and penalising for harm intended or foreseeably probable are just another retributive neurosis. What utilitarians regard as important is whether the penalty is severe enough to deter imitators and satisfy the victim and his sympathisers. If the offender is lucky enough to have done little or no harm, the sentencer can afford to be lenient unless the case is of a kind which will attract criticism from the news media. Cynical as it sounds, in practice this is how the severity of many sentences is determined.

HARM TO OFFENDERS OR THEIR DEPENDANTS

So much for harm to victims. Sentences are also modified, on occasion, to take account of the harm which the offenders or their relatives have suffered or will suffer as a result of the sentence, of what the offenders have done, or of stigma.

'Sensibility'

Even the eleventh century Laws of Cnut urged leniency – 'for the love and fear of God' – in the case of offenders who would suffer more than most from the usual penalty or penance. Bentham (1789) called this 'sensibility', the eighteenth-century equivalent of 'sensitivity'; and his principle of 'frugality' – no more severity than was needed to deter – meant that sensibility must mitigate. Nowadays fines are reduced for the poor. Prison sentences are reduced – sometimes not even imposed – because the offender is depressed, pregnant, about to emigrate, or young. The prison sentence of *Bibi* (1980) was reduced because as a Muslim wife she would suffer more than most in prison. (In contrast is the negative attitude of the Court of Appeal to pleas based on the dangers which will be faced in prison by offenders who are unpopular with other prisoners or whose health needs special medical attention. This will be discussed in chapter 13.)

Particularly interesting in this context is the guideline in *Howells and others* (1998). After indicating that good character may tip the balance against a custodial sentence (see chapter 7), Bingham LCJ said:

while the court will never impose a custodial sentence unless satisfied that it is necessary to do so, there will be an even greater reluctance to impose a custodial sentence on an offender who has never before served such a sentence.

The justification for this is not obvious. It is possible but unlikely that Bingham LCJ believed that a first custodial sentence increases the probability of recidivism. The much more probable alternative is that in his view someone who has not yet experienced a custodial sentence will, other things being equal, be likely to suffer more than someone who has.

Indirect Consequences of Conviction for the Offender

When a short custodial sentence seems likely a frequent plea is that it would lose the offender his job. If considerations seem finely balanced this may well tip the scales. Flood-Page's (1998) study of Crown Court sentences noticed that violent offenders with jobs were less likely to go to prison than the unemployed. She did not note a similar effect in the case of property offenders, perhaps because in their case the overriding factor was previous convictions, which fewer violent offenders have.

The consequences of the conviction itself may be serious for the offender. In *Richards* (1980), the defendant's prison sentence was reduced because his conviction for false financial claims would be 'the end of his whole [medical] career'. Even when the offence involves abuse of a professional position, the fact that the position will be lost sometimes weighs with the Court, although it is not usually sympathetic with breaches of trust. An example was *Fell* (1975), a mental nurse who had assaulted a refractory patient, and who would have to find some other profession (nine months' imprisonment were reduced to five). On the other hand, if the Court takes a very serious view of the offence or the offender's record a ruined career may not move it. The case of *Rees and Moss* (1982) demonstrates that the offender's record may tip the balance for or against this consideration. They were soldiers who had assaulted police in an effort to prevent the arrest of another soldier. They received sentences of one month's and four months' imprisonment respectively. When they appealed the Court was told that a custodial sentence meant almost automatic discharge from the Army, and that *Rees's* military record had been exemplary. They substituted a heavy fine. *Moss*, on the other hand, had previous convictions, and his appeal was unsuccessful, although discharge from the Army would mean that he, his wife and two children would lose their home.

Financial Harm

Financial penalties can occasionally mean more hardship for an offender or his family than a short custodial sentence. Loss of the matrimonial home is something which normally deters the Court of Appeal, especially when it is dealing with confiscation orders under section 71 of the Criminal Justice Act 1988. In *Taigel* (1998) it varied the amount of an order because it would have made the family homeless, making it clear that this was its policy but not 'an absolute rule'. No doubt a similar consideration would limit the amount of a fine; but I have found no case that says so. Fines must merely 'reflect' (not 'be commensurate with') the seriousness of the offence (s. 18(2) of the 1991 Act). The reason for the different wording has never been explained, but may have been the recognition that the amounts of fines must also take into account the offender's means, and that he must normally be given time to pay. It used to be said that the amount and the instalments should be such that the fine could be paid off within a year, but in *Olliver* (1989) Lane LCJ was less restrictive: '. . . a two-year period will seldom be too long, and in appropriate cases three years will be unassailable, again of course depending on the nature of the offender and the nature of the offence'.

The Effect of the Sentence on Others

A more awkward consideration of a retributive kind is the effect of a sentence on an offender's innocent dependants. The result of a fine or compensation order may be that they are deprived of more than he is. A prison sentence may mean hardship for children, who may even have to be taken into official care if it is their mother who is being removed. In *Parkinson* (1976) a mother's nine-month sentence was reduced for this reason, and she was released at once; and *Franklyn* (1981), a father, was released for similar reasons. In 1998 *Lynda Hier's* 18-month sentence for wounding with intent to cause grievous bodily harm was suspended because of its likely effect on her five children. If the sentence is very short, however, the Court may sound

fiercer: . . . 'as a matter of general interest' even if the offender is
'. . . a woman with a family, is in difficulty at home, and is living on
social security, that does not give her a licence in any way to commit
crime'. Ms *Botfield's* five days of imprisonment were upheld (1982).

'Natural Punishment'

Sometimes the offender seems to have already suffered enough as a
result of his offence. German jurists used to call this *poena naturalis*.
The Swedish penal code requires courts to 'consider to a reasonable
extent . . . whether the accused as a consequence of the crime has
suffered serious bodily harm'.[6] In England it is sometimes a consideration when a careless or dangerous driver has killed or seriously
injured a relative (see the guidelines in *Boswell* (1984)). In *Rimmer*
(1975) the Court of Appeal suspended a six-month prison sentence for
causing death by reckless driving because the defendant had spent six
months in hospital and, not having been insured, faced a large
financial claim. When *Conlon* (1998), who had been advised not to
drive because of his tunnel vision, was sentenced for causing a boy's
death the judge was told that the accident had plunged him into a
severe and chronic depression. Instead of four or five years' imprisonment she gave him a suspended sentence, saying 'I view your illness
at the present time to be your sentence'. The suffering need not
necessarily be the result of the offence. In *Campbell* (1995) the Court
of Appeal said – rather oddly – that 'he has punished himself in that
since he was sentenced [to imprisonment] his father, to whom he was
attached, has died'; and his sentence was reduced. Retributivists are
divided about the justice of regarding 'natural punishment' as a
mitigating factor, perhaps because it is a notion which seems to be
based, as I suggested in chapter 1, on humanity rather than desert.[7]
We shall see it at work again in chapter 10, when considering the
kinds of reasoning which influence the disposal of the mentally
disordered. It may be that it should be relegated to the status of
'reasons for mercy', which are discussed in chapter 14.

Stigma

Akin to 'natural punishment' are the stigmatising consequences of a
conviction, which may affect the offender's social and even familial

relations as well as his career. The 'shame and disgrace' of a schoolteacher's conviction for bestiality with a dog persuaded the Court of Appeal to cut short her prison sentence (*Pamela Jean P* (1992)). The Rehabilitation of Offenders Act 1974 was an attempt to reduce the damage by allowing a conviction to become 'spent' after a period, so that the offender could deny it[8] and even sue someone who referred to it. It was an ill-conceived piece of legislation, in several ways. The delay before a conviction becomes spent means that the offender is unprotected at the time when the news media are most interested in his case. The delay is short – six months – after an absolute discharge, but five years after a community punishment, seven years after a prison sentence of up to six months, and 10 years for a sentence of seven to 30 months. If the sentence is longer than that the conviction never becomes spent. The reasoning of the Gardiner Committee which recommended this elaborate provision was that 'the more serious the offence the longer it will be before one can be reasonably sure that the offender has reformed'. In fact the reverse is true: it is the less harmful offenders who are more likely to repeat their offences. What the Committee may have meant was that the *consequences* of a repetition by a seriously harmful offender would be worse, not that its probability was greater. But this sort of legislation does next to nothing to reduce probabilities: that is the aim of the measures discussed in chapters 5 and 6. In practice courts sometimes, but not often, reduce sentences to compensate offenders for stigma. An unusual example was cited in chapter 6: a judge's decision to reduce the prison sentence for a 41-year-old sexual offender in order to shorten the period for which his name would have to be on the police register of sexual offenders.

NOTES

1.   Different ways of achieving this were still being considered late in 1998.

2.   The amount has not changed since 1993.

3.   For an extraordinarily optimistic assessment of the harmlessness of indecent acts with children see Brongersma (1980).

4. If confirmation of this is needed Robinson's and Darley's (1995) experiments in the USA provide it.

5. I have the impression that this involves him in a modification of the theory of punishment offered in his 1986 book; but changes of position are not discreditable.

6. I am grateful to Andrew von Hirsch for this information.

7. Yet Kant tolerated the notion in his lectures at least.

8. The legislation allowed many exceptions: see Walker and Padfield (1996).

Chapter 9
Youth and Old Age

YOUTH

Youth must be the oldest reason for leniency, yet on occasion it can be an aggravation. Its history in England has not yet been the subject of a thorough study; but a brief account may explain the complexity of the current law.

So far as pre-Norman England is concerned we know only that youth protected lawbreakers until they reached their teens. The seventh century laws of Ine of Wessex say that a boy of 10 'can be privy to a theft'. The criterion was knowledge of right and wrong. The tenth century laws of Athelstan, drafted by a bishop, say that a robber caught with his booty is not to be spared punishment if he is over 12, and add that 'men should slay none younger than a fifteen winters' man'; but do not say why younger men should be spared. These minimum ages, which we may assume to have applied to other serious crimes, are remarkably high, especially when compared with those which eventually replaced them after the Norman Conquest.

The Roman Principle

The Normans did not interfere immediately with Saxon customary laws. Twelve was still a crucial age in Henry II's time, since a child could not be appealed of felony before that age.[1] Bracton's thirteenth century treatise talks of children as being protected by 'harmlessness of intention' (*innocentia consilii*), but does not specify a minimum age. (The protection by his time was the practice of pardoning convicted children rather than exempting them from trial, and this expedient persisted until at least the fifteenth century). For Spigurnel, a judge in the early part of the fourteenth century, the test was not harmlessness of intention but whether the child knew right from wrong. By that time the influence of the Church seems to have persuaded judges to adopt the approach of Roman law. This excused 'infants' under the age of seven, but if the wrongdoer was older allowed it to be asked whether he was 'capable of guile' (*doli capax*). This made sense to the Church, which regarded children over that age as fit to attend confession. Between seven and 12[2] the evidence of capacity for guile had to be very persuasive; after that he was 'more easily presumed to be *doli capax* . . . unless by great circumstances it appear that he is *incapax doli*', and at 14, the official end of puberty, he was tried as an adult.[3] It has to be remembered that these rules were designed to protect children from capital punishment, and may not always have protected them from lesser penalties.

'Capacity for guile' was interpreted as knowledge that conduct is seriously wrong in the moral sense. The rule had curious features. In recent years the presumption that the child was incapable of guile was sometimes rebutted, if no better evidence was available, by showing that his mental abilities were normal for his age, although the presumption was that children of that age were *not* capable of guile. Capacity to control one's behaviour was apparently not an issue. English lawyers and legislators are suspicious of defences based on weak self-control. Yet a child may know that stealing, vandalism or assault is an offence and still act from impulse.

Modern Modifications

The minimum age of criminal liability remained at seven until raised to eight in 1932[4] on the unchallenged recommendation of the Molony Committee (1927). By that time, however, it had become possible to deal officially, and without invoking a criminal court, with juveniles[5] of any age who seemed to need care, protection or control, and even to remove them from home to the 'approved schools' to which courts could send those whom they had found guilty of offences. This persuaded the Ingleby Committee in 1960 to recommend the raising of the minimum age to 12, and eventually to 14; but when legislators attempted this in 1963 the House of Lords forced a compromise at the age of 10, the current minimum.

The *doli incapax* rule was condemned by the Ingleby Committee (1960), partly because some courts already ignored it while others applied it in different ways, partly because the prosecution often found it impossible to prove guilty intention when official intervention was clearly desirable. The Law Commission were at that time in agreement, but by 1989 favoured the retention of the presumption. In 1994 a Queen's Bench judge very rashly said that it could be disregarded (*C (a minor)* v *DPP* (1995)); but the House of Lords pointed out that only a statute could abolish it (*C (a minor)* v *DPP* (1995)). The presumption – but not, as we shall see, the defence – was eventually abolished by the Crime and Disorder Act 1998.

Age, Duress and Provocation

As we saw in the previous chapter, the defendant's age is a 'relevant characteristic' when duress is being pleaded as a defence, and no doubt when it is pleaded in mitigation too. Chapter 11 will discuss the grounds on which provocation reduces murder to manslaughter. All that need be mentioned here is that age is relevant. In *Camplin* (1978) Lord Diplock said that the proper direction to a jury should explain that the 'reasonable man' for this purpose means

> . . . a person having the power of self-control to be expected of an ordinary person of the sex *and age* of the accused . . . (my italics).

Camplin's age was 15, and the implication was that a young person could submit that his self-control is weaker than that of an older person. It has not been made clear whether 'age' includes 'old age' when duress or provocation are pleaded, or whether the Court of Appeal really meant 'youth'.

Exemption from Adults' Penalties

Equally important has been the step-by-step exemption of the young from penalties to which adults can or could be subjected. They were

not exempted from corporal punishment until adults were; and even
the enlightened Prison Commissioner Alexander Paterson is on record
as authorising the flogging of a borstal inmate. The prime example of
leniency was of course the commuting of the death penalty. Until the
nineteenth century many a child of less than fifteen winters was being
hanged although judges had the power to prevent this. Exactly when
Home Secretaries began to advise sovereigns to commute the death
sentence on grounds of youth is not known; but the practice was well
established by the second half of the nineteenth century. In 1908, as
so often happens, this procedure was replaced by a statute. The
Children Act forbade the pronouncing or recording of a death
sentence on a person under 16; and the Children and Young Persons
Act of 1932 raised this minimum to 18. The prerogative continued to
be used as it had been, but to spare slightly older murderers, until the
virtual abolition of capital punishment in the 1960s.

Custodial Sentences

A commuted death sentence had to be replaced by some power to
incarcerate; and it was called 'Her Majesty's Pleasure'. It was of
course administered by the Home Secretary, and the 1908 Act
extended his power to juveniles sentenced for attempted murder,
manslaughter or intentional grievous bodily harm, allowing courts this
option when no other sentence seemed adequate. This form of
custodial sentence – which can be determinate or indeterminate –
allows the juvenile to be kept at first in whatever sort of establishment
seems suitable, but to be transferred to a prison if he is detained until
adulthood. The power is still preserved in section 53 of the consolidating 1933 Act, and has been extended to any offence for which the
maximum prison sentence is 14 years or more, as well as to indecent
assault on a woman or man and causing death by driving dangerously
or carelessly and under the influence of alcohol or a drug. It was
always optional, however, unlike the indeterminate sentence for a
juvenile murderer, and courts could, and still can, use other types of
custodial sentences for juveniles.

These have taken many forms. At first their only aim was to protect
the juvenile from adults by segregation, for example in the hulk
Bellerophon. Later, reformatory schools were meant to inculcate a
hard-working, law-abiding way of life. Twentieth century creations

were 'places of detention', later called 'remand homes', borstals, approved schools, detention centres, young offenders' institutions and, most recently, secure training centres.[5] Borstals, detention centres, young offenders' institutions and secure training centres were provided by the Prison Department, the others by local authorities or other agencies. Some had innovative regimes: some were simply renamed reincarnations. There were variations in eligible age-groups. Their aims varied too. Detention centres were expected to do little more than deter, and were sometimes called 'a short sharp shock'. Longer sentences were expected to alter attitudes to crime and fit inmates for law-abiding occupations: an expectation which has been labelled 'therapeutic optimism'.

Some Effects of Therapeutic Optimism

Therapeutic optimism led to important distinctions between custodial sentences for juveniles and their equivalent for adults. A minimum period (of two months) was specified for sentences involving young offenders' institutions, at a time when this was unheard of where adults were concerned;[6] and the minimum for 'detention and training' under the 1998 Act is to be four months. The rules for remission applied only to adult prisoners. Even a well-behaved young prisoner serving a determinate section 53 sentence could not count on remission. His release depended on the optimism or pessimism of staff about his progress. When the Parole Board had a say in his release it tried – not always successfully – to make sure that his fitness for release was considered as early as an adult prisoner's would be; but he had no *right* to this until the passing of the 1991 Act. A legacy of therapeutic optimism which still survives, however, is the absence of any power to suspend custodial sentences for juveniles or young adults. This was said to be justified by the benefits offered by the institutions. If the young offender needed them suspension deprived him of them. A striking example of the anomaly was the 20-year-old *Horney* (1990), sentenced to 18 months in a young offender institution for the manslaughter of his baby. The sentencing judge said that had Horney been an adult (i.e. a year older), he would have suspended the sentence. The Court of Appeal called the result a 'hardship', but felt unable to remedy it. The distinction between imprisonment and custodial sentences for the young is still defended by pointing out that suspension is now allowable only in 'exceptional circumstances'; yet most of the circumstances which the Court of Appeal accepts as exceptional in the case of adults (see chapter 7) can also befall the young. Once therapeutic optimism is abandoned, and custodial sentences are seen for what they are – more or less humane deterrents – the argument collapses. Meanwhile, in this respect youth is an aggravation.

The Options of Custody

For young offenders, as for adults, the all-important question is of course whether the sentence will be custodial or non-custodial, and the official criterion until recently has been the seriousness of the offence, as measured by the 'right-thinking' test. In practice the younger a juvenile is the more serious the offence has to be before a court will resort to custody. Even young adults in the Crown Court are slightly less likely than adults to be dealt with custodially (Moxon, 1988). Moxon noticed, however, that young recidivist burglars were *more* likely to get custodial sentences, probably because some of the adult burglars had their sentences suspended. Eventually, as we saw in chapter 4, the guidelines in *Howells* (1998) have acknowledged that seriousness is not the only criterion that may tip the balance:

> Youth and immaturity, while affording no defence, will often justify a less rigorous penalty than would be appropriate for an adult.

When the offence is of one of the 'grave' kinds which make the offender eligible for a section 53 sentence, the court may have difficulty in choosing between this and what will now be called 'detention and training' (see below). The considerations which it should have in mind have been summarised and brought almost up to date in the guideline cases of *Mills and others* (1998).[7] Long terms of custody are undesirable for juveniles; but serious offences by them call for sentences substantial enough both to punish and to deter, and sometimes to protect the public. The offence does not have to be of exceptional gravity to justify the use of section 53. It simply has to be one which calls for a term longer than the permitted maximum for juvenile custodial sentences (24 months). The court should not hesitate to use section 53 to impose a sentence which is not much longer than that maximum if, after careful thought, that seems to be 'appropriate'. When sentencing for two or more offences of which at least one calls for the use of section 53, courts may impose consecutive or concurrent terms which are shorter than two years; but consecutive terms should be avoided when the offender is under 16. A section 53 sentence does not necessarily mean detention in an institution run by the Prison Department: the juvenile can be allocated to one in the child care system, and in the 1980s this was the policy for those aged under sixteen and a half and not considered too dangerous or hard to manage. More recently, however, this policy has been frustrated by shortages of places.

Determinate custodial sentences are often shortened because of the offender's youth. The Court of Appeal shortened *Matthews's* (1998) sentence for raping a 14-year-old girl from 10 to eight and a half years solely because he was only 19. For murder the sentence must be indeterminate, as for adults, although it is officially not 'life' but 'detention at Her Majesty's pleasure'. For other crimes which carry 'life', indeterminate detention at the Home Secretary's pleasure is a possible choice. As we saw in chapter 5 the Court of Appeal does not normally approve of an indeterminate sentence unless the offender is mentally disordered or at least 'unstable', but approves of the occasional exception. The 16-year-old *Bell*, for example (1990), robbed a woman and then indecently assaulted her, threatening her baby with a knife. Psychiatrists did not label him mentally disordered or unstable, simply as likely to be dangerous for an unpredictable length of time; and his indeterminate sentence was upheld on appeal. In all probability it was the sexual assault which tipped the scale. When passing such sentences judges are not expected to specify minimum periods to be served before release. Usually, however, the sentence is determinate. In Moxon's (1988) sample the lengths of young adults' sentences did not differ much from the lengths of adults' sentences.

Longer-than-commensurate Sentences

When a section 53 sentence is imposed for a violent or sexual offence it can be a longer-than-commensurate sentence designed to protect the public (see chapter 5). So may a young adult's sentence to a young offender institution, or the new 'detention and training order' (see below). The 1991 Act, however, contained an odd little provision (s. 25) which debars a magistrates' court from committing an offender to the Crown Court with a view to such a sentence if he is under 21. It is not debarred, however, from committing an offender under 21 for trial for an offence which might lead to such a sentence; and if the offence is serious it would probably be obliged to do so.

Non-Custodial Measures

Courts' non-custodial measures were gradually adapted to deal with juvenile offenders. Powers to bind them over and to discharge them, absolutely or conditionally, remained unaffected. Supervision, originally the task of probation officers, was taken over by local authorities' social workers in the 1960s although juveniles between their 16th and 18th birthdays may be supervised by either. Supervision can include conditions such as curfews, residence away from the family, psychiatric treatment and special education. Attendance centres were created in the early 1950s and are now available for offenders under 20, if they are within travelling distance of one. Fines, compensation orders and orders for 'costs' must (with the obvious exceptions) be paid by parents if the offender is under 16 (and if he is aged 16 or 17 the court may order a parent to pay under section 57 of the 1991 Act).

Stigma

For most of this century it has been assumed that stigmatising young offenders is unjust or at least counter-productive. The Children Act 1908 excluded the public but not newspaper reporters from juvenile courts (and neither the press nor the public were excluded from Quarter Sessions or Assizes when a child was on trial). The 1933 Act (s. 49) still allowed the press into juvenile courts but forbade the publication of anything that would enable the child to be identified; and this applies to the modern youth court. It is allowed to make exceptions to prevent injustice, and to facilitate the arrest of a sexual offender, a violent offender or an offender whose crime carries a maximum sentence of 14 years. In the 1970s 'labelling theory' (Lemert, 1969) seemed to support the belief that stigmatising young offenders increased the likelihood of recidivism. The empirical evidence was weak, however, and the theory was eventually eclipsed by enthusiasm for 'naming and shaming', although the supporting evidence was no stronger. Late in 1996 the Conservative Government amended the Crime (Sentences) Bill so as to extend youth courts' discretion to cases in which publication would be 'in the public interest', a phrase whose convenient vagueness has already been mentioned. The main justification offered in the debate was the need to protect potential victims from persistent delinquents; but other speakers also claimed that shaming deterred.

This marked change of attitude towards the confidentiality of youth court proceedings was endorsed in the Labour Government's 1997 White Paper with the slightly menacing title, *No More Excuses*, and eventually a circular of 11 June 1998 from the Home Office and Lord Chancellor's Office provided youth courts with advice on the subject, making several points:

(a)   'very often the private nature of the proceedings discourages young offenders from facing up to the consequences of their behaviour', so that

(b)   'all victims should have the opportunity to attend . . . unless the particular circumstances of the case mean that it would not be in the best interests of justice';

(c)   'there is more scope for the public to attend . . . than is presently allowed – for example in cases where the nature of the young person's offending has impacted on a number of people or the local community in general'; but

(d)   this is 'unlikely to be appropriate at any stage in sensitive sexual offence cases';

(e)   'lifting reporting restrictions [on the news media] could be particularly appropriate in cases where the nature of the . . . offending is persistent or serious, or has impacted on a number of people or [the] local community in general, [or where] alerting others to the young person's behaviour would help prevent further offending by him or her'; but

(f)   'there will. . .be circumstances in which the lifting of . . . restrictions will not be in the best interests of justice': for example if naming the offender would identify a vulnerable victim, or put the offender or his family at risk, or if the offender is particularly young or vulnerable, or has shown contrition and readiness to accept responsibility.

None of the 1933 Act's restrictions on attendance or reporting applied to Quarter Sessions or Assizes unless the judge so ordered. They were trusted to use their powers of restriction sensibly, and this is still the position of the Crown Court. The result was that until 1997 protection from the stigma of trial was automatic for minor offences but exceptional when the offence is of the most stigmatising kind. The Rehabilitation of Offenders Act 1974, which allows convictions to be 'spent' (i.e. deniable: see chapter 8) after certain periods, shortens some of those periods where juveniles are concerned; but none of these protections of course prevents neighbours, schoolfellows and teachers from knowing about court appearances: that would be almost impossible. It is too early to generalise about the effect of the circular on the policies of youth courts. There is still a statutory presumption in favour of confidentiality, but it can now be rebutted by the magic phrase 'the public interest', which often means no more than 'the public's curiosity'.

The 1998 Act

The new Labour Government's innovations were even more radical and tough. The White Paper, *No More Excuses*, which heralded the Crime and Disorder Act 1998, took a firm utilitarian line. 'Concerns about the welfare of the young person' it said

> have too often been seen as in conflict with the aims of protecting the public, punishing offences and preventing offending . . . Preventing offending promotes the welfare of the individual young offender and protects the public . . .

But for the reference to 'punishing offences' this would have been wholeheartedly utilitarian. What the Act itself laid down was that:

> 37(1)   It shall be the principal aim of the youth justice system to prevent offending by children and young persons.
> (2)   In addition to *any other duty* to which they are subject, it shall by the duty of all persons and bodies carrying out functions in relation to the youth justice system to have regard to that aim.

The italics are mine. 'Any other duty' reminds sentencers of their obligations under such provisions as sections 1 and 2 of the 1991 Act, which:

(a)   preclude a custodial sentence unless the offence itself is serious enough to justify it or (in the case of a violent or sexual offence) a custodial sentence is needed to protect the public from serious harm from the offender; and

(b)   protective sentences apart, require the length of a custodial sentence and the restrictions on liberty imposed by a community sentence to be commensurate with the seriousness of the offence.

To what extent these 'other duties' will interfere with the 'principal aim' of the youth justice system remains to be seen.

Welfare and Prevention

Interestingly, although the White Paper mentions the offender's 'welfare' the Act does not. Section 44 of the Children and Young Persons Act 1933 required a court dealing with a juvenile to 'have regard to' his or her 'welfare', and has not been repealed. If this had been interpreted as meaning that his or her welfare must override considerations such as the protection of others against serious harm, or the need to deter potential imitators, it would have tied the hands of courts very tightly. It is not, however, as strongly worded as section 1 of the Children Act 1989, which makes the juvenile's welfare the 'paramount consideration' in non-criminal proceedings involving juveniles' upbringing. The Court of Appeal has confirmed that welfare does not exclude general deterrence as a competing consideration (when dealing for instance with a gang of young robbers, as in *Ford and others* (1976)). As for the protection of the public, judges have used their power to impose indeterminate detention on juveniles guilty of 'grave offences' without being seriously challenged on the ground that this is inimical to their welfare (for example in *Flemming* (1973)). Sentencers must have regard to welfare but need not treat it as paramount.

The Specifics of the 1998 Act

What the Act specifically did was four things.

1.   It finally abolished the rebuttable presumption that a child[8] aged 10 or older is *doli incapax* (s. 34). What it did not abolish was the possibility of defending a child on the ground that he did not realise

that the act was seriously wrong. The defence can no longer rely on a presumption, but must produce evidence – for example of learning difficulties – to support the contention.[9]

2.   It did not tackle the *irrebuttable* presumption that a child under 10 cannot be guilty of an offence; but it side-stepped it. Sections 11 to 13 provided magistrates' courts with a 'child safety order', which they can use if a child under 10 has committed an act which would have been an offence had he been old enough, or if he needs to be prevented from doing so, or if he has contravened a curfew[10] or 'has acted in a manner that caused or was likely to cause alarm or distress to two or more persons not of the same household as himself'. The child cannot be found guilty by a court, but can be made subject to compulsory supervision, with requirements designed to provide 'care, protection . . . support and . . . control' and to prevent him from repeating the behaviour. A child safety order is not quite as drastic as a 'care order' which gives the local social work department parental responsibilities and powers, and it remains in effect for only three months (12 in exceptional cases). It is being introduced cautiously, in areas selected experimentally. But it can be regarded as circumventing the irrebuttable presumption of innocence in a very utilitarian way. What matters is no longer culpability but preventability.

Cautioning, Reprimanding and Warning

3.   The Act overhauled the system known as 'cautioning' where juveniles are concerned (but left it intact for adult offenders). Early in this century the Liverpool police popularised the practice of warning selected young offenders instead of charging them. (The Metropolitan Police resisted the innovation until the 1960s.) Dwindling optimism about the efficacy of sentencing made this alternative more and more attractive, until by the 1980s the Home Office were encouraging police to 'caution' young offenders not only when first detected but repeatedly. A backlash in the 1990s forced a retreat from this policy; but even in 1996 more than 85 per cent of boys aged 10, 11, 12 or 13 who had been detected in offending were cautioned. During the rest of the teens the percentage was high, but decreasing. After 17 it fell sharply from 54 to 35 per cent, and to 26 per cent after 21. The choice between cautioning and prosecuting is obviously a crucial one. Even an appearance in a youth court can be stigmatising. Normally the

public is excluded, the juvenile must not be identified in the news media, and any 'finding of guilt' must not be called a 'conviction', but the news cannot be kept from the neighbours and the school. The rules for cautioning are nowadays clear. The evidence must be enough for a prosecution. The offender must admit his guilt, and consent to be cautioned. The offence should not – normally at least – be of so serious a kind that it is triable only on indictment.

The 1998 Act (ss. 65, 66) provides for the replacement of this fairly simple system with one which is more refined but also more complex, and which is being 'piloted' in selected areas before being used nationwide. Instead of cautions there will be reprimands and warnings for children and young persons (but not for adults). A mere reprimand is to be administered by a constable (of a rank to be specified by the Home Secretary) who has evidence 'such that . . . (there would be a realistic prospect of [the offender's] being convicted' of an offence. The offender must have admitted the offence, must not have previously been convicted of, reprimanded or warned for an offence, and the constable must be satisfied that prosecution would not be in the public interest.

A warning is to be used if the constable, following official guidance from the Home Office, considers the offence sufficiently serious, if the offender has not already had a warning within the last two years, and the offence does not seem serious enough for a charge. After a second warning there cannot be another. A warned offender must be referred to a 'youth offending team' for assessment, the result of which will normally be assignment to a 'rehabilitation programme'. If he is later convicted of an offence committed within two years of the warning, he is not to be let off with a conditional discharge unless the circumstances relating to the offence or the offender seem exceptional – an unusual attempt to compel courts to initiate positive action. Reprimands and warnings must be administered at a police station in the presence of a parent, guardian or other 'appropriate adult', and can be cited in any later criminal proceedings in the same way as convictions. Any failure to participate in a rehabilitation programme can be similarly cited. All this must be explained to the offender in ordinary language.

New Measures for Juveniles

4.   The Act did not interfere to any important extent with the courts' existing repertoire of measures, but it added some new ones:

(a) 'parenting orders' requiring parents or guardians of juvenile offenders, truants or children subject to child safety orders, sex offender orders or anti-social behaviour orders to comply with conditions which may include counselling or guidance sessions (ss. 8, 9 and 10);

(b) 'reparation orders', requiring young offenders to make specified reparation to a consenting victim or to the community. Although the Act does not say so it can be assumed that this does not include financial reparation, since the power to make compensation orders is preserved (ss. 67, 68);

(c) 'action plans', requiring young offenders to be under the supervision of 'a responsible officer' – probably a social worker or probation officer – and to participate in specified activities, no doubt similar to those which have hitherto been provided under supervision or probation orders (ss. 69, 70);

(d) 'detention and training orders' for juveniles between their 10th and 18th birthdays (ss. 73–79). These replace all other types of custodial sentence for this age group except those passed for murder or other grave offences under section 53 of the 1933 Act. If the offender is under 15 the court must be of the opinion that he is a persistent offender; and if he is under 12 that only a custodial sentence will be adequate to protect the public from him. (Detention and training centres will not at first be provided for children under 12.) Orders must be for 4, 6, 8, 10, 12, 18 or 24 months, and may be consecutive for separate offences, so long as they do not together exceed 24 months. The period of each order must be commensurate with the seriousness of the offence unless the need to protect the public justifies a longer sentence (but the protection provided by a 24-month sentence would be short-lived). The provisions for early release differ from adults' parole in some respects, and there are special provisions for post-release supervision. Detention and training orders are intended 'to be more effective in preventing further crime' (Home Office Circular 38/1998), but in practice may be served in young offender institutions, secure training centres, secure local authority homes, or other types of establishment, at the discretion of the Home Office, not the courts.

In one way detention and training orders will increase the flexibility of the system, by allowing the Home Office almost as wide a range of choices between places for the individual juvenile as it has for those under section 53 sentences (which, in theory at least, are not restricted to any category of establishment). On the other hand, the minimum period of detention, which used to be two months, is now to be four. Youth courts, hitherto unable to pass custodial sentences exceeding six months, are now able to pass sentences of lengths up to 24 months. Courts will still be prevented from suspending custodial sentences, even in exceptional circumstances.

The Act includes other innovations designed to reduce delays in dealing with young offenders, and to ensure that local authorities meet their obligations. This chapter, however, is concerned with what directly affects the severity of measures for the young.

If the Youth Justice and Criminal Evidence Bill is enacted in its original form youth courts will have a new power: to refer a juvenile to a 'youth offender panel' with a view to an agreed 'contract' between the panel and the offender. The power will be limited to offenders not previously found guilty or bound over. Proceedings before panels will be less formal, and victims will be allowed to participate, since the main aim will be reparation. 'Contracts' are already a popular device of social workers; but now the refusal or breach of a contract will lead to resentencing by the court. The Bill also improves the protection of juvenile offenders (and witnesses) against public identification – for example when the juvenile is merely a suspect.

Age-based Rules

The Act is less rigid than its predecessors in its attitude to birthdays, but could have been more flexible. A question which the Ingleby Committee overlooked was whether age-based legal rules governing children's liability to be found guilty are needed any longer. The presumption, for example, that *all* children below the age of 10 are incapable of committing *any* criminal act with *mens rea* is obviously unrealistic. It may be true of children with learning difficulties, or those who have been grossly deprived of normal schooling and upbringing, or who come from an isolated subculture. Otherwise, any shopkeeper will testify that children younger than 10 take articles without paying but with the intention of permanently depriving him of them, knowing this to be against the law. They are not necessarily the products of seriously disturbed homes or delinquent gangs.

Stealing is enjoyable risk-taking, especially if all that one is risking is being brought home by the police. A minimum age as low as seven or eight did little harm; but every year by which it is raised increases the scale of the problems which have to be swept under a carpet. The minimum age had the ridiculous result that when Mr and Mrs *Lunt* were prosecuted in 1951 for receiving a tricycle from their seven-year-old son, knowing that he had stolen it, it was held that they could not be guilty since the law conclusively presumed him incapable of theft. This need not have happened. The draftsmen of the 1932 Act could have provided that an under-age child could not be *prosecuted* for an offence; but they seem to have felt bound to reflect the common law by providing that he could not be *guilty* of one, from which it apparently has to be inferred that in a case of this kind there has been no *actus reus*. This might be called a 'constructive *non sequitur'*.

The 1998 Act's 'child safety orders' are a step in a sensible direction. A rule designed to save children from the death penalty is hardly needed to save them from the social services. Age-based rules for the use of special measures are open to the same objection, though in a weaker form. Some 11-year-olds will not be harmed by temporary removal from home, and some older boys or girls will. Ideally, sentencers and social workers could be relied upon to discriminate beneficially without age-based rules. In real life not all can. Age-based restrictions on what can be done with a child, however, are at least better than age-based presumptions about his state of mind.

OLD AGE

At the other end of life leniency is less frequent and never obligatory. 'Maturity' can even aggravate, as it did in *Walters'* case (1994). He was 54, and guilty of 'carnal knowledge' of an under-age girl. Sexual offences are often viewed with more than normal censoriousness. However that may be, the cautioning rate[11] begins to rise in the fifties age-group. When the accused is 'elderly' this is one of the 'public interest factors' which weigh against prosecution, according to the Crown Prosecution Service's Code. It is easy to see why prosecuting an elderly man is not in *his* interest, not so easy to see why it is not in the *public* interest. The Code may merely have had in mind that refraining from prosecution will be less detrimental to aims such as deterrence than it would be if the accused were younger. Or this may simply be an example of an attempt to rationalise mercy (see chapter 14). The cautioning rate reaches 65 per cent in the sixties age-group, after which the statisticians fall silent.[12] Some of the rise may be explained by an increase in the percentage of cases in which the offences are trivial or the offender ill; but the greater part of the explanation must be leniency to age.

It is less easy to say this about sentencing. When the *Criminal Statistics, England and Wales*, deal with sentences they do not subdivide adult offenders by age-groups, and as so often we must rely on newspaper reports and decisions of the Court of Appeal. In January 1998, for example, a man of 77 received an eight-year prison sentence, which will probably mean release when he is 81, for attempts to rape three young girls a quarter of a century ago when he was in his early fifties (*Daily Telegraph*, 10 January 1998). The judge said that had he been younger the sentence would have been 'in double figures'. (Italian penal law would have exempted a person of this age from imprisonment, with exceptions; and the lapse of time (see chapter 13) would almost certainly have meant that this case was not an exception.) *Adams* (1995) at 67 had his 10-year sentence for soliciting to murder reduced to eight years. As the Court said:

Ten years' imprisonment . . . may well result in his spending a substantial proportion, *if not all*, of his remaining life in prison. For that reason, and for that reason only we consider it appropriate to . . . reduce the sentence . . .

The italics are mine. In fact even if this had been a life sentence it is hardly likely that *Adams* would have been detained until death.

Where short sentences for less serious offences are concerned the Court of Appeal seems less likely to be moved by old age. *Aragon* (1995), who had received six months' imprisonment for claiming remuneration for immigration cases which he had not yet adjudicated, failed to persuade the Court to interfere merely because he was aged 68. More fortunate was Dr Helen *Sweeney* who in 1998 had been convicted of selling prescriptions for Rohypnol, to be sold on the black market. The trial judge said that this merited a five-year prison sentence, but substituted a suspended sentence of 18 months in view of her age and state of health. Her age was 62.

Expectancy of Life

The justification for leniency in the sentencing of the elderly is seldom
that they seem less culpable, although sometimes the onset of senility
has this effect. It is usually Bentham's 'sensibility'. When long
custodial sentences are reduced for the elderly it is nearly always
because any such sentence deprives them of a larger fraction of their
expectation of life, or because they are supposed to suffer more from
the conditions of imprisonment. The former is indisputable: the latter
is not. The young prisoner suffers more, and is more likely to attempt
suicide or escape than an elderly inmate. Old men too may be bullied
by inmates, but are treated with special consideration by staff. They
worry more about their health, but are more likely than the young to
be transferred to hospitals when ill, and most unlikely to be compelled
to work. They are less likely to feel missed by wives or children, and
less likely to hanker for outside activities. Their chief anxiety is about
their expectation of life after release. Disputes about their quality of
life, however, are not of the sort that can be settled by hard facts.

As for expectancy of life, when this is reduced by illness the Court
of Appeal regards this as a consideration for the Home Secretary, not
the sentencer: see the case of *Stark* (1992), who had AIDS. It has not
advised judges how to deal with the normal life expectancy of the
healthy. The oldest offender in recent sentencing reports of the Court
of Appeal was *Harold S* (1998). At the age of 82 he was convicted
of raping his 11-year-old granddaughter more than once. He was
one-eyed, deaf, arthritic, with high blood-pressure and other car-
diovascular disorders. The sentencing judge seems to have started
from the assumption that 12 years' imprisonment would have been
commensurate for a younger man, and that this would have accounted
for about one third of his expectation of life. He seems to have been
told or guessed that *Harold S* had not much more than five years to
live, and calculated that 21 months would be a third of that. Perhaps
because this result seemed over-lenient he decided that the defendant
had aggravated matters by trying to avoid trial and pleading not
guilty, so that he felt able to justify a three-year sentence. The Court
of Appeal disapproved both of his actuarial approach and of his
reasons for abandoning it, but having no formula of its own upheld
the sentence. Meanwhile the appellant was reported to be adjusting
well to his first experience of incarceration.

NOTES

1. Although the text sounds as though he could then be dealt with for a felony committed before 12, this may be due to an inadvertent ambiguity (Glanville, 1180ca).

2. Hale mentions lower limits, such as 11, in the early days, but by Lambard's time (the second half of the sixteenth century) it was 12. By Hale's time (in the late seventeenth century) it was 14.

3. There were exceptions: for example, if he was under 21, and if the offence was a misdemeanour, the court had to be careful before deciding that he was *doli capax*. When these exceptions became obsolete is not known.

4. By the Children and Young Persons Act 1932: the 1933 Act usually gets the credit but was merely a consolidating Act. The 1932 Act also abolished whipping as a sentence of the court, although corporal punishment continued in approved schools for another generation.

5. The first secure training centre was not opened until May 1998.

6. The Crime Sentences Act 1997 provided mandatory minimum custodial sentences for recidivist drug-traffickers and burglars: but these are special cases. Otherwise the only minimum for prison sentences is the five-day one specified in section 132 of the Magistrates' Courts Act 1980, simply to save the Prison Service from an administrative nuisance.

7. In summarising the guidelines I have omitted guidance which does not seem to fit the options created by the new 'detention and training orders'.

8. A 'child' is defined in that Act as a person under 14, a 'young person' as aged at least 14 but under 18. Confusingly, the Children Act 1989 defines a child as a person under 18. I shall use 'juvenile' to refer to persons under 18, unless the context calls for distinctions. A 'young adult' is aged at least 18 but under 21.

9.   This was confirmed by the Solicitor-General in the House of Lords on 16 December 1997 (*Hansard*, col. 596). Surprisingly, the Home Office's circular about the Act did not endorse what he had said, but merely explained that children in the 10–13 age group will 'be treated in the same way as other juveniles (14 to 17 year olds) when deciding [*sic*] whether or not prosecution is appropriate'. Does this mean that the CPS can rule out the possibility of a defence based on an individual child's failure to appreciate the serious wrongness of a particular act or omission ? Only an appealed case will decide. The wording of the clause was needlessly obscure. Meanwhile Spigurnel seems to confirm the commonsense view that there cannot be a presumption without something relevant to presume.

10.   Local authorities can make 'child curfew schemes' prohibiting children under a specified age (not above 10) from being in a public place after a specified hour unless accompanied by a responsible adult (ss. 14, 15).

11.   I.e. the percentage of identified indictable male offenders who are cautioned. The percentages for women are even higher.

12.   This was in 1994, the last year for which the *Criminal Statistics, England and Wales*, subdivided age-groups older than 21.

Chapter 10
Mental Disorder

The notion that insane offenders should be spared punishment is at least as old as the fourth century BC. Plato's *Laws* proposed that – homicide apart – they should pay for the harm done, but suffer no other penalty. His code was never adopted however by any of the Greek states, and it is not until the second century AD that we have firm evidence of the principle in practice. Marcus Aurelius laid down that insane parricides should not be punished. Since parricide was a 'worst possible case' he must have meant 'even parricides'. His reasoning was that 'they are punished enough by their madness'.[1] It is reasoning that was echoed occasionally by English lawyers until the seventeenth century, and is perhaps still at the back of some sentencers' minds. It is sometimes criticised as implying that the insane deserve punishment for their crimes. In fact Marcus Aurelius' logic may well have been subtler. He may have meant to sidestep the attribution of culpability by saying that *even if* the madman is culpable his madness is punishment enough: 'natural punishment' again.

The *Digest*, however, put Western Europe on another tack. It offered another reason: that the insane are not culpable because they do not will their crimes, and this eventually superseded Aurelius' approach. The early Christian writers were superstitious rather than scientific, and tended to regard madness as due to demonic possession. By the eighth century, however, bishops were persuading English kings to be merciful to the mad;[2] and after the Norman Conquest judges' reasoning was inspired by the *Digest*. Madmen lacked the will to harm (Bracton, ca1250): they were like 'wild beasts'.

Yet sometimes this was obviously not so. There are cases in which violence is clearly mad, yet clearly intentional. Exactly when judges began to recognise another criterion is not certain, and perhaps never will be; but early in the fourteenth century Spigurnel was talking of children's ability to tell right from wrong, and by the seventeenth century Dalton was writing that idiots lacked this ability. When was the 'right-wrong test' extended to deal with insanity? Again this is uncertain, but from what *Earl Ferrers* said in 1760 to the House of Lords at his trial for murder it must have been regarded as relevant by that date.

The M'Naghten Rules

Hadfield's trial in 1800 for firing a pistol at George III is usually treated as a landmark; but all it led to was legislation to ensure that insane felons were more securely detained than they had been. The landmark of the nineteenth century was the trial of McNaughtan[3] for fatally wounding a secretary whom he had mistaken for Peel, the Tory Prime Minister. He knew what he was doing, and that it was criminal, but was under the delusion that the Tories were persecuting him. His counsel's eloquence secured his acquittal; but a public outcry forced Tindal LCJ and his colleagues to frame a statement of the common-law criteria as they believed them to be. The defendant must, at the time of his act, have been suffering from a 'disease of the mind', such that either

(a)   he did not know 'the nature and quality' of the act [i.e. did not know what he was doing]; or

(b)   did not know that it was 'wrong' [what Tindal meant will be discussed later]; or

(c)   was under a delusion which, if true, would have justified his act.

Ironically, although these came to be known as the M'Naghten Rules (nobody having troubled to find out how he himself spelled his name), he would have been convicted had they been applied to him, since his delusion did not justify homicide. It was Tindal rather than McNaughtan who deserved to have the Rules named after him.

Even after the Rules had been publicly formulated they were criticised by other judges as an incomplete statement of the law; and there are records of trials in which it is clear that another criterion was sometimes used – at least by juries – to allow the accused a special verdict. This was weakness of self-control, and there were attempts to persuade the Government to widen the Rules so as to include it. An attempt which nearly succeeded was made by the Atkin Committee (1924) which recommended the addition of 'irresistible impulse'. Parliament, however, was persuaded that it would be too difficult, if not impossible, to distinguish between an impulse which the defendant could not resist and one which he simply did not resist, and the attempt failed. Other jurisdictions, however, saw more merit in the idea. The American Law Institute's Model Penal Code, for example, recognises 'lack of capacity to conform one's conduct to the requirements of law'. There is a difference, of course, between the notion of a transitory impulse which cannot be resisted and a non-transitory weakness of resistance. As we shall see, English criminal law eventually found a way of recognising the latter, at least when murder is the charge. Meanwhile, it is interesting to compare English lawyers' acceptance of, and indeed insistence on, 'loss of self-control' when the plea is provocation (see chapter 11) with their lack of enthusiasm for accepting irresistible impulse as part of the insanity defence.

Another feature of the Rules which is of interest is that they have been interpreted by the Court of Appeal as excluding the offender who knew what he was doing but whose disorder led him to believe that it was not morally wrong. The classic case is *Windle* (1952), who thought it was right to give his ailing wife a fatal dose of aspirin, but who reported himself to the police because he knew it was against the law. The Court insisted that Tindal must have meant 'legally wrong', and Windle's conviction was upheld. It is not at all certain what Tindal meant. The Victorian House of Lords talked of 'the laws of God and man' as if they were much the same. A 'choice theorist' could defend the Court of Appeal on the ground that if an offender knows an act to be criminal then – assuming he has the capacity to obey the law – what his conscience tells him is irrelevant. Some Commonwealth jurisdictions have taken the more liberal view. It is also relevant that, as we saw in chapter 9, a child under 14 can be defended on the ground that he did not know his act to be 'seriously wrong' in the moral sense. A mentally impaired offender is at least as likely as a 13-year-old child to fail to realise that an act is morally wrong. It is true that if so he is also unlikely to know that it is against the law. There have been offenders, however, who were well aware of the criminality of their acts but believed, because of their mental disorders, that they were justified: Sutcliffe, 'the Yorkshire Ripper', is said to have believed he was obeying God. He did not, however, offer an insanity defence, and the defence is now so rare that any inconsistency is academic. It is worth noting – although the textbooks do not – that the Home Office used the Prerogative of Mercy to commute *Windle's* death sentence to 'life'. It was one of those cases in which the courts would probably have been lenient if their interpretation of the law had allowed them.

Unfitness for Trial

Slightly less rare is the plea that the defendant's mental state is such that he cannot understand a trial sufficiently to make a proper defence (*Pritchard* (1836)). If the plea convinces the court it will postpone trial until the defendant is expected to be fit, or, if he seems unlikely to be fit within the foreseeable future, will proceed to have a 'trial of the facts', the result of which may be to exonerate him completely or to find that he did the act charged (s. 4A, Criminal Procedure (Insanity) Act 1984). Such a finding is not a conviction, since he might, if fit for trial, be able to offer a valid excuse (such as insanity or self-defence). It does, however, allow the court the same freedom in dealing with him as it has in the case of a successful insanity defence (see below). Illogically, amnesia for the crime is not sufficient to excuse a defendant from trial. (I tried to persuade my colleagues on the Butler Committee (1975) that it should, but did not receive enough support.) Interestingly, mental unfitness for trial is not listed in the Crown Prosecution Service's 1994 Code as a reason for non-prosecution.

Insanity as a Bar to Execution

An interesting rule of unknown origin[4] and somewhat academic relevance is that a person must not be executed if he is mad, even if he had been sane when he offended and sane enough to be tried. Authorities offered different reasons, some more impressive than others. The madman could not suffer as he should (Covarrubias, 1568). His example could not deter other madmen (Coke, 1644). He would not be spiritually ready for the next world (Hawles, 1685, at the trial of *Bateman*). If sane he might be able to give a reason for sparing him (Hale, 1736). He is punished enough by his madness (Blackstone, 1765, echoing Marcus Aurelius). From 1884 until the abandonment of capital punishment in Britain, prisoners under sentence of death were routinely examined to see whether they were insane; but the Home Office did not make public the criteria it regarded as relevant. The doctrine is still preached – if seldom honoured – in jurisdictions of the USA which retain capital punishment. Nobody has ever suggested that it should apply to lesser punishments such as imprisonment.

Partial Insanity

Even in the seventeenth century lawyers realised that there were mental states which did not qualify as insanity but were far from normal. A common example was melancholy. Hale (1736) dismissed such states of mind as corresponding to the mentality of a child of 14, and therefore as providing no defence. The result was that many a severely depressed murderer went to the gallows. In Scotland the Bluidy Mackenzie, in spite of the bigotry which earned him his sobriquet, had urged more tolerance, and in the middle of the nineteenth century the notion of 'diminished responsibility', which reduced murder to 'culpable homicide', was developed to save killers from the death penalty. A century later an English Royal Commission included it in its recommendations and was supported by a Scottish Lord Chancellor (Kilmuir (1964)). The Home Secretary rejected it, but having no other proposals was eventually persuaded to include it in the Homicide Act of 1957. Unlike the insanity defence, it applies only to murder, but it serves the purpose of allowing juries to take into account:

> such abnormality of mind (whether arising from a condition of arrested or retarded development of mind or any inherent causes or induced by disease or injury) as substantially impaired his mental

responsibility for his acts or omissions in doing or being a party to the killing (s. 3).

The effect of a successful plea is a verdict of manslaughter. It was not long before *Byrne's* case (1960) showed how wide a door had been opened. He was a 27-year-old voyeur who strangled and mutilated the girl who saw him peeping through her window. Psychiatrists testified that he was a sexual psychopath who found it difficult or impossible to control his perverted desires. The jury rejected his plea of diminished responsibility, but the Court of Appeal accepted it, ruling that 'abnormality of mind' was 'wide enough to cover the mind's activities in all its aspects' (which is more liberal than Scottish judges' interpretation of the term). The result has been that in cases of homicide the plea of diminished responsibility has almost completely replaced the insanity defence. The commonest diagnosis nowadays is what Hale called 'melancholy': depression accounts for about two in every five cases, but personality disorder accounts for one in five (Mitchell, 1997). The commonest situation is domestic.

The effects of the two verdicts are similar but by no means identical. When diminished responsibility converts murder to manslaughter the court can choose any sentence in its repertoire, from an absolute discharge to life imprisonment or commitment to hospital. An insanity verdict allows a narrower range of choices: committal to hospital, an order entrusting the offender to the guardianship of a responsible authority or person, a supervision and treatment order involving a social worker and a medical practitioner, and an absolute discharge. (In a summary trial its effect is a complete acquittal (*Horseferry Road Magistrates' Court, ex parte K (1997)*). The important difference from the effect of a manslaughter verdict is that imprisonment (or its equivalent for young offenders) is not an option. This is an attraction for a defence counsel who is very sure that he can satisfy the M'Naghten Rules; but if he fails to do so his client will receive a mandatory life sentence if the charge is murder. A plea of diminished responsibility, on the other hand, allows the prosecution to counter it with evidence of insanity.

Diminished responsibility can be pleaded only when the charge is murder, and not even when it is attempted murder. Lawyers defend this by pointing out that it is only a conviction for murder which debars a judge from mitigating sentence on psychiatric grounds. Yet it is arguable that the system needs a type of verdict that would compel him to do so whatever the offence.

There have been proposals to redraft section 2 of the 1957 Act so as to eliminate the reference to that chimerical faculty 'responsibility' (see chapter 3), and so as to equate 'abnormality of mind' with 'mental disorder' in the Mental Health Act 1983 (an example will be found in the Law Commission's Draft Criminal Code Bill of 1989). Whether there is any point in this is doubtful. The Act's definition of mental disorder is open-ended, including as it does 'any other disorder or disability of mind', so that it gives no real guidance as to the scope of the defence. And as we shall see in chapter 12 some women's groups object that the 'battered woman' syndrome which causes women to kill their partners is stigmatised by being labelled as 'abnormality of mind', and the stigma would be worse if it were equated with 'mental disorder'. In chapter 12 I shall suggest an amendment which would lessen the stigma.

Meanwhile in practice the verdict results in imprisonment for about 45 per cent of male defendants. (For women the percentage used to be around 17 during the sixties, seventies and eighties, but has fallen in the nineties to about 8 per cent.) It does not prevent the judge from making the custodial sentence a life sentence if the defendant seems dangerous enough (see chapter 5). Other disposals take the form of hospital orders (usually with restrictions on discharge: see below) or probation orders with a requirement of treatment; but suspended prison sentences are occasionally used.

Since the *Criminal Statistics, England and Wales*, show this sort of manslaughter verdict separately it is possible to see how the plea has fared since it was made possible. As the table [pages 162–3] shows it was at first a very common verdict, especially in the case of women. In the case of men its frequency declined slightly after the final suspension of capital punishment for all types of murder in 1965, and although the decline began a few years later in the case of women it has been very marked since the mid-eighties. It is particularly marked when its frequency is compared with that of murder verdicts, as it is in the percentage column of the table. Part of the explanation must be changes in the patterns of homicide. Homicides associated with diminished responsibility are usually killings of family members, lovers or friends, while the general increase in homicides is largely attributable to growing numbers of other types – for example in the course of robberies.

Verdicts of murder and diminished responsibility

Year	Murder verdicts		Diminished responsibility verdicts		Columns 3 and 4 as % of columns 1+3 or 2+4		Sentenced custodially		Sentenced to 'life'	
	Column 1	Column 2	Column 3	Column 4						
	M	F	M	F	M	F	M	F	M	F
1958a	27	3	22	3	*b*	*b*	12	1	9	–
1959	42	–	18	3	*b*	*b*	18	2	8	–
1960	42	–	17	6	34	80	17	4	9	2
1961	49	2	24	12	31	91	15	4	12	–
1962	30	1	26	8	37	90	12	–	8	–
1963	44	2	40	6	42	84	21	–	14	–
1964	44	–	40	6	47	87	12	1	9	1
1965c	56	1	39	8	45	87	15	1	11	1
1966	70	2	44	7	42	88	16	2	6	–
1967	62	1	37	12	39	87	11	2	–	–
1968	73	1	33	11	36	88	9	1	2	1
1969	74	1	30	17	32	93	9	1	6	–
1970	94	3	55	11	33	89	20	1	11	1
1971	94	3	53	15	35	86	20	3	11	2
1972	76	3	57	19	39	83	19	2	7	1
1973d	87	3	60	20	40	86	25	2	9	–
1974	108	4	63	16	40	85	32	2	17	2
1975	102	5	49	17	37	82	26	4	13	1
1976	104	–	70	22	37	86	39	3	20	–
1977	112	3	56	17	36	88	40	7	17	4
1978	101	4	65	14	38	83	36	3	20	1
1979	126	10	72	20	36	75	48	4	24	–
1980	167	2	66	14	34	74	34	–	14	–
1981	122	4	66	20	33	77	21	2	8	1

Verdicts of murder and diminished responsibility

Year	Murder verdicts		Diminished responsibility verdicts		Columns 3 and 4 as % of columns 1+3 or 2+4		Sentenced custodially		Sentenced to 'life'	
	Column 1	Column 2	Column 3	Column 4						
	M	F	M	F	M	F	M	F	M	F
1982	176	8	76	14	*31*	*77*	37	4	8	1
1983	127	5	68	16	*33*	*75*	26	4	4	–
1984	148	8	57	15	*31*	*68*	25	2	5	–
1985	166	9	49	16	*28*	*68*	19	1	3	–
1986	170	9	38	11	*23*	*62*	16	–	3	–
1987	159	7	44	6	*21*	*57*	19	1	6	1
1988	220	11	45	8	*19*	*48*	21	2	8	1
1989	179	10	36	4	*22*	*39*	11	1	4	–
1990	174	6	16	6	*15*	*40*	9	–	3	–
1991	190	11	20	1	*12*	*29*	13	–	6	–
1992	172	10	12	–	*8*	*21*	7	–	4	–
1993	197	15	25	5	*9*	*14*	8	–	2	–
1994	183	9	40	10	*12*	*31*	10	–	4	–
1995	197	17	41	3	*16*	*31*	13	2	6	–

Notes

a This was the first whole year in which diminished responsibility verdicts were allowable.

b To reduce the fluctuations in the small numbers these are 'rolling 3–year percentages'. For example, the percentages shown for 1960 are the averages for 1958, 1959 and 1960, and so on.

c This was the year in which the death penalty was finally suspended.

d Until 1973 the *Criminal Statistics* showed only sentences of more than 10 years without distinguishing life sentences; but probably most of them were.

That does not account, however, for the decline in actual numbers of diminished responsibility verdicts. Since 'family killings' have not become less frequent[5] at least one other factor must be at work. According to the *Criminal Statistics* there has been a decrease in the percentage of homicides in which the suspect was 'mentally disturbed' – from 12 per cent in 1983 to 6 per cent in 1995, although this is probably based on the results of trials rather than observation. Taylor and Gunn (1999) suggest that there has been a real decline in the numbers of psychotic homicides, and it is certainly possible that the percentage of 'family killers' suffering from 'abnormality of mind' has decreased as sharply as the numbers of verdicts suggests. Other factors, however, may have reduced the probability of a successful plea of diminished responsibility. One possibility is that the plea is nowadays being contested more often than it used to be. When Sutcliffe, 'the Yorkshire Ripper', was tried in 1981 for killing several prostitutes four psychiatrists reported in favour of diminished responsibility, and the Attorney-General did not propose to contest it; but the judge ruled that it must be contested in front of a jury, which in the event rejected it. The decline began soon after. The Crown Prosecution Service denies, however, that its policy in such cases has changed in any way that could explain it; and indeed it seems to have begun before the creation of the CPS. The most likely possibility is that it has become harder to find psychiatrists who are prepared to testify to a 'substantial diminution' of responsibility, especially when the diagnosis is 'personality disorder', which will be discussed later in this chapter. More will be said about the diminished responsibility of women (and about the plea of infanticide) in chapter 12.

Physical Disorders

Meanwhile there are also physical disorders which result in mental states that are accepted as reducing culpability. *Wooton* (1998) was a diabetic who had been convicted of attempted murder. Although he could not plead diminished responsibility because his victim had not died, the sentencing judge made clear his belief that *Wooton* had been suffering from the hypoglycaemia to which diabetics are prone, and that this 'may well have heightened [his] aggression'. This persuaded the Court of Appeal to reduce the sentence from 15 years to 12, presumably on the assumption that the heightened aggression was hard to control. Another condition sometimes accepted as having a similar effect is premenstrual tension in women, which is discussed in chapter 12.

Automatism

It was recognised as long ago as the fourteenth century that sleepers' bodies might do unfortunate things without their volition. Mothers might overlay babies. Monks might have seminal emissions. The Spanish bishop, Covarrubias (1558) declared them guiltless in his massive and influential treatise; and in most western jurisdictions 'automatism' of this and other kinds (for example diabetic) is accepted as an excuse justifying an acquittal. In England the prosecution may object that what led to the act was not an unforeseeable contingency but an internal condition (such as a brain tumour), in which case the verdict may be insanity ('insane automatism') instead, and the court will have the power to deal accordingly with the offender. The defence is rare.

General

Most of the excuses and mitigations which English law accepts from the mentally disordered are counterparts of those pleaded by the mentally normal. Automatism can be pleaded by a driver whose sneeze made him swerve disastrously. 'Not knowing the nature or quality of one's act' is a cognitive mistake, and can be pleaded by the man who takes my umbrella believing it to be his, or who shoots someone in a dark thicket believing him to be a deer. Even an insane delusion is a defence only when it would be a sane person's defence if it were not a delusion but true.

The correspondence is distorted when the disordered person's excuse is not knowing that the act or omission is legally wrong. In England the only sane people who are allowed the defence that they did not know their act or omission to be 'seriously wrong' are children under 14; and nowadays even they must offer evidence to this effect (see chapter 9). Older people are not allowed this defence even if their moral ignorance is attributable to mental disorder, although, as we saw earlier, Tindal may well have meant 'wrong' to mean 'morally wrong', not 'criminal'. It was the twentieth-century Court of Appeal

which decided that 'wrong' must mean 'criminal'; and some common-law jurisdictions have refused to be so strict.

Failure of self-control is another respect in which the culpability of
the sane and the disordered is approached untidily and perhaps not
quite logically. The English insanity defence – unlike some United
States versions – cannot rest on a lack of capacity for self-control:
only diminished responsibility is allowed to take this form. Neither
insanity nor diminished responsibility is allowed to invoke a sudden
'irresistible' impulse (in spite of the Atkin Committee's (1924)
recommendation that the insanity defence should). Yet, as we shall see
in the next chapter, this is exactly what the English defence of
provocation relies on as its excuse.

Behind the Legal Headlines

Nowadays it is only in the trial or sentencing of homicides and other
grave offences that the moral responsibility of the accused is likely to
be an issue. Even older – and commoner – is the custom which looks
to the madman's kin to see that he does no more harm. Plato's *Laws*,
Saxon custom and Henry II's laws treated this as the solution to the
problem. Madhouses later relieved families of some of this burden,
and until the nineteenth century even the detention of insane killers
was not treated as a matter for the court. When Charles Lamb's sister,
Mary fatally stabbed her mother in 1795 the coroner's jury found that
she had done so while insane, but it was left to her brother to put her
in a madhouse and eventually look after her when she was allowed to
leave it. Even if the offender was arraigned it was not until 1800 that
an Act obliged judges to commit offenders found insane by a criminal
court to be kept at His Majesty's Pleasure, usually in an asylum.
Magistrates could deal with petty offenders as pauper lunatics instead
of convicting and imprisoning them, although they needed to be
reminded of this by the Home Office. Eugenic enthusiasm inspired the
Mental Deficiency Acts, which allowed courts to commit 'defective'
adults and children to institutions or guardianship. It was not until the
Criminal Justice Act 1948 that the mentally ill as well as the defective
could be formally sent to mental hospitals by magistrates' courts.

The same Criminal Justice Act also made it respectable for both
higher and lower courts to do what some London magistrates had
been doing unofficially for over a decade, namely putting offenders

on probation on condition that they accepted psychiatric or psycho-
therapeutic treatment, for example from the Portman Clinic. The
offender has to consent to probation under this condition, and is likely
to be more severely dealt with if he refuses; but he cannot be
compelled to become an in-patient or an out-patient against his will.

The Mental Health Act 1959, on the other hand, provided a
properly planned system for the compulsory hospitalisation[6] of offenders by lower or higher courts. So long as the offence was 'imprisonable', and a hospital was willing to receive the disordered offender, he
could be compulsorily admitted to it on the evidence of two medical
practitioners, one of whom must be a psychiatrist on an official list. If
it seemed necessary to protect the public from the offender the Crown
Court could add a 'restriction order' to prevent medical staff from
discharging him or giving him leave without the Home Secretary's
authority (or, later, the authority of a local Mental Health Tribunal).
More has been said about such precautions in chapter 6. It was not
necessary for the court to consider the extent to which his disorder
affected his culpability: merely whether his condition 'warranted' his
admission to a hospital instead of a penalty. Psychiatric probation
orders were to be reserved for those whose condition did not warrant
compulsory hospitalisation, but this did not rule out probation orders
which involved voluntary in-patient treatment. In practice the distinction is by no means always honoured. Some consultants prefer the
informality of a probation order. It involves hardly any form-filling,
and the patient knows that his stay is voluntary, which makes for
better staff-patient relations. In theory if he does 'discharge himself'
against the doctor's wishes – as often happens – his probation officer
could bring him back to court for a breach of the order – as seldom
happens. Many probation officers are given no information about the
offender after treatment begins, and are not told when or how it ended.

The most important feature of both psychiatric probation orders and
hospital orders is their approach to culpability. The Percy Commission
(1957) whose report laid the foundations of the Mental Health Acts
were utilitarians, and had nothing to say on the subject. The Acts too
are silent, and do not mention the consideration of blame when a
hospital order is a possibility; but neither do they forbid it. It is true
that they have two minor features which look retributive. They do not
allow courts to make hospital orders if the offence is not imprisonable,
despite the fact that the offender could be compulsorily admitted to

hospital under civil powers. And a summary court is allowed to make a hospital order without convicting the offender if he is mentally ill or severely impaired and it is clear that he did what he is charged with. Both provisions, however, are legacies of earlier legislation (see Walker and McCabe, 1972), and were not part of the Percy Commission's grand design.

The judges, however, did not hesitate to regard culpability as relevant. In 1961 *Morris* a depressed and chronically anxious old man who had committed a 'mercy killing' of his wife, was found to have been of diminished responsibility; but the judge refused to make a hospital order and sentenced him to life, on the implausible ground that the hospital was not secure enough. Upholding this decision the Court of Appeal commented, *obiter*,

> Of course there may be cases where, although there is a substantial impairment of responsibility, the prisoner is shown on the particular facts of the case nevertheless to have some responsibility for the act he has done, for which he must be punished . . .

On the other hand, in cases in which the offender's disorder had nothing to do with his offence this did not preclude a hospital order. The first case to confirm this was *Hatt's* (1962). He was an eccentric mortuary attendant whose hankering for unnecessary operations had resulted in a prefrontal leucotomy. When a car theft led to a hospital order with a restriction order he – or his legal advisers – realised that he might be detained far longer than under a prison sentence, and appealed, but was told that the Act did not require any causal connection between the offence and the disorder.

This was the position for nearly a quarter of a century, until *M'Batha's* case in 1985. He was a 31-year-old manic-depressive who sexually assaulted more than one young woman. The trial judge accepted that there was 'a direct causal link' between his disorder and his offences, but decided that 'there was also a substantial element of criminality in this behaviour. It is clear that he knew what he was doing . . .'. He rejected a hospital order in favour of 'life'. After further psychiatric reports the Court of Appeal, with some hesitation, decided that a hospital order with a restriction order was 'the most suitable method of disposing of this case'. This was no flash in the pan, for in *Birch* (1989) Mustill LJ confirmed that

... the most recent decision in *M'Batha* strongly indicates that even when there is culpability the right way to deal with a dangerous and disordered person is to make an order under section 37 and 41 [of the Mental Health Act 1983].

This seems to say that – at least when the disordered offender is dangerous – utility overrides desert. It is true that *M'Batha* and *Birch* were decided before the passing of the Criminal Justice Act 1991, which includes a requirement to use a custodial sentence if the offence is serious enough to justify it. The Act also, however, requires that if an offender is, or appears to be, mentally disordered when a court which is considering a custodial sentence has obtained a pre-sentence report, it must obtain and consider a report by a duly approved medical practitioner on his mental condition before passing a custodial sentence (mandatory life sentences being excepted), and must consider the likely effect of a custodial sentence on his mental condition and on any treatment which may be available for it (s. 4). This was meant to discourage courts from imprisoning disordered offenders on the assumption that the Prison Service would either treat them or find hospitals willing to accept them on transfer. It comes close to saying that a custodial sentence is improper if it is likely to have an adverse effect on their mental condition or to interfere with treatment for it. It is true that if the offender is committed to hospital this cannot always be regarded as a mitigated disposal. Hatt (or his solicitor) realised that he would probably be detained longer than he would have been under an ordinary custodial sentence. If this prolonged detention is meant to protect others from serious harm it can be justified. One liberal nightmare is that some non-dangerous offenders are detained longer than they would have been in prison merely in the hope of improving their condition. There was a time when this was so; but nowadays overburdened hospitals have 'open doors' for such patients, and a more realistic complaint is that they leave prematurely, to the detriment of themselves or others.

Personality Disorders

One special group of disorders has presented a special problem. In the nineteenth and early twentieth centuries English psychiatrists and legislators were slower than others to recognise anti-social personality disorders which are not necessarily associated with delusion or stupidity (Walker and McCabe, 1972). It was American psychiatrists who used the term 'psychopathic' to denote this group,[7] and a Scottish alienist, David Henderson, who popularised it in Britain. The first, perhaps the only, British murderer to be saved from the condemned cell by this diagnosis was a Scot, in 1954.[8] It was not until later that, following the recommendation of the Percy Commission (1957), the Mental Health Act 1959 defined 'mental disorder' as including 'psychopathic disorder',[9] now (in the 1983 Act) defined as 'a persistent disorder or disability of mind (whether or not including significant impairment of intelligence) which results in abnormally aggressive or seriously irresponsible conduct on the part of the person concerned'. Nowadays the preferred term is 'personality disorder', but 'psychopathic disorder' is a category enshrined in the Act, and 'psychopath' is convenient shorthand for an offender of this sort. So many psychopaths, however, proved unresponsive to treatment that in 1975 the Butler Committee recommended an indeterminate but 'reviewable' sentence which would require their detention to be reviewed every two years. All that the new Mental Health Act 1983 did, however, was to rule out hospital orders for this category unless the court was told that treatment might improve the disorder or at least prevent it from becoming more serious. This did not solve the problem of the psychopath who has been optimistically accepted by a consultant only to prove unresponsive and dangerous, but who could not be transferred to prison because his sentence had been a hospital order. On the recommendation of the Reed Committee (1994) the Act was amended by the Crime (Sentences) Act 1997 (s. 46) to allow the Crown Court, when passing custodial sentences on psychopaths, to accompany the sentences with 'hospital directions' which meant that they must go first to hospital, and to prison (or a young offender institution) if and when they ceased to be responsive to treatment. This expedient was not welcomed by the Royal College of Psychiatrists. The problem presented by the violent or sexual psychopath who proves unresponsive to treatment is exacerbated by the reluctance of the judiciary to use a life sentence when the offence qualifies for one. The reviewable sentence not only sounds less Draconian but would guarantee earlier and more frequent reassessments. It was again recommended a quarter of a century later by the Fallon Report (1999), with only two important differences: that the initial sentence should be a determinate one, of 'tariff' length; and that a hospital order should not be an alternative. The Home Secretary has indicated his readiness to legislate on these lines.

It is when the diagnosis is 'personality disorder' that the culpability of the defendant is most controversial. It does not fit into Fletcher's theory of excuses (see chapter 3), since it suggests not that the defendant's action was 'out of character', but that it was very much 'in character'. A choice theorist is in slightly less difficulty. Some psychopaths, unlike most of us, often cannot choose to control their dispositions, and so cannot be wholeheartedly blamed unless one blames them for their dispositions. Others, however, can control their dispositions, but do not see why they should choose to do so if they can avoid the penal and social consequences of acting as they please. Most choice theorists would say that this makes them as culpable as the rest of us; and certainly it makes the condition sound very like that of the man in the street, be he taxpayer, financier, motorist, politician, plagiarist, book-reviewer, journalist or adulterer. The man in the street, however, has moral qualms which restrain him from obeying some of his desires, whereas some psychopaths – of the kind called 'conscienceless' – seem not to. They know what is against the law or the moral codes of their peers, and are capable of the necessary self-control when it is in their interests. What they are not capable of is feelings of guilt;[10] and since this seems pathological it reduces their culpability in some people's eyes. Choice theorists, however, would argue – as they would have in *Windle's* case – that since offenders of this sort know what the law requires and are capable of the necessary self-control they are fully culpable, and their incapacity for guilt is irrelevant. It may have been thinking on these lines which has made psychiatrists less ready to testify to diminished responsibility.

At the Grass Roots

Most of this chapter has been concerned with decisions that are recorded either individually in law reports or collectively in the *Criminal Statistics*. They are massively outnumbered, however, by the cases in which magistrates' courts are faced with petty offenders who seem to be mildly disordered, and deal with them leniently but without committing them to psychiatric treatment – usually because none is offered. Non-prosecution is still an option, although not nowadays for such grave offences as Mary Lamb's. The *Code for Crown Prosecutors* says:

> A prosecution is less likely to be needed if the defendant . . . is, or was at the time of the offence, suffering from significant mental or physical ill-health, unless the offence is serious or there is a real possibility that it may be repeated . . .

Even so, magistrates are often faced with mildly disordered or eccentric offenders for whom psychiatric facilities have either no diagnosis ('no apparent disorder') or no room, and whom the court can only discharge or bind over if it wants to be lenient. There have been no recent attempts to estimate the scale of this problem, but in 1981 a survey by Salem[11] made it possible to estimate that some 3,000 such cases were dealt with non-punitively, by discharges or bind-overs. In that same year there were only three successful insanity defences, 28 findings of unfitness for trial, 83 verdicts of diminished responsibility, some 900 hospital orders, and some 1,200 psychiatric probation orders. What seems to have escaped notice in the grass roots has been the slow decline in courts' use of both probation orders and hospital orders as a means of ensuring psychiatric treatment or care for offenders. The frequency of both types of orders reached peaks in the late 1960s (1,566 psychiatric probation orders in 1968 and 1,438 hospital orders in 1966). By the middle of the 1990s only about 450 psychiatric probation orders and 700 hospital orders were being made, in spite of the substantial increases in convictions.[12] Several factors have probably contributed to the decline. One must be the diversion from prosecution of petty offenders who in earlier decades might have been made subject to psychiatric probation orders; but that cannot have had much effect in the Crown Court. Another must have been the increasing reluctance of hospitals and out-patient clinics to accept offenders as patients, especially when their disorders were complicated by addictions or uncooperative and disruptive personalities. There may also have been a decline in the optimism of probation officers, psychiatrists and sentencers about the efficacy of the two kinds of order. A possibility is that the development of forensic psychiatry as a special expertise has resulted in greater selectivity. However that may be, judges seem to have shown an increasing preference for custodial sentences, in the knowledge that if such sentences were long enough the offenders could be transferred to hospitals with restrictions on their discharge.

Psychiatric Evidence

There is no rule of law that requires medical evidence when the defendant is pleading insanity, unfitness for trial, automatism or diminished responsibility; and in the nineteenth century a jury occasionally found in favour of obviously disordered defendants without it. Nowadays both judge and jury would be too sceptical. For a hospital order or a prison sentence with a 'hospital direction' the written or oral evidence of two medical practitioners – one of them on the Home Office's list – is required by statute, together with the information that a named hospital is willing to receive the offender. A report from one medical practitioner, not necessarily with special qualifications, is all that is statutorily required for a probation order with a requirement of medical treatment.

Rationales

The point has been made that mental disorder does not always have a mitigating effect on the disposal of the offender. Indeed where a discretionary life sentence has been passed the Court of Appeal is less likely to disapprove if the offender is mentally ill, psychopathic or 'unstable' (see chapter 5). When disorder does mitigate, however, the rationale is not always the same. Although Marcus Aurelius' reasoning is no longer explicit, magistrates often feel that the hapless schizophrenics who appear before them for petty thefts or breaches of the peace are 'punished enough by their madness'. Sometimes the consideration is plain utility – the optimistic hope that treating the offender instead of fining or imprisoning him will improve his behaviour or at least his quality of life. Often the health services are simply unable to offer any help. It is when the harm he has done or attempted is serious that retributive assessments of culpability sometimes override utility or humanity.

NOTES

1.   'Satis furore ipso puniatur': see Justinian's *Digest, 48.9.9.* Like some other humanitarian sentiments this may belong to the Stoic

philosophy, although my efforts to confirm that have so far failed. Certainly the Stoic Cicero asked, 'What can be a greater penalty than madness?' and Marcus Aurelius himself was a Stoic. (I am grateful for the help of Peter Stein in tracing the doctrine beyond the *Digest*.) In classical Greece it was commonly believed that madness was a divine punishment (and therefore sufficient). Moses asked Jehovah to use it punitively. Early Christians more often blamed devils.

2. Although surprisingly the eleventh century Laws of Cnut do not mention madness in their list of categories deserving of leniency.

3. We now know that he spelled his name thus.

4. Its origins are probably to be found in mainland Europe, where it was the subject of ecclesiastical dispute in Covarrubias's day (1558). It was certainly a common-law rule in Henry VIII's time. Lady Rocheford tried to escape execution for treasonable complicity in the Queen's adultery by feigning madness; but the king quickly enacted that the rule did not apply to treason. She was executed, but his Act was repealed under Elizabeth (Walker, 1969).

5. See Table 4.4 in the *Criminal Statistics. England and Wales*.

6. Or guardianship. But guardianship orders could be made only if someone offered facilities for them, as local authorities were expected to do. Few did. As a method of dealing with disordered offenders they are negligible, and are neglected accordingly in this chapter.

7. Psychopathic' had been used freely – and more vaguely – by European psychiatrists for a collection of non-cognitive disorders.

8. My source is personal involvement. He was released about 10 years later, and committed another impulsive murder.

9. The other categories are 'mental illness', deliberately left undefined; 'severe mental impairment', defined as 'a state of arrested or incomplete development of mind which includes severe impairment of intelligence and social functioning and is associated with abnormally aggressive or seriously irresponsible conduct on the part of the

person concerned'; 'mental impairment', defined similarly, but as 'not amounting to severe impairment'; and 'any other disorder or disability of mind' without a definition. An example of the last which was given during the passage of the 1959 Bill was senile dementia, although nowadays this might well be regarded as 'mental illness'. I have not come across a modern case in which this residual category has been discussed. One reason may be that it is not a category which qualifies the patient for compulsory admission to a mental hospital, civil or criminal. If he is not suffering from mental illness, mental impairment or psychopathic disorder, his admission must be voluntary even if he is an imprisonable offender.

10.   More precisely still, some do not seem to experience feelings of guilt in any circumstances, while some have specialised consciences which feel uncomfortable only about certain types of conduct.

11.   The survey was commissioned by the Home Office, and the Research Officer was Shirley Salem. Her report was admirably precise and detailed, and it was regrettable that she had to go on to other successful research without producing a publishable version. A copy of her report is held by the library of the Cambridge Institute of Criminology.

12.   Sources: the annual *Probation and After-Care Statistics, England and Wales*, and the annual *Criminal Statistics, England and Wales*.

Chapter 11
Revenge and Provocation

Lawyers try to distinguish revenge and provocation, usually treating the former as an aggravating motive, the latter as mitigation.

Wild Justice

Francis Bacon called revenge 'a kind of wild justice', and it has a lot in common with retribution. Human beings are the only primates which practise either. The object of both is a person (although in more primitive societies it may be an animal or even an inanimate object that has caused injury). Both consist of the deliberate infliction of harm to the person or to property, which may take talionic or symbolic forms. Both avengers and punishers want the offender to understand why he is being made to suffer. Both punishments and revenges can be criticised as excessive or inadequate. Long delays raise doubts about the propriety of both (see chapter 12). Both are usually regarded as justified by those inflicting them. Revenge is tolerated by official justice if it does not take the form of an offence or a tort (an example is an unfair but non-libellous review). When it takes a criminal form the avenger may plead that his action was justified or at least extenuated by what had been done to him. If the court does not agree it is called 'taking the law into one's own hands', and is usually regarded as a reason for increasing the severity of the sentence: see the Court of Appeal's remarks in *Wilson and others* (1996). Yet if the revenge is not too long delayed it can mitigate the sentence. In *Haley* (1983) a 45-year-old man with a clean record had been in hospital as a result of a traffic accident. On leaving he had learned that his wife had formed a sexual association with another man. He went to this man's home with a knife, and when the door was answered stabbed his wife's lover in the chest, back and arm. The victim made a good recovery, but *Haley* was sentenced to three years' imprisonment. The Court of Appeal's reasoning was almost wholly utilitarian:

> First of all there is no need to deter the appellant. He will never do anything like this again. Secondly it seems to us that *ex hypothesi* this is not really a case where the deterrence of others comes into play, for obvious reasons. Sufficient punishment must be imposed upon a person such as this for two purposes: first of all to allow [*sic*] this man to expiate his own offence, and secondly of course to mark the disapproval of society of this sort of behaviour.

His sentence was reduced to 18 months, nine of which were suspended, allowing him to be released almost immediately.

In *Haley's* case the Court did not use the word 'provocation'; but it did in *Tracy's* (1993). Tracy had had acid thrown at him by a gang, and a week later threw acid back at them. He was dealt with leniently by the Court, which called his motive 'delayed provocation' rather than 'revenge'. A few years later similar leniency was shown to *Wadha* (1996), a Syrian who had been subject to racially motivated violence from three youths. Driving away from the hospital about three hours later, after treatment for his injuries, he saw them in the street and deliberately drove into them, injuring two. The Court of Appeal reduced his sentence from three years to two, making it clear that the racial element of the attack on him was the main consideration. No doubt the fact that the delay was only a matter of hours helped the Court to reason in this way; but an example of considerably delayed provocation was *Conton* (1993). He was a black youth who had been regularly persecuted by a Nazi-type gang, led by one Rogers, and had seen a friend of his fatally stabbed by them. One evening, coming across Rogers alone in a railway station, he punched and stabbed him. The Court of Appeal emphasised that this could not be tolerated 'whatever the provocation', but reduced his custodial sentence from six months to four. In *Brookin* (1995) there was no racial element. He had been told by telephone that a known tearaway called Larway-Carter had attacked his girlfriend in a public-house. He hastened to the spot with a hammer, and found Larway-Carter, who had been arrested, in a police car. Larway-Carter shouted abuse at him, and he hit him with the hammer. The Court of Appeal was sympathetic, and regarded the circumstances as exceptional enough to justify suspending his custodial sentence.

Provocation Proper

These cases, however did not result in deaths. It was the law of homicide, and the automatic sentence of death for murder, which developed the notion of provocation as a mitigating plea, and, as we shall see, the courts are stricter when the victim dies. The notion that there could be special circumstances in which revenge could be regarded with sympathy instead of condemnation developed in the sixteenth century out of distinctions between murder and manslaughter.[1] In earlier times 'hot blood' and the *chaude mêlée* had been recognised as reducing culpability for homicide; but by Anne's reign the distinction had become more sophisticated. A brawl over a woman in a guardroom led to a fatal stab which was discussed as thoroughly by the judges of the Queen's Bench as it would be in today's Court of Appeal. The result was Holt's famous judgment in *Mawgridge* (1707), in which he was able to define four quite distinct situations. In modern terms they were as follows:

A suffers a physical insult (nose-pulling is Holt's example);
B witnesses or learns of an assault on a friend or kinsman;
C witnesses a person being wrongfully deprived of his liberty;
D finds his wife committing adultery.

The underlying justifications for violence in these situations seem to have been either outrage (in the case of A and C) or 'honour' (in the case of B and D). Honour mattered as much to the English gentleman in Elizabethan and Stuart times as it did to the heroes in the *Iliad*. If B and D did not respond with angry violence they would have been thought to lack a proper sense of honour, or at least to be cowards.

The Proportionality of the Violence

In Holt's day potentially fatal violence was probably not regarded as an excessive response to the situations which he described. Duelling was a common response by gentlemen to affronts to their honour, and if a quarrel led to an immediate duel (but not a postponed one) a fatal outcome was mere manslaughter. As for the nature of the provocation, Holt makes it clear that insulting words or gestures are not enough: the situations he described involved actions. It was not until the middle of the twentieth century that words came to be recognised by statute as sufficient provocation to reduce murder to manslaughter. Holt did, however, cite seventeenth century cases in which it had been held that the fatal violence was an excessive response (for example killing a thief or a trespasser): he himself uses the word 'proportionate'. The notion of a disproportionate response was developed in *Welsh* (1869) by the introduction of the notion of 'a reasonable man': until then the question seems to have been less objective (i.e. whether the provocation was enough for the accused). After *Welsh* the provocation had to be enough, as the Homicide Act 1957 put it, 'to make a reasonable person do as [the accused] did'. The reasonable person used to be someone without any special characteristics, but now – since *Camplin* (1978), who was a 15-year-old boy – he can be a reasonable *doppelganger* who shares 'such of the accused's characteristics as [the jury] think would affect the gravity of the provocation'; and 'the question is not merely whether such a person would in like circumstances be provoked to lose his self-control but also whether he would react to the provocation as the accused did'. Individual peculiarities can be taken into account not only if they make the provoking acts or words more provocative but also if they make the defendant more provokable, as a reasonable man might be if severely depressed (*Smith* (1998)).

Loss of Self-control

He must, however, have 'the power of self-control to be expected of an ordinary person of [his or her] sex and age'. Holt, interestingly, did not stipulate that the accused must have lost his self-control. Yet loss of self-control is mentioned in the earlier case of *Walters* (1688), where the relevant anger is described as 'an ungoverned storm'. By the eighteenth century it is being called a temporary loss of reason, or even 'brief insanity'. The Criminal Law Commission of 1834 seems to have regarded loss of self-control as a necessary condition of acceptable provocation, and in *Duffy* (1949) Devlin J made it clear, and Goddard LCJ confirmed in the Court of Appeal, that the necessary condition is 'a sudden and temporary loss of self-control', without 'time for cooling'. This was strict, not to say 'harsh' (the Court of Appeal's word in *Camplin* (1978)); but it did enable Devlin J to draw a clearly visible line between provocation and revenge, since the latter involves some degree of premeditation. Devlin J's definition made it difficult for judges to deal with 'cumulative provocation' – a history of repeated assaults, insults or infidelity – unless the killing had been an immediate response to a final act or insult. Mrs Duffy's was a case in point. After the final quarrel she changed her clothes, got a hammer and a hatchet, and did not kill her husband until he had gone to bed. A prosecutor, however, would sometimes agree to a charge of manslaughter instead of murder in cases of this sort and, if he did not, a sympathetic judge and jury would sometimes ignore Devlin. In *Wright's* case (1975) a man-slaughter plea was accepted by the prosecution because he had had to put up with his younger wife's open hatred and repeated sexual activities with boyfriends over a period of years. He chose a wedding anniversary, and took a hammer with him when he brought her a cup of tea in bed. The sympathetic judge was apparently able to gloss over the absence of a provocative act immediately before the killing by attributing it to depression. It sounds as if *Wright* could have pleaded diminished responsibility. As we shall see in the next chapter this is the plea most likely to succeed when a wife gives way to cumulative provocation without an 'on-the-spot' act or insult. Loss of self-control received statutory recognition in the Homicide Act 1957 (s. 3), but without the adjectives 'sudden and temporary':

> Where on a charge of murder there is evidence on which a jury can find that the person charged was provoked (whether by things done or by things said or by both together) to lose his self-control, the question whether the provocation was enough to make a reasonable man do as he did shall be left to be determined by the jury; and in determining that question the jury shall take into account every-thing both done and said according to the effect which, in their opinion, it would have on a reasonable man.

The inclusion of 'words or things done' was a relaxation: the common law, as summarised in *Duffy*, had required an act or acts. Taunts or gestures could now be taken into account. It is worth noting that the 1957 Act does not require that the 'things' must be said or done immediately before the killing: it simply insists on loss of self-control. What tends to be assumed is that there cannot have been loss of self-control unless the provocation had been given very shortly before the killing. Loss of self-control is easier to assert than to prove, and English lawyers have been very suspicious of the notion in other contexts. In spite of the fact that eighteenth-century writers and judges talked of it as if it were 'brief insanity', it was not included amongst the possible forms of insanity in the M'Naghten Rules; and the Atkin Committee's attempt in 1924 to extend the insanity defence so as to include it was rejected. When provocation is the plea, however, it is now regarded as sufficient if the defence, or indeed the judge, points to anything – words, actions or circumstances – that suggests loss of self-control. The onus is then on the prosecution to rebut the suggestion beyond reasonable doubt. Just how sudden or temporary the loss must be is no longer clear, but a lapse of time between the provocation and the retaliation – sometimes called 'cooling-time' – can cast doubt on its genuineness, although it is not conclusively negative evidence. The Law Commission's (1989) recommended rewording section 3 of the Homicide Act 1957 was

A person who, but for this section, would be guilty of murder is not guilty of murder if – (a) he acts when provoked (whether by things done or by things said or by both and whether by the deceased person or by another) to lose his self-control; and (b) the provocation is, in all the circumstances (including any of his personal characteristics that affects its gravity), sufficient ground for the loss of self-control.

The reasonable man has been written out of the script, simply leaving the jury to decide whether the provocation was sufficient ground for the loss of self-control. Nor is there any requirement that the loss should be sudden and temporary. The Law Commission's Code, however, is not yet law. Provoked homicide by 'battered women' is discussed in the next chapter.

Non-homicidal Violence

It is of course illogical that the Homicide Act 1957 deals only with provocation which results in a killing. The Law Commission said that its rewording should also apply to attempted murder, and that there should be an offence of attempted manslaughter. In practice this particular illogicality hardly matters, since the sentencer can use his discretion to allow provocation to mitigate. What does matter is the uncertainty as to the application of the definition of provocation in homicide to non-homicidal offences in general. For example, in *Cunningham* (1959) Parker LCJ said that 'there is no suggestion that words alone except under the Homicide Act 1957 are sufficient to found a defence of provocation'. Many years later, however, in (*Camplin* (1978) the Court of Appeal said that section 3 of the Homicide Act was intended to mitigate the harshness of *Duffy*, and that it 'abolishes all previous rules of law as to what can or cannot amount to provocation'. Even so, as we have seen, it cannot be assumed that courts will approach the plea in exactly the same way when the violence is not fatal. Certainly there does not seem to be the same insistence on sudden loss of self-control. The more trivial the retaliation the more likely is provocation to mitigate to a substantial extent. *Keeling* (1998), a huntsman who bruised a saboteur with a whip, was let off with a conditional discharge by the Norfolk magistrates because the saboteur's actions had been provocative. The magistrates even timed the conditional discharge so that it ceased to apply when the new hunting season began – with the implication that they would be equally sympathetic if there were a repetition.

Delayed Provocation or Revenge?

Most important, however, is the courts' apparent willingness to recognise 'delayed provocation' when the violence does not result in death. It is not easy to point to something that distinguishes delayed provocation from revenge, especially when the delay is a matter not of hours but of a week, as in *Tracy*. Would his acid-throwing have been mitigated if it had been delayed a week or two more? Or was it the talionic nature of his action – acid for acid – that persuaded the Court to be sympathetic? Perhaps what is needed to arouse the necessary sympathy is a feeling that the crime, although not exactly justified, is to some extent proportionate to a deliberate act of the victim: what Bacon called 'a kind of wild justice'. But once courts abandon Devlin's insistence that there must be no vestige of premeditation – harsh as it now seems – it is not easy to offer them an equally clear distinction.

Proposals for Change

The increasing liberality with which the courts have interpreted provocation has not prevented them from being strongly criticised. The most vocal critics have been sympathisers of women who have been convicted of murdering their partners after long histories of domestic violence, but in circumstances which did not appear to the courts to come within the definition of provocation. To meet their need Horder put a simple suggestion to the House of Commons' Home Affairs Committee when it was reporting (in 1993) on domestic violence. He proposed that section 3 of the Homicide Act 1957 should be amended by adding that 'there is no rule of law that a provoked loss of self-control must be sudden as well as temporary'. In everyday language, a woman's (or indeed a man's) self-control could be gradually overwhelmed. The Home Affairs Committee's report did not discuss this solution, perhaps because they hesitated to pronounce on a proposal which would have radically altered Devlin's definition of provocation. This and other solutions offered to solve the special problem of domestic provocation will be discussed in the next chapter. There have been more radical proposals, which would not necessarily widen the scope of the plea. Von Hirsch and Jareborg (1987)[2] make the point that the current concept of provocation is an uneasy combination of two necessary conditions – loss of self-control and justifiable resentment. If the cause of the resentment is such as to make retaliation pardonable, why insist that it must be done in a state of lost self-control? Conversely, if self-control has been lost is it fair to insist that the resentment must be justifiable? Logic suggests that there should be two independent pleas, one based on justifiable resentment, the other reserved for cases in which the resentment may have been unjustified but self-control has been lost. As von Hirsch and Jareborg realise, neither plea would be any easier to assess than at present. Whether self-control had really been lost would be just as hard to judge, and all they can suggest is that courts should be stricter (which might require a shift of the burden of proof). At present courts need not be too strict because the defence must also show that the retaliation was what could be expected of a reasonable person; but if this requirement were removed the diagnostic criterion of lost self-control would become all-important; and that is a problem which the English law dealing with mental disorder has not yet solved. Even when self-control is the basis of the plea of diminished responsibility, what is required is a lasting weakness of self-control, and not merely a temporary loss.

Horder's 1992 book had also favoured a one-legged plea of 'righteous indignation', but had argued against a plea of lost self-control. His objection to it was not the difficulty of diagnosing it. In his view it amounted to no more than violent anger, which he regarded as morally no better than lust or greed. (One must grant that all three are among the deadly sins.) However puritanical this may sound, it poses a question which cannot be lightly brushed aside. It does seem to be the case that sexual desire or avarice can overwhelm a person's normal self-restraint. Yet pleas based on these weaknesses are not usually acceptable. Why should anger be given a privileged status? Why should it command more sympathy than any of the other deadly sins? If it were simply an idiosyncrasy of our culture's morality the question would be an awkward one. But there is more to be said about that later. Nor would a plea of righteous indignation or justifiable resentment be without problems. Could a firm line be drawn between it and revenge? What sorts of provocation would make physical retaliation a not too wild kind of justice? Von Hirsch and Jareborg recognise the difficulty, especially when the provoking action was not criminal but merely infringed commonly recognised standards of decency:

> Where civil law recognises the wrongfulness of such conduct (for example by providing a tort remedy) the answer may be straight-forward enough. The difficulty arises when the conduct is reprehen-sible but not illegal at all – as are various personal calumnies and betrayals. Here, the victim's actions may still be plainly wrong by any commonsense assessment, but fashioning a standard of wrong-doing for the courts' guidance will be no easy matter . . .

As for conduct that is merely insulting, they are inclined to rule this out as the basis for a justifying grievance. This would rule out the taunts and gestures that were made acceptable by the Homicide Act 1957, and would thus put one clock back. Here again the difficulty has become acute only because the other leg of provocation – lost self-control – has been amputated. So long as a jury has to ask itself whether the accused showed signs of lost self-control it is not necessary for the judge to tell them what sorts of conduct can or cannot provoke reasonable people. As for Horder's question – why should anger have a privileged status? – the answer must be that it is given such a status only because it is a special kind of anger. It is anger roused by things done or said which the accused regarded as intended to harm or at least insult him. This notion of a special kind of anger thus limits as well as supports a mitigating plea. So long as it is coupled with an insistence on some degree of justification it is possible to see why it will serve the purpose. Nor is anger the only example of an emotion which can be given this special status: fear is given it when the plea is self-defence. Lust can be mitigated if deliberately stimulated by the victim (as *Wilbourne* (1982) demonstrated: see 'Temptation' in chapter 7). The interesting question, however, is what a plea of *righteous* anger (or justified resentment, to use von Hirsch and Jareborg's phrase) would sound like. No doubt it would be founded on evidence of harm done to the accused by the victim (or at least reasonably attributed to the victim by the accused). It sounds as if the accused would then be required to establish that his resentment was 'righteous'. It is not clear why this is needed, and why it would not be sufficient merely to persuade the court that it was natural (or 'understandable'). The accused is not being charged with unjustified resentment. The defence's task would be to show why the defendant's culpability *for translating his resentment into violent retaliation* should be regarded as reduced. Whether a person's resentment is justified or not is a question for his conscience. And since the plea is not to involve lost self-control the question for the court would be how culpable he is, not for giving way to the resentment, but for what he chose to do by way of retaliation. The court would not be deciding whether the choice was justified, but simply how excessive it was, having regard to the harm suffered by the defendant. What the new plea would have to be founded on would not be justified resentment of harm but the *proportionality* of the retaliation prompted by the resentment. Since homicide would almost always be regarded as disproportionate, defendants to the charge of murder would have to claim loss of self-control, as before.

Defending the *status quo* is not one of my habits; but it is arguable that the purists are exaggerating its defects. Two-legged provocation is able to maintain its balance precisely because it is not trying to stand on one leg. It is not confused about its legs, but uses each to remedy the weakness of the other. And there is a utilitarian consideration. Resentment may be justified. The retaliation which it prompts may be proportionate. But it may be of a kind which the law prohibits for the sake of public order. To refrain from penalising it, or to penalise it less severely, because it seems proportionate and understandable would be to rate private feelings above the public interest, and would weaken deterrence. To mitigate or forgo the penalty only when the retaliator fulfils certain strict conditions – such as loss of self-control – is much less dangerous.

NOTES

1.   See Green (1976) and Horder (1992). The latter is particularly interesting when discussing notions such as outrage and honour, and I am indebted to him for some of my historical information.

2.   They were following up a tentative comment by Ashworth (1983).

Chapter 12
Women's Situations

Long before statisticians interested themselves in the sentencing of women it was known that courts dealt with them more leniently; and in earlier chapters we have already seen what seem like examples. In 1953 Goddard LCJ said irritably in *Williams and Williams*:

> Why it seems so often to be considered, where a man and woman are involved, that the woman should always receive a less sentence than the man, I do not know . . .

His disapproval has been echoed by the Court of Appeal from time to time. In *Hancock* (1986) it said plainly that 'the courts must in most cases treat women offenders on the same basis as men', and it refused to reduce her sentence of 12 months' youth custody for indecent assaults on boys.

This is a good example of a failed attempt at retributive consistency. 'Failed' because it assumes that men and women suffer equally from equal terms of imprisonment. No doubt there are some men and women of whom this is true; but as a general assumption it is probably not true. Most women are more upset than men by separation from parents, children or partners. Long separation from a partner is more likely to mean the loss of the partner. A woman's choice of companions in custody is limited. Because fewer prisons are needed for women they are less diversified, and therefore less suited to any special psychological or other needs. They are less likely to be within visiting reach of family and friends.

It is not at all certain, however, that sentencers are in fact ignoring this. Sample after sample[1] has shown that when allowance has been made for variables such as age, previous record and type of offence, women and girls are less likely to receive custodial sentences, and that when they do the sentences are shorter than in the case of men. They are three times as likely as men to have prison sentences suspended, even now that suspension is confined to 'exceptional circumstances (see the table in chapter 7). A possibility is that these differences are fully accounted for by differences in the seriousness of the offences. Offence-types are such broad labels that 'theft', for example, covers pilfering from Boots at one extreme and lucrative embezzlement at the other. When Hedderman and Dowd (1997), however, studied shoplifting of the most minor kind – a single theft by someone with no previous convictions, dealt with at a magistrates' court outside London – they still found differences in the pattern of sentencing. No women were imprisoned, whereas 3 per cent of men were. More men than women were fined, no doubt because women are less likely to be earners. More women than men were simply discharged, absolutely or conditionally. On the other hand, women with clean records convicted of violence (at higher or lower courts) were as likely as men to be dealt with custodially, although the percentage was only 3 per cent. Excluding cruelty to children made no great difference. It was only when the violent men and women had previous records that the courts were more lenient to women (possibly because greater severity provided more scope for leniency).[2] In general the only women who could claim to have been dealt with more severely than they would have been if they had been men, were those who were given community service because their finances persuaded the courts not to fine them. Otherwise there was no evidence of discrimination against women.

Some feminists still believe, however, that women are more likely, other things being equal, to be imprisoned. In 1977 an amateur statistician noticed that higher percentages of women prisoners had no previous convictions, and inferred that if they had been men they would not have received custodial sentences . As I pointed out, this inference is a statistical fallacy. Men and women prisoners are samples drawn from different populations. A much higher percentage of males who are not in prison have previous convictions (the percentage is around 30 per cent by the age of 30 if teenage findings of guilt are counted). Consequently if a man and a woman are imprisoned for the same offence, or for an offence of the same degree of seriousness, the man is much more likely to have a criminal record. Nothing can be inferred from this about discrimination in sentencing. It is as if epidemiologists noticed that lower percentages of women admitted to casualty departments had records of previous admissions, and inferred that casualty departments were discriminating, when the simple explanation is that more men incur injuries. The amateur statistician probably did not realise that the percentages of offenders with no records are higher among women *whatever the sentence*. But the fallacy dies hard, and is resurrected from time to time – in 1992 by a well-known QC (Kennedy, 1992) and in 1997 by the National Association of Probation Officers.

Gelsthorpe's interviews with 189 lay and stipendiary magistrates at five courts disclosed that they tended to divide women offenders into 'the troublesome and the troubled'. The mitigating factor most often mentioned was a woman's responsibility for dependants, especially for children (see chapter 8); but even when she had no dependants some magistrates were reluctant to resort to imprisonment simply because of her sex. If she had a job the court did not want the sentence to be the cause of her losing it. If she had a partner – preferably a husband – that was more encouraging than living alone.[3]

Battered Women

When the offence is murder a special problem is presented by the woman (rarely a man) who has suffered violence for weeks, months or years from a partner, or whose children have suffered it, and who finally kills him, but in a situation which does not quite fit the courts' definition of provocation. This was the defendant's position in *Duffy*, 1949. She had suffered brutality from her husband, and on the night of the crime they had quarrelled and exchanged blows, mainly because her husband would not let her take the children away. Unfortunately she left the room, changed her clothes, and waited until her husband was in bed. She then came in with a hammer and a hatchet, using both to dispatch him. The insistence of the judge, Devlin J, on the need for sudden loss of self-control, without time for cooling, and with no sign of premeditation (see chapter 11), led the jury to convict her of murder. His direction was upheld in the Court of Appeal, and indeed praised by Lord Goddard, so that from time to time it has been treated as a guideline. What the textbooks do not add is that the jury had been sufficiently impressed by Mrs Duffy's situation to recommend mercy, and her death sentence – like *Windle's* – was commuted to 'life', from which she was released after slightly less than 3 years.[4]

The Homicide Act 1957 relaxed the criteria of provocation by accepting 'things done or said' as possibly provocative; but it was silent about self-control, and it did not interfere with the common law's insistence that this should be 'sudden and temporary'. In cases of non-fatal violence, as was said in chapter 11, even the Court of Appeal is sometimes prepared to treat revenge as a mitigating circumstance by calling it 'delayed provocation' if it is not too long delayed; but where the crime is homicide it applies the official criteria more strictly. Its only concession to women and girls is Lord Diplock's ruling in *Camplin* (1978) that the defendant's sex is relevant when the question is how much self-control a reasonable person would have in the circumstances. For this purpose, he said, 'the reasonable man' means:

> . . . a person having the power of self-control to be expected of an ordinary person of the *sex and age* of the accused . . . (my italics).

As we saw in chapter 9 he did not mean that there are some things said or done that might be more provoking for a boy of 15 (i.e. *Camplin*) than for a man: he simply meant that a boy's self-control might be weaker. What did he mean when he inserted 'sex' into his ruling (which the case did not require)? That, other things being equal, a woman's self-control is *likely* to be more easily overcome than a man's? Or, less dogmatically, that when the defendant is a woman the jury must be reminded of this *possibility*?

However that may be, Crown Court judges and juries can be very sympathetic to battered women. Helena Kennedy (1992) cites several unreported cases from daily newspapers in which women clearly benefited from the empathy of juries rather than the law. A striking reported case was *Susan Harrison* (1992). After suffering years of ill-treatment and humiliation from her partner she hired a man to kill him, and lured him to a convenient place for the purpose. Her jury accepted her plea of provocation, and when sentenced to seven years' imprisonment she appealed; but the sentence was upheld.

It is true that the defence has only to offer a single piece of evidence which suggests provocation in order to saddle the prosecution with the need to produce evidence which negatives it. All that is required, however, to create scepticism or at least doubt is evidence that the accused had been heard on some earlier occasion to talk of killing her partner, or had sharpened the knife shortly before using it, or that the victim was asleep. All three of these kinds of evidence were presented in *Sarah Thornton's* trial in 1990, so that her plea failed. So did her first appeal in 1992. Her case became a *cause célèbre* and the Home Secretary was pressed to refer the case again to the Court of Appeal in 1993. After an initial refusal he did so in 1995. The Court of Appeal thought it possible that fresh evidence about her personality might be relevant to the plea of provocation, and ordered a retrial, in which the jury acquitted her of murder but convicted her of manslaughter. The judge said that he was sentencing her on the basis not of provocation but of diminished responsibility. His sentence of five years meant her immediate release.

Diminished Responsibility?

Normally the battered defendant has more chance of success if she pleads diminished responsibility (see chapter 10). More and more psychiatrists nowadays recognise a mental state which they call 'the battered woman syndrome'. *Jane Gardner* (1994), a woman of 52, had been involved for some years with a man who constantly beat and persecuted her. She sometimes retaliated, and on the final occasion she stabbed him several times, so that he died. She was found guilty of manslaughter as the result of provocation, but sentenced to five years' imprisonment (the lower end of the scale for such manslaughters). The Court of Appeal, however, was told by a psychiatrist (Dr Mezey) that the attacks and persecution had led to 'a cumulative state of hopelessness, helplessness and depression, . . . a battered woman syndrome', which persuaded the Court to substitute probation. As her counsel had pointed out, the plea could equally well have been diminished responsibility.

That plea is not popular, however, with some feminists, who object
that it 'medicalises' the woman's excuse, stigmatising her as suffering
from 'an abnormality of mind' even if her violence is an understandable response to an intolerable situation. This may have contributed to
the puzzling decline in the numbers of diminished responsibility
verdicts over the last decade and a half. It is possible that self-defence
and provocation have become more popular pleas. But, as we saw in the
table in chapter 10, the decline in diminished responsibility verdicts has
also been a feature of homicides by men. The explanations do not have
to be the same, but may be, in which case speculation must continue.

Solutions

There seem to be six possible solutions to the problem of the battered
woman who kills. An obvious one would be the relaxation of the rigid
statute which makes 'life' the only permissible sentence for murder,
allowing judges the same wide choice of sentence as they have for
manslaughter – ranging from 'life' to absolute discharge – so that they
could take mitigations into account. Home Secretaries, as we saw in
chapter 5, have resisted a reform of this sort; but so many committees
have advocated it that it must be somewhere over the horizon. It
would of course open a door that would be wider than is needed
simply to deal with battered women; and it would not protect them
from the stigma of being labelled 'murderess'.

A narrower loophole has already been outlined in the chapter on
provocation: Horder's simple proposal that the loss of self-control
should not have to be sudden. The difficulty about it is that a slow
loss of self-control sounds like a contradiction in terms. Losing one's
self-control is like losing one's balance – not something that happens
gradually. It is more realistic to recognise that one may lose self-
control with the same person time after time until the final loss leads
to serious violence.

A better expedient would be to repopularise diminished responsibility by 'demedicalising' it. The definition in the Homicide Act 1957
could be slightly altered by inserting the words I have italicised:

an abnormal *state* of mind (whether arising from a condition of
arrested or retarded development of mind or any inherent causes or
induced by disease or injury *or ill-treatment*) . . .

These insertions would mean that it would no longer be necessary for witnesses to talk as if the defendant's condition was an inherent or lasting 'abnormality', and it would be allowable to attribute it wholly to 'ill-treatment'. In practice this is what psychiatrists already do when they use the notion of the battered woman syndrome. They do not mean to imply that the woman suffers from an inherent or lasting abnormality: merely that her recent state of mind was not her normal state of mind. And they are attributing it not to any of the causes listed in section 3 of the Homicide Act 1957 but to ill-treatment. It is a pity that – as was mentioned in chapter 10 – the Law Commission has favoured amendments which tie diminished responsibility even more closely to 'mental disorder'. There is no indication, however, that the Draft Criminal Code will receive Parliamentary time in the near future.

Women who benefit from a verdict of diminished responsibility are usually made the subjects of hospital orders or probation orders with a requirement of psychiatric treatment. They are less likely than men to receive a prison sentence, and when they do their sentences are much shorter. They are hardly ever sentenced to life. This cannot confidently be attributed to gender-bias: it is more likely to reflect differences in diagnoses and the situations leading to homicide.

A new Defence?

What most women's groups want, however, is a defence which will vindicate rather than partially excuse. A solution which has already been discussed (in chapter 11) is to replace the plea of provocation – or supplement it – with a new plea of 'righteous indignation' (Horder, 1992) or 'justifiable resentment' (von Hirsch and Jareborg, 1987). This would not insist on 'sudden loss of self-control', and could not be negatived solely by evidence of preparation. Journalists have dismissed it as 'a licence to kill'; and if it is to escape this criticism it must be drafted with great care. Otherwise it would simply be left to the accused and her counsel to persuade a jury that her partner's treatment of her justified her violence, and, as we have seen, some juries are more sympathetic than others. It would no doubt be open to the prosecution to raise the question whether the accused had no non-violent alternatives; and the worse the history of abuse by her partner the more difficult she would find it to explain why she had not left him. The plea need not be restricted to female defendants, and a few male defendants might be able to make it plausible. Logically it ought to lead, if successful, to a complete acquittal, since it argues that the violent act was justified, not merely to some extent excusable.

Self-preservation

Another radical solution was discussed by the Home Affairs Committee of the House of Commons in 1993: a new plea of 'self-preservation', intended to reduce murder to manslaughter. In its latest version (Radford and Kelly, 1997) the accused would have to establish that the victim had been at the relevant time in a familial relationship with the accused; had subjected him or her to continuing sexual or physical violence; that the accused believed that but for his or her action his or her life, or the life of some other member of the family, would have been in danger; and that he or she had no alternative but to kill or cause grievous bodily harm.

The Committee rejected this on two grounds. One was traditional: that such a defence is unknown to English law. The other was less of a knee-jerk:

> . . . now that the courts recognise that a history of abuse can result in diminished responsibility the new defence would imply that the killing was a rational choice.

So it would; but that would not make the plea unique. The use of force in self-defence can be a rational choice. There have even been cases in which a decision to use it pre-emptively, before the apprehended attack begins, has been held to be justified. In *Beckford* (1988), for example, Lord Keith said that ' . . . a man about to be attacked does not have to wait for his assailant to strike the first blow: circumstances may justify a pre-emptive strike'. (Beckford was a Jamaican policeman who shot a gunman he was chasing after the man had ceased to fire at him.) But pre-emptive action is 'lawful' only if one's life is in 'immediate jeopardy' (Lord Milmo in *Cousins* (1982), where the defendant's pre-emptive *threat* to kill was held unlawful for that reason). As for the objection that in most cases the endangered woman has the alternative of leaving the home, and taking any children with her, two points need to be made. One is that the law of self-defence no longer insists that the defender should have retreated if retreat was possible. The other is that it would usually be very difficult for the woman to put herself completely beyond the reach of a vengeful partner.

The proponents of a plea of 'self-preservation' did not suggest, however, that it should lead to a complete acquittal. They proposed it merely as a partial justification, leading to a manslaughter verdict. No doubt too they had in mind that it would be more likely to receive serious consideration if proposed merely as a *partial* justification, like provocation. The notion of a 'partial' justification is not irrational, if applied to actions which are motivated by justified emotions but which are more drastic than they need have been. In the chapter on provocation I discussed von Hirsch and Jareborg's proposal for a plea of 'justified resentment', which also looks like a proposal for a partial justification, since it would, I argued, allow a court to decide that the defendant's resentment had been justified but that his action had been disproportionate. 'Self-preservation' could be regarded as claiming that the defendant's *fear* was justified, and as raising the question 'How *excessive* was the killing?'.

When this is seen to be the crucial question the solution seems to be one already offered in the Law Commission's Draft Criminal Code Bill of 1989:

Use of excessive force

59.   A person who, but for this section, would be guilty of murder is not guilty of murder if, at the time of his act, he believes the use of the force which causes death to be necessary and reasonable in the circumstances to effect a purpose referred to in section 44 [which includes 'to protect himself or another from unlawful force or unlawful personal harm'] but the force exceeds that which is necessary and reasonable in the circumstances which exist or (where there is a difference) in those which he believes to exist.

A successful defence of this kind would result in a verdict of manslaughter. If the force was not judged excessive it would of course be an acquittal. As with the present plea of self-defence it is what the defendant genuinely, even if not reasonably, believes that would be all-important, although of course a jury is more likely to be convinced that the belief was genuine if it was reasonable. The clause would thus cover situations in which the defendant genuinely believed that a pre-emptive killing was the only way of saving herself or her children from 'unlawful personal harm'. It is unlikely, however, to be enacted until Parliamentary time is found for the whole of the Law Commission's Bill. Meanwhile diminished responsibility seems to be serving, with help from psychiatrists, as a fairly safe plea for most 'battered women', so that the demand for a new vindicating plea is unlikely to enlist enough political support to reach the statute book by itself. It may be one of those ironic situations in which there are so many possible solutions that no single one will attract sufficient support.

Infanticide

The pleas so far discussed have been open to men as well as women, even if they were designed for women. There is one plea, however, which is expressly confined to women, and in very special circumstances. The juncture at which any woman is most likely to kill someone is after childbirth, and the most likely victim is the baby, although the mother may also kill other children, and then perhaps herself. In the days when illegitimacy was disgraceful, and contraception an occult science, infanticide was a common resort. The courts of mediaeval Europe regarded it as a particularly heinous form of murder, and sentenced the mothers to hideous forms of death. Even the enlightened *Code Napoléon*, which eschewed capital punishment for most crimes, retained it for the killing of children whose births had not been registered, because a special deterrent was needed for a crime so easy to conceal. In England the same argument was urged by a judge (Baron Bramwell) to the Capital Punishment Commission in 1865.

In practice by this time it was acknowledged that most infanticides following births were committed in disordered states of mind, often attributed to puerperal fever or lactation (but now more often explained as the result of disturbances of the endocrine system). Home Secretaries commuted the mothers' death sentences almost automatically. From 1872 onward there were attempts to promote Bills to save them from the death sentence (or, as a cynic once put it, to save the judge from the harrowing experience of pronouncing it). Most of them relied on the notion of loss of self-control; but the version which eventually reached the statute-book in the Infanticide Act 1922 used wording drafted by Lord Birkenhead: 'disturbance of balance of mind' as a result of giving birth to a 'newly born' child. The effect was to reduce murder to manslaughter for sentencing purposes. At first 'newly born' was interpreted very strictly (in *O'Donoghue* (1927) it was held to exclude a five-week-old baby). Eventually the Act was amended in 1938 so as to cover killings within 12 months of the birth. The most important feature of the defence, however, was that it did not require any pronouncement as to whether the mother knew what she was doing, recognised its illegality, or could have restrained herself. All that was needed was an assurance, preferably from a doctor, that the 'balance of her mind' was 'disturbed'. It was an unsophisticated forerunner of 'diminished responsibility', but its very lack of sophistication has protected it from the attacks to which the latter has been subjected.

It was still limited, however, to the child to which the mother had given birth. If, as sometimes happens, she killed any other child that was murder, and she had to rely on the Prerogative of Mercy. It is not clear whether this curious feature was intentional or simply due to ignorance of the facts. When the Homicide Act 1957 introduced the plea of diminished responsibility, the mother who killed two or more children within 12 months of giving birth could plead infanticide in respect of the baby and diminished responsibility in respect of the rest; but the position was – and still is – scarcely defensible. A verdict of diminished responsibility requires the jury to estimate that the mother's responsibility was 'substantially impaired'. Infanticide requires no such precision. Both concepts are hard enough to handle without coupling them together. The Butler Committee (1975) thought that the defence of infanticide could be abolished, leaving diminished responsibility to deal with all such cases; but the Criminal Law Revision Committee (1980) disagreed, with the support of the Royal College of Psychiatrists. What the Criminal Law Revision Committee had in mind were '. . . the tragic cases in which the social and emotional pressures on the mother consequent on the birth are so heavy that her balance of mind is disturbed and she gives way under them . . .'; and the Committee proposed that the Act be amended so as to cover not only disturbance of balance of mind as a result of giving birth but also disturbance due to 'circumstances consequent on that birth'. This proposal found its way into the Law Commission's

Draft Criminal Code; and there, for the moment, it rests, like so many other worthy proposals. No neat amendment has been proposed to meet cases in which the mother kills not only her last-born child but others as well. The only recent development worth note is the tentative suggestion (e.g. by Mackay, 1995) that the stresses experienced by some fathers should be accorded some recognition of a similar kind.

Unlike the verdict of diminished responsibility, 'infanticide' is not usually preceded by the stigmatising charge of 'murder'. The prosecution is almost always persuaded by the psychiatric evidence to charge the mother only with infanticide, so that no issue is left to the jury. The usual disposal is psychiatric – a hospital order or a probation order with a requirement of treatment. Occasionally – once or twice in a decade – the mother is sent to prison (or a young offenders' institution). These may be cases in which the prosecution had accepted the plea but the judge was less impressed by the evidence of 'disturbed balance of mind'. Less probably they were cases in which the prosecution brought evidence to rebut 'disturbed balance' which persuaded the judge but not the jury. In 1998, for example, *Tina Jamadar* received a three-year prison sentence for two infanticides, after two separate births, having disguised them as 'cot deaths'.

What is certain – and hard to justify – is that if the mother merely injures the baby she risks a substantial custodial sentence. *Inez Isaac* (1998), who had fractured her baby's legs by twisting them, was sentenced to three years' imprisonment in spite of evidence that she had been recovering from a difficult birth and suffering from post-natal depression. It took an appeal to have this sentence varied to a psychiatric probation order.

Premenstrual Syndrome

Finally, although premenstrual tension ('PMT') or premenstrual syndrome ('PMS') is regarded as a recent diagnosis, Edwards (1984) cites several cases from the first half of the nineteenth century which show that women's moods at this stage of the menstrual cycle were occasionally pleaded either in mitigation or as 'insanity' (which in 1851 saved a woman from the death sentence). In 1960 Dalton revived interest in the diagnosis as an explanation for aggressiveness or abnormal carelessness (for example in female shoplifters). Sceptics have questioned her hormonal explanation (e.g. Ussher, 1989), but by

1978 courts took it seriously as a mitigating consideration. In November 1981 a Mrs English was reported by the newspapers to have founded a successful diminished responsibility plea on it; and in the same year *Craddock* (1981) did the same. Next year, her doctor having reduced her injections of progesterone, she uttered threats to kill a policeman, and in court – under the name of *Smith* (1982) – offered PMT as a complete defence, calling it a kind of automatism or irresistible impulse. She failed to satisfy the trial judge, and the Court of Appeal confirmed that it could not be a complete defence, but did not rule it out as a mitigating factor, or as a factor which might diminish responsibility for homicide.

Marital Coercion

It remains to mention a third plea which only women can offer, and that only if they are married. The English common law used to allow a wife the rebuttable presumption, if she was charged with an offence other than murder or treason, committed in the presence of her husband, that she had committed it as a result of his coercion, and must therefore be acquitted. Like the *doli incapax* presumption in the case of a juvenile (see chapter 9) it could be rebutted by the prosecution – for example by evidence that her husband could not have been present. It was a legacy of the old Roman attitude to the authority of the head of the family (see the next chapter). The common-law defence was abolished by the Criminal Justice Act 1925 (s. 47), but a substitute was provided:

> . . . on a charge against a wife other than treason or murder it shall be a good defence to prove that the offence was committed in the presence of, and under the coercion of, the husband.

Since there is no longer a presumption in her favour it is the wife who must produce evidence of coercion (which the prosecution can of course seek to discredit); but she has only to tilt the balance of probability in her favour. The coercion need not amount to violence or threats of it (that would be duress). It is possible, however, to make a mess of the defence. *Gary and Ann Richman* (1982) were charged with making fraudulent insurance claims. He pleaded guilty, but his wife offered the defence of marital coercion. There was evidence that her husband was a domineering man, but her description of the coercion was that 'He begged me to sign [the claim] and told me to trust him, so I did it'. This did not sound like coercion, and the jury convicted her. The defence has been described as an anachronism, and the Law Commission's 1989 Draft Criminal Code would abolish it. Certainly a modern version would have to recognise the frequency of unhallowed unions, and perhaps of coerced men. Nevertheless the defence does acknowledge a politically unwelcome fact: that sexual partnerships can involve domination such that the dominated partner can be induced to do things for which she (or he) cannot be regarded as completely to blame. A case of this kind will be described in the next chapter. It is equally true that there are relationships of other kinds which can involve equally powerful domination, and it is strange that a defence derived from Roman law did not include paternal coercion. (I can recall a case in which a mother coerced her teenage son into shooting her brutal husband; but since she was not charged with any offence I must not name her.) There is no obvious place for drawing the line. Arguably it is less discriminatory to treat coercion in any kind of relationship as a case for mitigation rather than as a defence. This was the course taken, for example, by Mrs *Rainford's* counsel (1998), who persuaded the judge that her fraudulent claims for about £7,000 in social security benefits were made under 'duress' from her even more fraudulent husband (but probably not 'in his presence'). She was allowed a conditional discharge.

NOTES

1.   The best studies are by Hedderman and Hough (1994), a review which includes studies of the Crown Court, and Hedderman and Gelsthorpe (1997), which took samples from magistrates' courts. The samples were large enough to make it highly unlikely that inter-gender differences were wholly attributable to chance.

2.   The sentencing pattern for drug offences was too complex to summarise here.

3.   Farrington and Morris (1983) also found that a woman's marital status was an important consideration for their magistrates.

4.   I am indebted to the Home Office for the information.

Chapter 13
Unfashionable Mitigations

This chapter is about three pleas in mitigation which are either seldom heard in English courts or, if heard, seldom encouraged by the Court of Appeal, but which raise interesting questions: superior orders, staleness and the dangers of imprisonment.

In 1944, when 35 German soldiers were ambushed and killed by Italian partisans, Colonel Otto Priebke took 352 Italian hostages and had them shot in the Ardeatine Caves, acting on orders from 'Berlin'. At the end of the war he escaped to Argentina, where he lived an apparently untroubled life until he was extradited to Italy 52 years later, at the age of 83. An Italian military court found him guilty, but took into account his plea of 'superior orders' and the staleness of the crime, with the result that it imposed no penalty for what he did. Outrage in Rome led the *Corte di Cassazione* to order a retrial by different judges, who sentenced him to 15 years' imprisonment (effectively reduced to five by the provisions of successive amnesties). In 1998 another appeal resulted in a life sentence. What should interest British readers, however, are the two mitigations invoked by the original court, which would carry little, if any, weight in an English court.

SUPERIOR ORDERS

Even academic lawyers in England pay little attention to superior orders as an exculpation nowadays.[1] It is sometimes referred to in passing while discussing duress, since disobedience may have serious consequences. Obedience, however, may be the result of respect for authority rather than fear. The authority may be supernatural or human. Aeschylus made Orestes act under supernatural orders when he killed Clytaemnestra. Roman lawyers argued that 'an act is not regarded as willed if done in obedience to the order of a father or a master' (Justinian's *Digest*), and another argument of classical authors was that that the responsibility for the ordered act devolves wholly on the ordering authority (Daube, 1956).

The defence was offered by some of the 'regicides' after the Restoration. An example was *Axtell* (1660), commander of the guard at Charles I's trial, who was accused of inciting his men to cry 'Justice, justice: execution, execution':

> Axtell: I am to serve and obey all my superior officers, that is my commission: if I do not I die by the law of war.
>
> Court: You are to obey them in their just commands; all unjust commands are invalid. If our superiors should command us to undue and irregular things (much more to the committing of treason) we are in each case to make use of the passive, not active, obedience.

The Lord Chief Baron's distinction between lawful and unlawful orders sounds very modern, and was followed by nineteenth-century English courts and the British *Manual of Military Law*.

Modern English Law

The defence of obedience to a superior's orders is still recognised in many modern penal codes, but English lawyers have accepted it only when the situation was such that the order negatived *mens rea* – for example by misleading the subordinate as to the facts. An exception was made for wives who committed non-homicidal felonies or misdemeanours in their husbands' presence, on the Roman presumption that they were 'under their man's rod' (*sub virga viri*: Turner, 1961); and as we saw in the previous chapter the Criminal Justice Act of 1925 preserves the spirit of this defence. As for public servants they could not use this excuse because they were servants of the King, and since he could do no wrong they must be the wrongdoers.

That fiction does not seem to have been relied on by the Scots, who have less respect for sovereigns. Baron Hume (the Scottish equivalent of Blackstone) wrote sympathetically about soldiers who committed homicide in doing what they thought to be their duty. He was quoted to a Scottish jury in 1941 when a soldier, *Sheppard*, was tried for culpable homicide. The private had been escorting a deserter, whom he had been told by his lance-corporal to shoot if he tried to escape, and did. The jury took the judge's hint and acquitted him. The case raised an interesting question. Would he have thought he was doing his duty if the lance-corporal had not left him with instructions to shoot? Is there a material distinction between 'doing one's duty' (as one sees it) and obeying what one regards as a lawful order from a superior?

However that may be, early editions of the British *Manual of Land Warfare* treated soldiers who obeyed orders as justified 'so long as the orders . . . are not obviously and decidedly in opposition to the law of the land . . .'. It was not until late in the 1939–45 war that the *Manual* took the different view that such obedience, if criminal, was not an excuse but merely a mitigating factor; and in the following year the Nuremberg Declaration took the same line in regard to 'war crimes'. This is what a realist once called 'the doctrine of intelligent bayonets'. It expects soldiers trained in obedience to discriminate between legitimate and illegitimate orders.

It is not only servants of the sovereign who may be given illegal orders. In 1975 a magistrates' court acquitted a private security officer of wilfully obstructing traffic by checking vehicles, on the ground that he was obeying his employer's instructions. On appeal Lord Widgery ruled in the Divisional Court that 'this was no sort of lawful excuse' (*Lewis* v *Dickson* (1976)). Yet John Smith (1989) was able to draw attention to the strange civil case of *Janaway* (1988) in which the Court of Appeal seems to have reasoned as if there was such an excuse. It seemed to assume that a doctor's secretary would have been able to plead 'superior orders' had she typed a letter arranging an abortion which she knew to be illegal. This is particularly interesting because most criminal codes which accept the defence do so only if the *actus reus* was not obviously illegal. A mild case of *incuria*?

Milgram's Experiment

In real life anyone who has been in the armed services, the merchant Navy or the police will be aware of situations in which orders are expected to be obeyed instantly, and without questioning their legality. Even undisciplined civilians can be successfully ordered to act in potentially homicidal ways, as Milgram's (1963) experiments demonstrated. He recruited nearly 1,000 men for what was ostensibly an attempt to improve people's learning by giving them electric shocks. The 'learners', invisible to the participants, were really his accomplices, and the shocks were not real. Each time a 'learner' pretended to fail in his task the 'subject' had to give him an increasingly strong shock. His protests and cries of pain could be heard. Some subjects refused to continue, but the experimenter's insistence compelled two-thirds to carry on, administering the most severe shocks of which the apparatus was ostensibly capable, even in the face of a sign which warned that the level was dangerous. They were extremely worried, even guilty, about having to do this, but felt that the experimenter was in a position of authority, and that the responsibility was his. This was a vivid demonstration of the fact that even people who are not members of disciplined organisations can be manoeuvred into situations in which they feel obliged to obey illegal orders.

As a plea in mitigation, obedience to superior orders is rare in England, but in *Bosomworth* (1996) the Court of Appeal accepted something like it. Mr Bosomworth, JP, was involved in an accident while driving with excess alcohol in his blood. He ordered his wife to tell the police that she was the driver, and she complied; but their passenger later betrayed her and she was jailed for perjury. The Court of Appeal reduced her sentence on being told that 'she was ruled with a rod of iron and always had to obey'. The language is almost Roman (*sub virga viri*) and it is not clear why she did not offer the old defence of marital coercion, which was discussed in the previous chapter.

Less explicitly a court will sometimes deal more leniently with an accomplice to a planned crime on the ground that he was acting under the influence of a ringleader. No doubt the role of the ringleader is often merely that of a tempter who offers reward; but that hardly lessens the culpability of the accomplice. It is only when the influence comes close to orders that leniency makes moral sense.

The State of Mind

What is the state of mind which is supposed to justify leniency in cases in which the offender knew his act to be criminal but was acting solely because he had been ordered to? In some cases it may be close to duress. Mrs Bosomworth may have feared the consequences of disobedience. Priebke said that he feared being shot if he refused to carry out the orders from Berlin, and he may have been realistic. Cicero, had he been in Priebke's position, would have felt that obedience would be justified because all the moral responsibility for the deed lay with the ordering authority. Milgram's subjects may well have felt the same. Both these justifications are retributive. A utilitarian, however, might justify leniency on the pragmatic ground that someone who knowingly breaks the law only when ordered to by an authority which he recognises is unlikely, once convicted, to repeat his offence.

STALENESS

The 'staleness' of an offence can be a bar to prosecution. The trial of a summary offence (but not of one triable either way) must take place within six months of the date on which the magistrates' clerk's office was first given information about the offence, except in the rare cases[2] in which the statute dealing with the offence allows a longer period (s. 127, Magistrates' Courts Act 1980). There are also three indictable types of offences which can be prosecuted only within time-limits: sexual intercourse with a girl under 16 (sch. 2, Sexual Offences Act 1956, which also allows 12 months); certain homosexual offences (s. 7, Sexual Offences Act 1967, which allows 12 months); and offences under the Trade Descriptions Act 1968, which allows three years).[3]

In many jurisdictions there are more comprehensive 'statutes of limitation' which lay down maximum periods for the prosecution (or in Sweden the penalising) of different categories of offences. The underlying reasoning is usually that long delay can make it difficult or impossible for the defendant to assemble a defence. Certainly this is the reason usually given for the time-limits laid down for civil actions in the Limitations Acts, where the standard period is six years, though with exceptions as short as three years (for personal injuries) and as long as 12 years (for the recovery of land). This raises an obvious question. Why are defendants in most types of criminal cases treated as if the lapse of time does not create similar difficulties for them? The answer is presumably that potential plaintiffs in civil actions can be expected to identify the appropriate defendant and make up their minds whether to sue within a finite time; but that the State's *prima facie* duty to prosecute crime is not affected by the lapse of time, and that it can be trusted to take into account the defendant's problems in assembling his case after the lapse of time. Yet if so, what special considerations justified the exceptions in the Sexual Offences Acts and the Trade Descriptions Act?

The question is now of historical interest only, since the Crown Prosecution Service (which did not exist when these Acts were passed) has a declared policy:

Regard must be had not only to the date when the last known offence was committed, but also the length of time which is likely to elapse before the matter can be brought to trial. The Crown Prosecutor should be slow [*sic*] to prosecute if the last offence was committed three or more years before the probable date of trial, unless, despite its staleness, an immediate custodial sentence of some length is likely to be imposed. Less regard will be paid to staleness, however, if it has been contributed to by the accused himself, the complexity of the case has necessitated lengthy police investigation or the particular characteristics of the offence have themselves contributed to the delay in its coming to light. Generally, the graver the accusation, the less significance will be attached to the element of staleness.

The quotation comes from the 1992 edition of the CPS's Code. The 1994 edition has rather less to say. It lists 'common public interest factors' for and against prosecution, and among the latter is '. . . a long delay between the offence taking place and the date of the trial, unless

the offence is serious;
the delay has been caused in part by the defendant;
the offence has only recently come to light; or
the complexity of the offence has meant that there has been a long
investigation . . .'.

Neither edition of the Code explains why it should be in the public
interest not to prosecute after the lapse of a long time. The Code refers
respectfully to Hartley Shawcross' statement in the House of Commons in 1951 about the Attorney-General's policy as regards prosecutions, which lays great emphasis on the public interest; but he said
nothing to explain why long delay should weigh against prosecution.
The reason cannot be the increasing weakness of evidence, since the
Code is careful to deal separately with that problem. It may simply
be political: after a considerable lapse of time the public – or more
precisely the news media – are unlikely to make a fuss about
non-prosecution unless the offence is serious, which is the first
exception mentioned in the Code.

So much for pragmatism: what about retributivism? Staleness is not
an excuse of the kind which secures acquittals (unless the court can
be persuaded that the delay in prosecution was a deliberate means of
harassment); but it can be a ground for mitigating sentence. Unfortunately it does not fit at all well into most of the varieties of retributive
theory which were outlined in chapter 1. Kant's duty to punish is
timeless. As for 'debts to society', they are metaphorical, but unless
they are quite unlike civil debts they should increase with time, not
diminish. 'Penalty' theories, which regard punishments as evening the
score in the game of life, could perhaps be stretched to accommodate
the idea, for example by ruling that after a certain lapse of time
scoring begins afresh: but why? In any case what seems to be wanted
is a theory that will allow desert to decay, like radioactivity, rather
than suddenly vanish. As for 'symbolic' theories, most are crypto-
utilitarian, since they envisage some advantage from the symbolism,
whether that advantage is moral education, moral satisfaction or the
denial of impunity. Only Nozick's theory seems free of this taint,
since for him the essential function of punishment is 'connecting' the
sinner to the moral values of his society, whether or not this has
any beneficial effect. He could hardly suggest, however, that as time
goes by the quantum of punishment needed to achieve 'connection'

decreases. It would be more plausible to suggest that it might have to increase. Only intuitionists need be in no difficulty, because what is intuited needs no explanation. It is worth noting, however, that Moore, a modern intuitionist, appeals to feelings of guilt as evidence that there is such a thing as desert. Although he does not make the point, feelings of guilt certainly fade with time. But that does not prove that desert does.

The usual explanation of fading is simply that after a long lapse of time the offender is 'not the same person' (see, for example, Stally-brass, 1945). Even lawyers – in Europe at least – will offer this justification, although they would not use it to contest a contract or a will. It was offered to me in correspondence about Priebke's case by Professor Ugo Genesio of the Institute of Humanitarian Law; and Priebke's priest told journalists that 'men change: he's no longer the same man as he was so many years ago' (*La Stampa*, 15 April 1997).

The mere lapse of time, however, is not what makes someone 'a different person'. Exactly what does is a question that is at least three hundred years old. Locke's answer in 1690 was remarkably discriminating. One deserved reward or punishment for an act if one was conscious of doing it or having done it.[4] To punish a man for what he did in his sleep would be like punishing his twin. What Locke did entertain, though only as a theoretical possibility, was the notion of multiple personality:

> But if it be possible for the same man to have distinct incommuni-cable consciousness at different times, it is past doubt the same man would at different times be different persons . . .;

and this, thought Locke, was why a man should not be punished for what he did when mad. Certainly we do not blame Morton Prince's Sally Beauchamp or Thigpen's Eve in their normal states for their actions when they were 'taken over' by other 'personalities'. Nor do we blame people for what they do in their sleep, or in other kinds of automatism. In both cases, however, there is an obvious and sharp discontinuity between the person's normal state and the state in which they committed the act. Amnesia makes the discontinuity even more convincing. In the case of the typical offender there may be a discontinuity of mood – for example between the rage in which he struck a blow and the remorse which follows the rage. Remorse is often claimed as a plea in mitigation. Sometimes counsel will offer evidence that the act was 'out of character'. It may well be true, too, that after a decade or so a relevant trait of the offender, such as a taste for violence, has weakened, or even vanished. None of these pleas, however, amounts to a claim that mere lapse of time has literally made the offender a different person. It is obviously a metaphor; but what is its literal implication? That it is present character rather than past conduct which deserves? As we saw in chapter 3 this is not the assumption on which sentencing is based.

It is when a child has been an offender that it is most persuasive to say that when grown-up he has become 'a different person'. It would be more precise, however, to say that *some* children grow out of *some* of their antisocial characteristics. Not all bullies remain bullies: only some. There are jurisdictions in which the records of juvenile findings of guilt are 'sealed', and cannot be mentioned when they appear in court as adults. However desirable this may be for other reasons it does not settle the question whether an adult should be excused punishment for something which he did when he was 10. Something makes us say 'Yes'; but it is probably the belief that young children are not fully responsible for their misdoings, or perhaps the pragmatic experience which tells us that punishment long delayed is ineffective.

Forgiveness

Yet is there perhaps an increasing duty to forgive? Certainly duties can increase in importance (as for example a duty of care becomes more important when risks increase); and there are duties which can make us feel guiltier as time passes: unkept promises and unpaid debts are examples. Forgiveness of wrongdoers is regarded by Christians as a duty, or at least as a virtuous state of mind. Until recently it was discussed only by preachers and theologians, but has figured in latter-day writings about what is called 'restorative justice', and has even been measured after a fashion (see Estrada-Hollenbeck, 1996). Its relevance for sentencers is still questionable. In the first place, it is arguable that only those who have suffered from the wrongdoing are entitled to forgive the wrongdoer (see for example, Murphy and Hampton, 1988). Others, who have not suffered, may manage to neutralise their indignation and condemnation, but that should be called 'quasi-forgiveness' (Benn, 1996). Even if sentencers are allowed quasi-forgiveness, however, it does not follow that this should make them more lenient. To forgive is not to be convinced that the wrongdoer deserves no punishment or less punishment (as theologians such as Moberly (1978) have pointed out).

A victim's forgiveness, however, is something which sentencers are sometimes asked to take into account. The forgiveness may be the result of the offender's demonstration of remorse, but it may be attributable to nothing more than his good luck in his choice of victim, as *Tunstall's* case[5] vividly demonstrated. He had caused the death of two of his passengers by dangerous driving. The parents of one victim forgave him (and told the judge so): the parents of the other did not. In the 1980s the Court of Appeal sometimes took into account the forgiveness of those concerned for utilitarian reasons:

> . . . forgiveness can in many cases have an effect, albeit an indirect effect . . . It may reduce the possibility of reoffending, it may reduce the danger of public outrage which arises where a defendant has been released . . . unexpectedly early, and it may enhance the evidence of provocation by the victim . . . (*Darvill* (1987)).

And as we saw in chapter 8 the Court sometimes infers from the victim's forgiveness that the harm (of rape in *Hutchinson* (1993)) was less than it might otherwise seem to be.

More recently the Court of Appeal has taken a more strictly retributive line:

> The opinions of the victim or the surviving members of his family about the appropriate level of sentence [for causing death by dangerous driving] did not provide any sound basis for reassessing a sentence. If the victim felt utterly merciful toward the criminal, as some did, the crime had still been committed, and must be punished as deserved . . . Otherwise cases with identical features would be dealt with in widely different ways (*Nunn* (1996)).

Yet in *Collyer* (1996) the Court simply declared, without giving reasons, that:

> when the victim of a grave offence has made plain a forgiving attitude towards the appellant, that is something which the Court

should take into account in fixing the appropriate level of sentence
. . . it is the Court not the victim that decides the sentence: *but it
is a relevant consideration* (my italics).

This sounds like general guidance which supersedes *Nunn*. What the
Court has never said, however, is that sentencers themselves should
be forgiving, still less that this is a duty which becomes more pressing
with the lapse of time.

When Staleness is All[6]

As for mere staleness, English judges are seldom moved by this plea.
It is typically offered when young victims of sexual abuse grow up
and successfully accuse the abuser; but in such a case (*Tiso*
(1990–91)) the Court of Appeal said that 'whilst any factors which
have positively emerged in the time between the offence and the trial
are open to the court to be taken into consideration, the mere passage
of time cannot attract a great deal of discount by way of sentence
. . .': a dictum which was quoted with approval in *Nicholson* (1992).
In neither case did the Court explain why it did not altogether
disregard 'the mere passage of time'. One is left with the impression
that it did not want to commit itself, or perhaps more precisely had
not given the point much thought.

It is easier for utilitarian reasoning to make sense of staleness.
When an offender provides us with evidence that what he did was 'out
of character' – for example because he was under duress, or excep-
tionally provoked – we can regard this as relevant because it seems
to make him less culpable. This is Fletcher's 'theory of excuses' (see
chapter 3), and although Fletcher himself did not discuss staleness his
theory can be used to make sense of it. It is arguable that the longer
the time that has passed since the offence – always assuming that the
offender has not repeated it in the interval – the less justifiable it is to
infer from it that he is 'the sort of person' who is capable of repeating
it. Whether or not Fletcher's theory makes retributive sense it would
certainly have made sense to Bentham. His principle of 'frugality'
would have suggested that the staler the offence the less likely it is
that a penalty is needed to correct or deter. This draws attention to an
important difference between the implications of the utilitarian and
the retributive approach to staleness. For retributivists staleness is

either irrelevant or – if they believe that desert does fade – a reason for scaling down the severity of punishment. This is how the Court of Appeal seems to have reasoned in the case of *Meyers* (1996), who had twice escaped from custody, but had lived a law-abiding life for eight years under an assumed name. His sentences, totalling nine years, were halved. For utilitarians on the other hand the passage of time is merely of possible relevance when they are assessing the probability that any penalty is needed. Either it is or it isn't; and the amount of time that has elapsed since the offence is at most relevant only to the confidence with which this can be decided. It may of course be irrelevant. There will be cases such as Priebke's in which the offender himself is no longer in a position to repeat his crime, or no longer disposed to do so, but in which a penalty seems called for to deter potential imitators and signify moral condemnation.

THE DANGERS OF IMPRISONMENT

Some sentencers take into account not only the psychological harm that incarceration seems likely to inflict on the vulnerable (see chapter 8) but also its physical dangers. Nowadays, however, the Court of Appeal is more likely to take the line that it is for the Home Secretary to use his powers (or the Prerogative of Mercy) to release prisoners if, for example, their life expectancy is short (as in the case of *Stark* (1992) who suffered from AIDS). The plea that in prison the offender will have to be segregated for his own safety was rejected in *Kirby's* case (1979) by Lord Chief Justice Widgery, as 'a matter which can properly be put before the Parole Board in due course . . .', yet a similar plea not long afterwards persuaded three different judges to suspend the sentence of *Holmes* (1979). They even said that the court was 'under a duty' to take his situation into account. In 1997, however, the Court admitted in *Bernard's* case that these decisions were 'not easily reconcilable', and enunciated principles which sound like guidelines:

(i)   a medical condition which may at some future date affect either life expectancy or the prison authorities' ability to treat a prisoner satisfactorily may call into operation the Home Secretary's powers of release by reference to the Royal Prerogative of mercy or otherwise but is not a reason for this Court to interfere with an otherwise appropriate sentence . . .

Nowadays the Royal Prerogative is hardly ever used to free sick prisoners. Section 36 of the Criminal Justice Act 1991 was devised for compassionate releases. Except in emergencies it involves consultation with the Parole Board, and the process is not speedy. It has the advantage over the Prerogative that it can be reversed if the illness turns out to have been fictitious. The Court continued:

(ii)   the fact that an offender is HIV positive, or has a reduced life expectancy, is not generally a reason which should affect sentence . . .

We saw in chapter 9 that the Court's attitude to life expectancy where the elderly are concerned is at best ambivalent.

(iii)   a serious medical condition, even when it is difficult to treat in prison, will not automatically entitle an offender to a lesser sentence than would otherwise be appropriate . . .

This takes a stern line. Bernard himself, however, convicted of importing a large quantity of cannabis, was aged 63, had a narrowed oesophagus (which made swallowing difficult), diabetes and hypertension, and was at risk of a heart attack and a stroke. The Court made a small concession:

(iv)   an offender's serious medical condition may enable a court, as an act of mercy in the exceptional circumstances of a particular case, rather than by virtue of a general principle, to impose a lesser sentence than would otherwise be appropriate.

In other words the Court is so reluctant to accept physical ill-health as a mitigating consideration that it will do so only as an exceptional act of mercy (which in *Bernard* merely reduced the defendant's prison sentence from five years to three and a half). Whatever one thinks of the guideline, it raises a general question of considerable interest: whether there should be 'acts of mercy' which are contrary to policy as regards mitigating considerations, and this is discussed in the next chapter.

NOTES

1. Surprisingly, Hart and Honore's *Causation in the Law* does not discuss this sort of causation, although the index implies that it does.

2. For example section 6(2) of the Road Traffic Offenders Act 1988 sets a limit of three years for cases in which late availability of evidence prevented prosecution within six months.

3. The prosecution of offences Act 1985 merely enabled the Government to set time-limits (by regulations) for the preliminary stages of prosecutions. It did not make it permissible to limit the time between the commission and the prosecution of an offence.

4. If Locke really meant to exculpate anyone who simply could not remember committing his crime he was being generous. He would have had to excuse quite a few muggers, burglars and 'ethnic cleansers' who have committed so many crimes that they cannot remember all of them. And at the extreme there are people who are so shocked by their crime (usually domestic violence) that they repress the memory. Drunkenness too can result in amnesia, as can concussion. Perhaps such things were outside Locke's experience. Modern philosophers are less generous: see the review by Glannon (1998).

5. See the Daily Telegraph, 16 March and 13 May 1998. I am indebted to the office of the Lord Chief Justice for a copy of the transcript of this unreported case. Tunstall's original sentence was lenient – community service. The trial judge was not told of the unforgiving attitude of the other victim's parents; but it is unlikely that this influenced the Court of Appeal. The Attorney-General's reference (number 16 of 1998) resulted in three and a half years' imprisonment, the Court taking into account several aggravating features of the case, which included Tunstall's drunkenness and his claim that he was not the driver.

6. What has not been tested is the attitude which the Court of Appeal would take to a sentence imposed after a crime has ceased to be a crime. I cannot, for example, find records of any post-1967

prosecutions for pre-1967 homosexual acts of the kind which ceased to be offences in that year: probably there were none. But if there had been, a Kantian purist would say that it was proper to punish for an act which was an offence when it was committed. Probably the modern Court of Appeal would take a more utilitarian line. But the relevance of this issue to staleness is tenuous.

PART IV
SOME POINTS OF PRINCIPLE

Chapter 14
The Quiddity of Mercy

Mitigation must be distinguished from mercy. In strict juridical theory criminal courts can only mitigate (or of course aggravate) the measures they impose. Mercy – in some jurisdictions known by other names, such as 'clemency', or '*la grace*' – is exercised by non-judicial authorities. In the USA 'executive clemency' is exercised by the President or a state governor, and in other countries by the head of state. In England it is in theory the 'prerogative' of the sovereign. In practice he or she is (by a tradition established by Peel in young Victoria's reign) obliged to exercise it only as 'advised' by the Home Secretary, who considers the advice of his civil servants, but is not supposed to consult the Prime Minister or Cabinet.

The Prerogative of Mercy has a long history. Originally it was used more often for technical or political than for compassionate reasons. When mediaeval juries found that a person had killed another but was insane, the administrative problem of what to with him had to be solved by the king's mercy. (It is ironical that when Victoria persuaded Gladstone to make the verdict 'guilty but insane' she was ridiculed: see Walker, 1969). Royal pardons for treasons and felonies were frequently sought and granted in the Middle Ages in order to placate. In modern times its best-known function was the commutation of the death penalty. In chapters 10 and 11 we saw how it was used to commute the death sentences in *Windle* and *Duffy* when the courts had no power to do so. In Victorian and Edwardian times, before the creation of the Court of Criminal Appeal, it was used to reduce sentences of penal servitude which seemed excessive. Its functions tend to be taken over by statutes. Youthful murderers were eventually saved from the gallows by statutory age-limits, and infanticidal mothers by the Infanticide Acts. The compassionate release of very ill prisoners is now authorised under section 36 of the Criminal Justice Act 1991. Remission and parole also originated in the Prerogative.

More often nowadays it is other authorities which take decisions that - can be called 'merciful'. The Crown Prosecution Service may, as we have seen, refrain from prosecutions for a variety of reasons. It does not call this 'mercy', but employs the conveniently ambiguous phrase 'not in the public interest'. A prison governor may allow a prisoner home leave to attend a death-bed or some happier event. The pertinent question for sentencers, however, is whether it is proper for a criminal court to go further than is justified by a plea in mitigation, and act mercifully in the strict sense of the word, whatever that may be. As we saw at the end of the previous chapter (in the case of *Bernard's* ill-health), the Court of Appeal thinks that this is sometimes proper, although at other times it uses 'mercy' more loosely. 'The sentences are properly described as lenient or merciful' it said in *Spencer* (1996). It tends to resort to what it calls 'mercy' when it has a vague compassion for the offender but cannot articulate a precise justification for reducing the severity of the sentence.

Mercy and Discrimination

If mercy is something different from justified mitigation does that make it nothing more than unfair discrimination in favour of lucky individuals ? If not, what is its 'quiddity', to use the old scholastics' word? Theology is outside the scope of this book, but it is worth noting that divine mercy was something that worried mediaeval theologians. Could God be both just and merciful to sinners? 'God acts mercifully' wrote Aquinas (1270 ca) 'not by going against his justice but by doing something more than justice; thus a man who pays another two hundred pieces of money though owing only one hundred does nothing unjust . . .'. It is interesting that Aquinas should resort to the analogy of a debt to deal with punishment; but in this context it is an even more unconvincing analogy than usual. God's role is nearer that of the creditor than that of the debtor.

This chapter, however, is about penal mercy; and it was the jurists of the Enlightenment who questioned the justice of it. Beccaria (1764) argued that it is the penal code itself which should be lenient, not its agents. If the code were perfect mercy would be unnecessary. Filangieri, the Sicilian nobleman (1785), was blunter. If a pardon is just the law is wrong, but if the law is not wrong the pardon is. It is this point which troubles modern philosophers: Smart, Murphy, Card, Moore and Harrison.

Kant's Mercy

Kant (1796) was not altogether consistent about mercy. It belonged, he thought, not to criminal justice but to private relations between individuals, who could act mercifully when suffering civil wrongs. The sovereign was under a duty *not* to pardon crimes, but could properly pardon treason, since it was a wrong which was personal to him. Yet the values of Kant's culture persuaded him to make odd concessions even where homicides were concerned. Murderers must die, but not duelling officers (because they were defending their honour) or mothers who killed their illegitimate babies (because the babies were beyond the protection of the law).[1] And as a rare concession to expediency he allowed the sovereign to commute the death penalty in cases in which it would excessively deplete the number of his subjects. Kant was a citizen of a rather small state, which needed all its manpower.

Smart's Mercy

Anselm had another good question. If God is merciful to some sinners, why not to all whose sins are similar? (If he had been writing today he might have talked of discrimination.) But it was the unpredictability of mercy rather than its inconsistency which worried Beccaria. Utilitarians, unlike retributivists, have no need to worry about inconsistency unless it reduces the acceptability of the criminal justice system to a damaging extent.

The credit for recognising that there is a jurisprudential problem here probably belongs to Alwynne Smart. Certainly her article in

Philosophy in 1968 expressed surprise at the way in which it had been ignored by theories of punishment. She pointed out that using the word 'mercy' to include such things as mitigation and proportionality distracts us from its genuine and more interesting sense. A sentencer who did *not* take mitigation and proportionality into account could be called 'unjust', whereas genuine mercy is 'deciding not to inflict what is agreed to be the just penalty, all things considered'. It is justice, not mercy, for example, to deal leniently with an offender whose offence has already caused him suffering.

She went on to specify conditions under which mercy could be said to be unjustified: if it causes suffering to an innocent person, is detrimental to the offender's welfare, harms the authority of the law, or if it is clear that the offender is unrepentant or unlikely to reform. Not everyone would agree with some of these conditions, for example the last. It has a utilitarian flavour, and Smart was a retributivist. However that may be, her view was that mercy must do more good than harm if it is to be justified. I am not sure what she would have said about situations in which prisoners are released to save the lives of hostages. The motivation is altruistic but it is arguable that it would 'harm the authority of the law'. She does not discuss mercy motivated by expediency or favouritism: she was writing before Nixon's pardon. More about that sort of mercy later. She saw the force, however, of Anselm's second point. Acts of mercy may discriminate unfairly between similar cases. Inconsistency always worries retributivists, and we have seen the lengths to which the Court of Appeal will sometimes go in order to avoid it.

She devoted quite a lot of time to what she saw at first as a candidate for the status of 'genuine mercy': leniency motivated by staleness; but she concluded that this is justice rather than mercy. 'Since the real offender no longer exists, or fully exists, we are not in a position to show him mercy . . . There is something odd about showing mercy to someone who is not an offender'. This was overstated, as we saw in chapter 13 where it was pointed out that it is only metaphorically true to say that the offender is a different person. If justice does not require this, perhaps she should not have dismissed it after all?

However that may be, her quest for genuine mercy had a happy ending. Offenders are sometimes dealt with leniently, as we saw in chapter 8, because the just penalty would entail suffering for innocent dependants. The sentencer's duty, she thought, is to prevent this. So mercy is justified only when it is demanded by the claims of other obligations. To which Claudia Card (1972) objected that mercy should be discretionary, not obligatory, but does not say why. Certainly it is novel to regard mercy as obligatory; but it is a point that needs discussion later. Murphy's (1988) objection was that mercy 'must be based on a compassionate concern for the *defendant's* plight; but this too seems to be merely an appeal to the traditional conception of *misericordia*.

Murphy's Mercy

Murphy himself believed at first that mercy is incompatible with justice: 'tempering is tampering'. Later in the same book he borrows and develops one of Kant's ideas. Private individuals can be merciful to each other, for example over debts. (Portia's famous plea to Shylock was for mercy in claiming a debt.) If punishing is the state's right but not its duty (as some modern retributivists hold), a judge or head of state may show mercy

> . . . if (and this a very big 'if') it can be shown that such an official is acting not merely on his own sentiments, but as a vehicle for expressing the sentiments of all those who have been victimised by the criminal and who, given those sentiments, wish to waive the right each has that the criminal be punished . . .

This would be readily accepted by Islamic jurists, familiar with codes which allow victims to forbid death sentences or amputations. Western jurists would distinguish more sharply between private actions to remedy wrongs and criminal prosecutions of conduct which is assumed to threaten society as well as individuals. Some would also argue that mercy should not depend on mere luck, and that an offender whose victims wish him not to suffer the proper penalty is lucky indeed. Murphy's solution, too, would confine mercy to extremely unusual situations in which all the victims are identifiable, alive, and have had an opportunity to make their feelings known.

He might reply that the infrequency of such situations is not an objection. He was not after all trying to find a large niche for mercy, only one that would allow it some position in criminal justice. Yet there is something fishy at the back of this niche, and Harrison (1992) puts his finger on the fish. Agents of the state cannot properly act on behalf of private individuals. The state is supposed to be impartial, rational and consistent. Its laws should be flexible, but flexibility should be exercised for reasons, without partiality, and only in ways that can become precedents: that is, in rule-following ways. A rule should be part of the penal law, part of justice.

Card's Mercy

Claudia Card, too, had a solution. She wrote as a retributivist of the classical kind, who saw the infliction of desert as a duty; but she occasionally treats it as a mere right:

> Mercy may be seen as an attempt on the part of the more fortunate to compensate the less fortunate for their undeserved suffering, when a significant part of that suffering is due neither to injustice in the laws nor to the fault of the offender himself, by imposing less than the deserved punishment which they have a right to exact.

Like Murphy's idea this is neat but oddly restrictive. It confines mercy to a special class of case, although one which is more vaguely defined. What is clear, however, is that offenders who are not 'unfortunate' cannot expect mercy from Card, and that the reason for granting it to the unfortunate will not be connected to the offence: not, for example, to its staleness.

Harrison's Mercy

Yet her objection to Smart's version of mercy was that it was obligatory. We must conclude that mercy for 'unfortunates' must be discretionary, and discretion creates the possibility – indeed the probability – of discrimination and inconsistency. This brings us face to face with Harrison's uncompromising position, which finds no place for mercy in the criminal justice system of a properly run state. Such a system must operate both impartially and rationally. Rationality means that its impartiality must not be simply whimsical (for example, mercy on birthdays) or random (mercy by dice-throwing), but based on reasoning; and reasoning must lead to similar decisions in similar cases. (Anselm, Smart and Murphy would have agreed in their own ways.) But mercy, says Harrison, must be unconstrained, and so cannot survive amongst the rules of a rational and impartial criminal justice system.

Card does not explain why mercy 'seems basically something we have no obligation to give'. She writes as if this were axiomatic, and may simply have taken for granted the tradition that the Royal Prerogative – and its equivalent in the United States – is not subject to the law. Harrison takes the same view, but sees that it needs arguing. If one is following a rule when coming to a lenient decision, it must, he thinks, be part of the penal code. It may be required by statute, regulation or case-law, but the difference does not matter: it is 'justice'. And mercy cannot be merely part of an enlightened justice, which is why, like Beccaria, he can find no place for it.

Yet this prompts the question, 'Why should not mercy be a useful term for special kinds of leniency even if they are rule-governed?'. After all, resort to the Royal Prerogative is rule-governed. In the days of capital punishment the Home Office had a precedent-book which recorded the reasons why it had been invoked. There were occasional innovations (as when it was decided that borstal inmates' unpaid fines should be remitted to make life easier for them after release); and occasional breaches of precedent (as, for example, when Maxwell Fyfe, as Home Secretary, refused to commute the death sentence on *Bentley*, contrary to precedent[2]). But the rules were respected.

Criteria for Mercy

This does not make it much easier, however, to answer the question posed by Alwynne Smart. Where does the boundary lie between mitigation and mercy? If we are trying to decide whether mercy is a fictitious animal or merely an endangered species, we ought to take a look at the wide range of reasons which sometimes prompt heads of state or sentencers to exercise leniency. Most have already been discussed in earlier chapters. Others – such as amnesties – are listed in Sebba's (1977) fascinating international survey. Sebba himself shared Beccaria's view that mercy was needed only because of the imperfections of penal codes, and might some day become obsolete. But his interest was in the variety of procedures for exercising it – executive clemency, parole and so forth – and not in what distinguishes it from mitigation.

A review of the practices and the literature suggests five criteria:

(a)   compassion for someone must be the main motive for mercy (a criterion which distinguishes it from mitigation);

(b)   it must not be whimsical or random, but consistent (which means rule-following);

(c)   it must not be improper in other ways. (There are quite a lot of other ways. Leniency can be the result of a bribe, of intimidation, of favouritism, whether shown to friends, co-religionists or members of a political party, ethnic group, trade union or other association.) It may even be superstitious, as when a magistrate tempers his sentences at Christmas;

(d)   it should not be leniency of a kind required by justice (which would exclude most but not all of the reasons for leniency which have been discussed in earlier chapters);

(e)   it should not be motivated solely by expediency (which would exclude bargains with hostage-takers, leniency in exchange for pleading guilty or turning Queen's evidence', economising in scarce resources, such as prison places, or granting diplomats immunity from prosecution). This is not a condemnation of expediency: simply a distinction.

Amnesties

Amnesties are a kind of leniency which is usually prompted by expediency rather than compassion. They may take two forms: a promise of immunity from prosecution, or the remission of an already incurred penalty (usually imprisonment). Some amnesties are merely celebratory, like the one granted in Belgium when its king married: but most are prompted by expediency. Draft dodgers in the USA during the Vietnam war were eventually granted an amnesty to heal political wounds. English amnesties have been rare. Edward II promulgated a pardon for all felons and traitors, except the Bishop of Winchester. Charles II offered immunity to everyone involved in his father's execution, if they applied for it within four days (but he allowed Parliament to make exceptions, among whom was the unfortunate Captain Axtell who unsuccessfully pleaded 'superior orders': see chapter 13). Nowadays English amnesties seem to take the form of a promise not to prosecute: a 1995 example was an attempt to persuade fraudulent claimants of social security benefits to confess and desist. Although granted to whole categories of offenders they can result in injustice. An obvious instance is the release of prisoners irrespective of the time they have served. Some US draft dodgers had been imprisoned, some had managed not to be.

Genuine Mercies

This leaves a very few kinds of leniency as candidates for the status of genuine mercy. The commonest is probably Alwynne Smart's: a response to an obligation which is held to override the right or duty to punish, the most frequent examples being the quashing or reduction of a parent's prison sentence in the interests of her (or more rarely his) children. Another is the repatriation of prisoners to serve their sentences in their own countries, a practice made possible by the Convention on the Transfer of Sentenced Prisoners and other international agreements. A third is the notion of 'natural punishment' – the consideration that the offender 'has suffered enough'.

A fourth is rare. When Britain still used capital punishment murderers under sentence of death were spared because Parliament was debating the abolition of the sentence: for an example see the story of Simcox in chapter 5. The underlying principle was that an offender should not suffer a penalty which is or may be on the point of becoming obsolete. It can be argued that this is a compassionate principle: the offender would be eligible for pity if he suffered merely because of the date of his crime.

A case might be made out for a fifth sort: leniency exercised because of meritorious conduct unconnected with the offence or with remorse for it. The striking examples given in chapter 7 cannot easily be regarded as 'justice'. More precisely it is hard to see how a retributivist could justify them, except on the crude basis of 'moral bookkeeping'. On the other hand they were not motivated by compassion. Perhaps they should simply be categorised as 'improper'?

Rules for Mercy

Harrison's point about rules has still to be considered. His assumption is that if the reason for leniency is capable of being stated in the form of a rule that rule is – or at least should be regarded as – part of the penal code. This can be granted for the sake of argument, since the more important question is whether there can be acceptable 'leniency rules' which are not required by retributive justice. If so, it hardly matters whether they are labelled as part of the penal code or not. And as has already been said there is no reason why mercy should not be rule-governed: no reason for saying that there cannot be a kind of rule which is best called 'merciful'. In this context rules are simply a device for ensuring consistency.

The candidates which have been offered for the status of mercy seem capable of being applied with some degree of consistency, and even of being expressed as rules. Italy's penal code exempts from imprisonment (with exceptions) mothers of very young children and offenders over a certain age. The eligibility of prisoners for repatriation is governed by legislation (in Britain the Repatriation of Prisoners Act 1984).

There may well be difficulties in framing constitutive rules. How meritorious must an action be if it is to be a reason for leniency? What kinds of prisoners can be repatriated without risk? Risk of what? (See *Hansard* (Lords) for 5 March 1984, col. 18, for what the Home Secretary's reasoning would probably be.) The intention may be clear but its application unclear. This may be what the Court of Appeal had in mind when it said that there are classes of cases in which the circumstances 'vary so infinitely' that it is 'difficult, if not impossible' to lay down guidelines (*Lindsay*, 1993). It may be that in some cases we must be content with a rule for which constitutive rules are 'difficult if not impossible' to express – what Dworkin called a 'principle' (1977).

Utilitarians' Mercy

The views so far discussed have taken for granted a retributive view of punishment. Beccaria apart, it always seems to be assumed that utilitarian sentencers or heads of state would not be interested in mercy or indeed in any kind of leniency which goes beyond Bentham's (1789) principle of 'frugality': the principle that punishment should be no more severe   than is necessary for its utilitarian purpose. In this unsophisticated scenario – accepted, it seems, by Smart (1968) and Bean (1981) – utilitarians would punish A less severely than his accomplice B only if in each case they believe that they are applying the minimum severity needed to achieve their aim (not being retributivists they would not be troubled by inconsistency). Leniency motivated by compassion would be ruled out.

This scenario, however, relies on two assumptions:

(a)   that utilitarian sentencers *know* what sort of sentence will maximise the effect they want;
(b)   utilitarians will not be content with anything less than *maximisation*.

In real life, as Bean the penologist must have known, (a) is by no means always the case. Indeed it is usually the case only when precautionary detention is the wanted effect. Otherwise, sentencers are often faced with choices between measures without the means of knowing which will be more effective, and are thus free to choose the less severe. This is no more than the application of 'frugality' in conditions of uncertainty. But there may also be situations in which they can be fairly sure that measure X will be more effective than Y, but by a narrow margin. When this is so only a utilitarian who insists on maximising his utilities is obliging himself to choose the more severe penalty. Yet one can have utility as one's aim without always trying to maximise it. So non-maximising utilitarians can be merciful, provided that their reasons fit the criteria for mercy.

NOTES

1.   Why were they beyond the law? What did Kant mean? He did not say. It is interesting that the *Code Napoléon* of 1810 (which deserves its title no more than Justinian's *Digest*) took the opposite line. Infanticidal mothers – unlike most other murderers – must be executed because their crime was so easy to conceal that the maximum deterrent was needed.

2.   Bentley and Craig were two young burglars who were cornered by police. Craig had a revolver and shot a policeman fatally, after (it was said) Bentley had shouted, 'Let him have it' – meaning what?). Maxwell Fyfe's civil servants argued that Bentley, who had been unarmed, should not be hanged, especially since the firer of the shot, Craig, was below the legal age for hanging (18). Maxwell Fyfe's own autobiography (Kilmuir, 1964) did not disclose that his refusal to invoke the Prerogative was contrary to official advice and precedent, but a later Home Secretary breached the traditional *omerta* and told Parliament.

Chapter 15
The Next Step

What must have struck the reader of earlier chapters is the number of reasoned decisions by the Court of Appeal which are difficult, if not impossible, to reconcile with each other. Some of them have already been the subject of scattered and tactfully worded criticism in professional journals. When they are assembled in a book, however, they make a dispiriting collection. Sometimes the explanation is that their dates are wide apart, and that minds have changed. If that were all it would be reassuring. Sometimes, however, the explanation is simply that the decisions were taken by different sets of judges, for none of whom sentencing was a specialty.

While this book was nearing completion the Crime and Disorder Act 1998 reached the statute-book. Among its many innovations were two requirements. In future, when hearing an appeal against a sentence the Criminal Division of the Court of Appeal must consider whether its guidelines for that category of case need review, and, if it has not yet issued relevant guidelines, whether it should do so. The Lord Chancellor is required to set up a Sentencing Advisory Panel, which the Court of Appeal must consult when framing or revising guidelines, and which can of its own initiative propose the framing or revision of guidelines (ss. 80, 81).

When framing or revising guidelines the Court of Appeal must have regard to

(a)   the need to promote consistency in sentencing;
(b)   the sentences imposed by English and Welsh courts for offences of the relevant category;
(c)   the cost of different sentences and their relative effectiveness in preventing reoffending;
(d)   the need to promote public confidence in the criminal justice system;
(e)   the views of the Sentencing Advisory Panel.

Consistency

The Act gives pride of place to consistency. Not the visionary 'commensurateness' of the 1991 Act: only the more attainable goal of consistency. Like commensurateness, however, it belongs to the world of the retributivist. (Utilitarians worry about it only if it makes decisions too unpredictable or discredits the system to an extent that reduces its efficacy.) Even retributivists who believe that there is more to desert than mere rule-following (see chapter 1) are troubled by the sort of rule-breaking which is involved in inconsistent sentencing.

There are several sorts of inconsistency, some more serious than others. As we saw in chapter 7 the Court of Appeal is usually concerned to prevent unjustifiable differences between the sentences of accomplices in the same offence, in case these give rise to a sense of injustice which discredits the system in the offenders' eyes. It is understandably less worried by small or even moderate differences between sentences for unrelated offences. These everyday inconsistencies are occasionally noticed and featured by the news media, but are usually unobserved and disturb nobody (except perhaps academic retributivists who are aware that they must be occurring).

More troubling – at least for retributivists – are inconsistencies not between sentences but between the principles on which they are determined. Several examples have been cited in earlier chapters. One was the contrast between *Bradley* and *Spence* (see chapter 7 under 'Intoxication'). In *Bradley* Lord Chief Justice Lane had said that 'the day is long past' when intoxication could mitigate an offence, but two years later two other judges allowed it to reduce *Spence's* sentence for a violent rape. In chapter 5 we saw the Court deciding in *Richart* that a threat to kill is not a 'violent offence' for the purpose of a LTC sentence, but later deciding in *Wilson* that it is, without overlooking *Richart* but also without distinguishing the cases.

The Court used to defend volte-faces of this sort. When *De Havilland* (1983) appealed against his life sentence on the ground that no medical evidence of his dangerousness had been adduced, and cited cases in which the Court had insisted on such evidence, his dangerousness was so obvious that the Court delivered a much-quoted rebuke to his unfortunate counsel:

> . . . decisions on sentencing are not binding authorities in the sense that decisions of the Court of Appeal are binding both on this court and on lower courts. Indeed they could not be, since the circumstances of the offence and the offender present an almost infinite variety from case to case . . . The vast majority of decisions of this court are concerned with the particular facts and circumstances of the case before it, and are directed to the appropriate sentence in that case. Each case depends on its own facts.

This was extraordinarily sweeping. There had been decisions which the Court plainly regarded as binding. An example was the doctrine in *Faulkner* (1972) as to when sentences should or should not be consecutive, which, as we saw in chapter 7, was later expressly called 'binding' by Lord Chief Justice Lane (even if it was not always followed by the Court). More recently, in *Ozair Ahmed* (1994) the Court seemed to have forgotten the *De Havilland* doctrine altogether:

> . . . it is unfortunate that the learned judge did not seem to have been referred to the appropriate authorities . . . if he had been we would have hoped that he would have passed a more appropriate sentence . . . We would urge members of the Bar when mitigating on sentence to draw the sentencing judge's attention to appropriate decisions of this Court on sentencing.

This rebuke was all the more striking because Ahmed's appeal was based not on a principle but simply on the fact that his 21-month sentence for mortgage frauds was much longer than the norm.

It raises doubt as to whether Dunn LJ had really meant what he said in *De Havilland*. All that he needed to concede was that the Court's normal insistence on medical evidence was subject to an exception when the offender's dangerousness was obvious without it. He did not have to assert that none of its sentencing decisions was binding.

Not only is the Court expected to lay down guidelines: it admonishes judges who depart from them without good reason, as it did in *Johnson* (1994). The judge who sentenced Johnson had said, 'Much as I respect their Lordships, I do not agree with their principles and I do not mind saying so and I am not going to act upon their principles'. The Court of Appeal's comment was that incidents of this sort created an appearance of injustice:

> In such special cases the judge should indicate clearly the factor or factors which in his judgment allow departure from the tariff set by this court. What a judge must not do is to state that he is applying some personal tariff because he considers the accepted range of sentences to be too high or too low.

Interestingly the Court made it clear that but for the judge's remarks it would not have interfered with the seven-year sentence for what had been a violent mugging. As it was, Johnson was the lucky beneficiary. His sentence was reduced by two years, apparently lest he feel that he had suffered an injustice.

What the Court could still point out is that in many cases the decision as to the severity of the sentence has to balance a multiplicity of aggravating and mitigating factors, the exact mixture of which can for practical purposes be regarded as unique. 'For practical purposes' because even if by chance it were replicated in another case it would be unreasonable to expect a court to know of this. Something like this may be what the Court had in mind when it talked of classes of cases in which the circumstances 'vary so infinitely' that it is 'difficult if not impossible' to lay down guidelines (*Lindsay*, 1993). This is much less sweeping than the *De Havilland* doctrine.

To sum up, when it is the aggravation or mitigation of sentences that is involved, there are several sorts of decisions which it would make sense to treat as binding, or at least as binding in non-exceptional circumstances (what might be called 'elastic binding'):

(a)   interpretations of crucial statutory terms (such as 'violent offence' when a longer-than-commensurate sentence is in question), or of non-statutory phrases such as 'abuse of trust';

(b)   definitions of situations such as those which justify making sentences consecutive;

(c)   decisions that considerations of certain kinds should *not* mitigate (or should *not* aggravate);

(d)   procedural decisions: for example, when and how to test the credibility of mitigations.

Some decisions of these kinds have been the subject of guidelines. Yet a glance at Appendix B will reveal how few there are. As I have said, consistency is more important to retributivists than to utilitarians, but it is unlikely that the Court of Appeal would offer this as an excuse.

Everyday Sentencing

The 1998 Act's second requirement recognises that the cases which reach the Court of Appeal are not typical. They are examples of sentences which seem to the offender's lawyers – or to right-thinking Attorney-Generals – to be outside the normal brackets for the offence and the circumstances. Even when the Court of Appeal upholds the sentence this probably means only that it is just within the brackets. The requirement to study the normal sentencing habits of the English and Welsh courts will call for research beyond the *Criminal Statistics*, whose categories of offences are too broad to be of any use for this purpose. They do not distinguish attempts from successes (murder apart), first convictions from nth convictions, multiple from single offences, longer-than-commensurate from other custodial sentences; and these are only a few examples.

Cost and Effectiveness

The third considerations specified by the Act are refreshingly utilitarian – cost and effectiveness. At present we know more about cost than about effectiveness, and what we do know about the latter is not encouraging. That precautionary detention works is obvious, but what courts need, as we saw in chapter 5, is expert advice as to when it is advisable. Chapter 6 emphasised that the unreliability of non-custodial measures as precautions is not yet fully appreciated. As for correction, routinely published statistics are misleading. As we saw in chapter 2, research statistics tend to show only small differences between the effectiveness of custodial and non-custodial sentences in reducing recidivism; but this may be because they are usually comparing sentences and not regimes. General deterrence depends on success in two difficult tasks: convincing potential offenders that the probability of conviction is high when it is not, and convincing them that the consequence will be a substantial custodial sentence, which is certain only for a few types of offences. The people who are more likely to be convinced are potential rather than actual offenders because the latter are too experienced to be deceived about these probabilities.

Public Confidence in the System

The Court of Appeal's attitude to public opinion has become more respectful. 'The Courts do not have to reflect public opinion' said Lawton LJ a quarter of a century ago in *Sargeant* (1974). 'On the other hand courts must not disregard it. Perhaps the main duty of the court is to lead public opinion.' Just over ten years ago it made a less grudging concession when it approved the remarks of the sentencing judge in *Broady* (1988):

> Judges are not here to gain approval or disapproval from the public, and thus decide their sentences perhaps on the lowest common denominator of public opinion. But at the same time public abhorrence of behaviour like the defendant's [baby-battering] should not be and must not be disregarded by the courts, who also have a duty to pass judgment in a way which is generally acceptable among right-thinking, well-informed persons . . .

This does not mean, suggests Shute in a closely reasoned article (1998), that sentencers must be guided by opinion polls. The 'right-thinking, well-informed person' must be 'a kind of ideal type', a hypothetical person who not only embodies sound moral values but also knows everything pertinent about the case and is also able to think rationally about it. Shute concludes that this amounts to little more than saying that sentencers should double-check their own reasoning.

What is even more interesting is the question why the courts make these occasional bows in the direction of public opinion. It can hardly be that they feel in need of confirmation that their sentences are retributively right – 'commensurate with the seriousness of the offence'. That would expect too much precision, even from a right-thinking, well-informed person. The answer is probably what the Court said in *Williams* (1997):

> . . . it is important if confidence in the rule of law and the administration of justice is to be maintained that offenders committing this kind of offence [robbing schoolchildren] are, and are seen to be, severely punished by the courts . . .

This, at any rate, is what section 80(3)(d) of the 1998 Act requires the Court of Appeal to have in mind: 'the need to promote public confidence in the criminal justice system'. It is a consideration, however, which can be given too much weight when what is under discussion is judges' sentencing policy, especially if it is interpreted as an encouragement to increase the use of imprisonment (as it was in *Williams*). There are other features of the system which have a more damaging effect on public confidence. Low detection-rates, high acquittal rates and other miscarriages of justice are only a few examples.

It is true that the typical man in the typical street is punitive. Survey after survey has found that the majority of respondents believe that sentencers are too lenient. In fact many respondents are underestimating courts' severity; but even the better informed minority tends to be of the same view.[1] It is to be hoped, however, that the Court of Appeal will not take s. 80(3)(d) to mean that it must try to *satisfy* the Draconian man in the street. It will be sufficient if its policies do not alienate him.

In fact the man in the street does not study sentencing statistics or the *Criminal Appeal Reports (Sentencing)*. He forms impressions from the cases which the news media select to stimulate his interest. Even so, it is seldom the precise sentence which interests him,[2] unless it is presented as an example of unjustifiable leniency – for example a non-custodial sentence for causing death by dangerous driving. In theory the Attorney-General's power to refer to the Court of Appeal sentences which seem to him unduly lenient ought to reassure the man in the street. In practice the news of a referral may simply confirm his distrust of sentencers; and it would be useful to know if it has this effect.

What research has found, however, is that

... when members of the public have a level of information [about a case] that is comparable to that which is available to a judge in a court, the public respond in a way that is fairly consistent with judicial practice (Hough and Roberts, 1998).

It follows that, if the aim is the modest one of minimising avoidable loss of public confidence in sentencing, increasing severity is not the only way of achieving it. The news media could be given fuller explanations of sentences which seem *prima facie* lenient.

The Effect of Section 80

Whether section 80 will stimulate the drafting of a lot of new guidelines remains to be seen. Bingham LCJ himself has expressed doubts in an interview (Rutherford, 1997):

... It may be that the guidelines panel will find that far from there being huge areas of criminal activity that are uncharted in terms of guidelines there are relatively few such areas where there could reasonably be full guidelines. Furthermore there are some offences, such as manslaughter, for which it would be virtually impossible to construct a guideline that would be of any value.

His impromptu example was not well chosen, since there are several guideline cases dealing with manslaughter in different circumstances (see Appendix B). More important, it made clear that he was thinking only of guidelines which deal with types of offences, and not of the other sorts which I have discussed under the heading of 'Consistency', and which seem particularly needed to deal with aggravation and mitigation, not to mention mercy.

NOTES

1.   This is one of the unpublished findings of the 1996 British Crime Survey (a personal communication from Michael Hough).

2.   When respondents are asked about cases which interested them they are usually unable to remember the sentence (Walker and Marsh, 1984).

Appendix A
Serious Offences

'SERIOUS' ENOUGH FOR A CUSTODIAL SENTENCE

As chapter 4 must have made clear, there is no official list of types of offences which are regarded by the judiciary as 'serious' enough, without aggravating features and unless considerably mitigated, to justify a custodial sentence. There can be little or no doubt about offences involving fatalities, or injuries resulting from intentional violence (although deaths caused by careless driving are an exception: see chapter 8). The same is true of the sexual offences listed in schedule 9 to the Criminal Justice and Public Order Act 1994 (see the next part of this appendix), and one or two other sexual offences of which examples are cited below. Robberies, burglaries of occupied dwellings, blackmail, damage by arson or explosions and dishonesty which abuses a position of trust, or is extremely lucrative, almost always earn custodial sentences, even when somewhat mitigated.

There are a number of offences, however, about which this can be said with confidence only after studying examples in the *Criminal Appeal Reports (Sentencing)* or in *Current Sentencing Practice*. The examples which follow are unaggravated, and in some cases have mitigating features which make it all the clearer that the offence itself was regarded by the Court of Appeal as serious enough to justify imprisonment or one of its juvenile equivalents. Most of the cases were decided after section 1 of the Criminal Justice Act 1991 came into effect.

abortion, illegal: *Scrimaglia* (1971) 55 Cr App R 280
aggravated vehicle taking: *Sealey* (1994) 15 Cr App R (S) 189
animals, importing prohibited species of: *Sperr* (1992) 13 Cr App R (S) 8
assault on a police officer: *Moore* (1992) 14 Cr App R (S) 273

bail, failing to surrender to: *Uddin* (1992) 13 Cr App R (S) 114
bankruptcy, managing a company during: *Thompson* (1993) 14 Cr App R (S) 89
bigamy to evade immigration control: *Cairns* [1997] 1 Cr App R (S) 118
bombs, hoaxes involving: *McLennon* (1994) 15 Cr App R (S) 17
buggery, false allegation of: *Cunningham* (1993) 14 Cr App R (S) 383
burglary of a dwelling: *Lewis* (1993) 14 Cr App R (S) 744

cannabis, offences involving (except for personal use): Current Sentencing Practice
cheating in casino (at roulette): *Webb* (1995) 16 Cr App R (S) 486
children, cruelty or violence to: *Masters* [1996] 2 Cr App R (S) 159 (Attorney-General's reference 57 of 1995); *Houghton* 1992 13 Cr App R (S) 11
children, possessing indecent photographs of, for distribution: *Dash* (1994) 15 Cr App R (S) 41
contempt of court: Current Sentencing Practice B8–33
coroner, concealing corpse from *Godward* [1998] 1 Cr App R (S) 385
corruption: Current Sentencing Practice B 9–13
counterfeit money, offences involving: *Derbyshire* (1992) 13 Cr App R (S) 126; *Dickens* (1993) 14 Cr App R (S) 76
counterfeiting computer programmes: *Lloyd* [1997] 2 Cr App R (S) 157
credit cards, stealing with a view to fraud: *Bumrunpruik* (1993) 14 Cr App R (S) 98

disorder, violent: *Sturton* (1992) 13 Cr App R (S) 116
driving-test, arranging for impostor to take: *Prince Adebayo* [1998] 1 Cr App R (S) 15

drugs in Class A, any offence involving them, including possession for personal use: *Cox* (1994) 15 Cr App R (S) 216

elector, procuring personation of: *Brindley* [1997] 2 Cr App R (S) 353
escaping from lawful custody: *Clarke* (1994) 15 Cr App R (S) 825
evicting tenant unlawfully: *Madarbakus* (1992) 13 Cr App R (S) 542
explosives, illegal manufacture or use of: Current Sentencing Practice B 7–33

false imprisonment: *Brown* (1994) 15 Cr App R (S) 337
false insurance claim: *Bedding and others* (1995) 16 Cr App R (S) 101
false name, using at arrest and trial, to conceal record: *Lomax* [1996] 2 Cr App R (S) 20
financial deposits, neglect in taking: *Lawrence and Ian Reuben* [1996] 1 Cr App R (S) 79
firearms, most illegal uses of: Current Sentencing Practice B 3–33
flying log-book, making false entries in: *Grzybowski* [1998] 1 Cr App R (S) 4
fraudulent trading: *Colin and Anthony Palk* [1997] 2 Cr App R (S) 167

handling stolen goods commercially: *Rogers* (1994) 15 Cr App R (S) 245
harbouring escaped prisoner: *Taylor* (1994) 15 Cr App R (S) 893

immigration, assisting illegal: *Goforth* [1997] 1 Cr App R (S) 234
indecent material, importing: *Travell* [1997] 1 Cr App R (S) 52
Inland Revenue, concealing income from: *Ford* (1981) 3 Cr App Rep (S) 15

kidnapping, for any purpose: see Current Sentencing Practice B3–43

noxious thing (Temazepam), causing to be taken: *Hogan* (1994) 15 Cr App R (S) 834

passports, using improperly; using false passports: *Takyi* [1998] 1 Cr App R (S) 372; *Olorunnibe* [1998] 2 Cr App R (S) 260
peregrine falcons, unlawfully keeping and selling: *Canning* [1996] 2 Cr App R (S) 202
perjury, suborning perjury: *Vianna* (1994) 15 Cr App R (S) 758
perverting the course of justice: *Kelly* (1992) 14 Cr App R (S) 170

prostitution, living on earnings of: *Kirk* (1995) Cr App R (S) 895
proxy voters, forging details of: *Lewis* [1998] 1 Cr App R (S) 13

railway passengers, endangering: *Mullaly* [1997] 2 Cr App R (S) 343
rape, attempt to: *Diggle* (1994) 16 Cr App R (S) 163
rape, false allegations of: *Gregson* (1993) 14 Cr App R (S) 85
reckless or dangerous driving of motor vehicles (without injury):
     Hourihane (1992) 14 Cr App R (S) 357; *Vickers* (1993) 14 Cr App
     R (S) 317
'road rage' common assaults: *Fenton* (1994) 15 Cr App R (S) 682
robbery or attempts to rob: *Sunderland and Collier* [1996] 2 Cr App
     R (S) 743 (Attorney-General's references 60 and 61 of 1995)

'stalking': *Smith* [1998] 1 Cr App R (S) 138
steroids, unlawfully dealing in: *Wileman* [1997] 2 Cr App R (S) 326
suicide, aiding: *Osborne* (1991) 13 Cr App R (S) 225

theft when in a position of trust: *McCormick* (1994) 16 Cr App R (S)
     134; *Clark* [1998] 2 Cr App R (S) 95
threatening to kill: *Brown* (1991) 13 Cr App R (S) 239
trade description offences: *Booth* [1997] 1 Cr App R (S) 103

video cassettes, illegally copying: *Gibbons* (1995) 16 Cr App R (S)
     398
violence aboard an aircraft: *Beer* [1998] 1 Cr App R (S) 248
violent disorder in prison: *Mahoney* (1993) 14 Cr App R (S) 291

waste, unauthorised dumping of: *Garrett* [1997] 1 Cr App R (S) 109
witness, intimidating: *Williams* [1997] 2 Cr App R (S) 221
witness, refusing to give evidence as: *Montgomery* (1995) 16 Cr App
     R (S) 274

OFFENCES ELIGIBLE FOR LONGER-THAN-COMMENSURATE SENTENCES

Section 31 of the Criminal Justice Act 1991 (as amended by the
Criminal Justice and Public Order Act 1994, sch. 9, paragraph 45, in
respect of sexual offences) defines the sorts of offences which are
eligible for longer-than-commensurate sentences of imprisonment
under section 2(2)(b) of the Act as follows:

'sexual offence' means any of the following—

(a)   an offence under the Sexual Offences Act 1956, other than an offence under sections 30, 31 or 33 to 36 of that Act [i.e. rape, procuration by intimidation or deception, abduction for sexual purposes, having or promoting sexual intercourse with girls under 16 or mental defectives, incest, buggery, gross indecency between men in certain circumstances, indecent assault, causing prostitution; but not living on a prostitute's earnings, controlling or abetting her or keeping a brothel];

(b)   an offence under section 128 of the Mental Health Act 1959 [sexual intercourse with a mentally disordered patient];

(c)   an offence under the Indecency with Children Act 1960 [gross indecency with or towards a child, not amounting to a more serious sexual offence];

(d)   an offence under section 9 of the Theft Act 1968 of burglary with intent to commit rape;

(e)   an offence under section 54 of the Criminal Law Act 1977 [inciting a sister, daughter or granddaughter under the age of 16 to have sexual intercourse with oneself];

(f)   an offence under the Protection of Children Act 1978 [involving indecent photographs of children];

(g)   an offence under section 1 of the Criminal Law Act 1977 of conspiracy to commit any of the offences in paragraphs (a) to (f) above;

(h)   an offence under section 1 of the Criminal Attempts Act 1981 of attempting to commit any of those offences;

(i)   an offence of inciting another to commit any of those offences.
. . .

'violent offence' means an offence which leads, or is intended or likely to lead, to a person's death or to physical injury to a person, and includes an offence which is required to be charged as arson (whether or not it would otherwise fall within this definition).

and Section 31 adds that

In this Part any reference, in relation to an offender convicted of a violent or sexual offence, to protecting the public from serious harm from him shall be construed as a reference to protecting members of the public from death or serious personal injury, whether physical or psychological, occasioned by further such offences committed by him.

'SERIOUS OFFENCES' QUALIFYING FOR OBLIGATORY LIFE SENTENCES

Section 2 of the Crime (Sentences) Act 1997, which (with exceptions) makes a life sentence obligatory for a second or subsequent conviction for a 'serious offence', lists the following as 'serious offences' if committed in England and Wales (and also lists their equivalents in Scotland and Northern Ireland):

(a)   an attempt to commit murder, a conspiracy to commit murder or an incitement to murder;

(b)   an offence under section 4 of the Offences against the Person Act 1861 (soliciting murder);

(c)   manslaughter;

(d)   an offence under section 18 of the Offences against the Person Act 1861 (wounding, or causing grievous bodily harm, with intent);

(e)   rape, or an attempt to commit rape;

(f)   an offence under section 5 of the Sexual Offences Act 1956 (intercourse with a girl under 13);

(g)   an offence under section 16 (possession of a firearm with intent to injure), section 17 (use of a firearm to resist arrest) or section 18 (carrying a firearm with criminal intent) of the Firearms Act 1968; and

(h)   robbery where, at some time during the commission of the offence, the offender had in his possession a firearm or imitation firearm within the meaning of that Act.

OFFENCES QUALIFYING FOR HOSPITAL ORDERS WITH RESTRICTIONS

Section 41 of the Mental Health Act 1983 does not exclude any imprisonable offence. The Crown Court simply has to be of the opinion that a restriction order is 'necessary for the protection of the public against serious harm'. In practice, offences such as theft, criminal damage and public order offences as well as violent and sexual offences sometimes result in restriction orders. Civil, sentenced and remand prisoners who are transferred to mental hospitals by 'transfer directions' are also usually the subject of restrictions on discharge etc. under sections 48 and 59 of the Act, irrespective of any assessment of their offences or their dangerousness.

Appendix B
Guideline Cases

Courts are guided by a number of cases in which the Court of Appeal has not merely upheld or varied the sentence which was the subject of an appeal, but has indicated what factors sentencers should take into account by way of aggravation or mitigation. Some of these cases are expressly called 'guideline cases', but many are not, even when their advice is as detailed as it is in the sketchier guideline cases. The important cases are:

aggravated vehicle-taking: *Bird* (1993) 14 Cr App R (S) 343

amphetamines, importing unlawfully: *Wijs and others* [1998] Crim LR 587

arson: *Calladine* (1975) Current Sentencing Practice, B7–12001; *Priest* (1980) 2 Cr App R (S) 68; *Hoof* (1980) 2 Cr App R (S) 331

assisting law enforcement, evidence of: *X* (1999) Times Law Reports, 3 February

attempted murder: *Ellis* (I995) 16 Cr App Rep (S) 773

breaches of financial trust: *Barrick* (1985) 7 Cr App Rep (S) 142; *Clark* [1998] Crim LR 227

buggery between adults in a public place: *Tosland* (1981) 3 Cr App R (S) 364

buggery of youth by adult: *Willis* (1974) 60 Cr App Rep 146 burglary of a dwelling: *Brewster and others* [1998] 1 Cr App R (S) 181

cannabis, importing: *Aramah* (1982) 4 Cr App R (S) 407; *Ronchetti and others* [1998] Crim LR 227; *Maguire* (1997) 1 Cr App R (S) 130; *Wagenaar and Pronk* (1997) 1 Cr App R (S) 178

causing death by dangerous driving: *Boswell* (1984) 6 Cr App Rep (S) 257: *Willetts* (1993) 14 Cr App Rep (S) 592: *Shepherd and Wernet* (1994) 15 Cr App Rep (S) 640 (Attorney-General's references 14 and 24 of 1993)

cocaine dealing: *Aranguren* (1994) 16 Cr App Rep (S) 211

concealing income from Inland Revenue: *Ford* (1981) 3 Cr App Rep (S) 15

counterfeiting: *Crick* (1981) 3 Cr App R (S) 275

criminal damage: *Ward and others* (1997) 18 Cr App R (S) 442

custodial sentences for juveniles: *Mills and others* [1998] 1 WLR 363; [1998] 2 Cr App R (S) 128

custodial sentences, when to shorten: *Bibi* (1980) 2 Cr App R (S) 177

disqualifying company directors: *Griffiths and others* (1997) Times Law Reports, 29 December

drugs, Class A, offences: *Aramah* (1982) 4 Cr App R (S) 407; *Martinez* (1984) 6 Cr App R (S) 364; *Bilinski* (1987) 9 Cr App R (S) 360; *Singh* (1988) 10 Cr App R (S) 402; *Aroyewumi* (1994) 99 Cr App R 347; *Hurley* [1997] Crim LR 840

Ecstasy, importing: *Warren and Beeley* [1995] Crim LR 838

evidence, refusal to give: *Phillips* (1983) 5 Cr App R (S) 297; *Montgomery* (1995) 2 Cr App R 23

exceptional circumstances for the purpose of obligatory life sentences for serious offences: *Kelly* [1999] Crim LR 240

excise duty evasion on imported alcohol and tobacco: *Dosanji* [1999] 1 Cr App R (S) 107

explosions, conspiring to cause: *Martin* [1999] Crim LR 97

explosive devices, planting: *Byrne* (1975) 62 Cr App Rep 159

false statements about a company's financial position: *Feld* [1999] 1 Cr App R (S) 1

firearm, real or imitation, unlawful possession or use: *Sheldrake* (1985) 7 Cr App Rep (S) 49; *Avis* [1998] Crim LR 428; Hill (1999) *Times* Law Reports, 13 April

frauds, petty: *Bibi* (1980) 2 Cr App R (S) 177

gross indecency between men: *Morgan and Dockerty* (1978) Current
Sentencing Practice, B4–92001

handling stolen goods: *Wilson* (1980) 2 Cr App R (S) 196
heroin dealing: *Aramah* (1982) 4 Cr App R (S) 407; *Martinez* (1984)
6 Cr App R (S) 364
hospital and restriction orders: *Gardiner* (1967) 51 Cr App Rep 187;
Birch (1989) 11 Cr App R (S) 202

illegal entry, facilitating: *Le and Stark* [1999] Crim LR 96
ill-health of defendant: *Bernard* [1997] 1 Cr App R (S) 135
incest: *Attorney-General's reference No 1 of 1989* (1990) 11 Cr App
R (S) 409
indecent assault: *Bibi* (1980) 2 Cr App R (S) 177; *Wellman* (1999)
Times Law Reports, 6 January
infanticide: *Sainsbury* (1989) 11 Cr App Rep (S) 533
Inland Revenue, false statements to: *Ford* (1981) 3 Cr App R (S) 15

kidnapping or false imprisonment: *Spence and Thomas* (1983) 5 Cr
App Rep (S) 413

living on immoral earnings: *Farrugia* (1979) 69 Cr App Rep 108;
El-Gazzar (1986) 8 Cr App R (S) 182
LSD, possessing with intent to supply: *Hurley* (1998) 19 Cr App R
(S) 299

manslaughter by knife-carriers: *Latham* (Attorney-General's reference
No 33 of 1996) (1997) 18 Cr App R (S) 10
manslaughter in a fight: *Coleman* (1992) 13 Cr App Rep (S) 508
manslaughter in cases of diminished responsibility: *Chambers* (1983)
5 Cr App Rep (S) 190
minimum periods of detention for discretionary lifers and their
juvenile equivalents: *Furber* (1998) 19 Cr App R (S) 208
miscarriage, illegally procuring: *Scrimaglia* (1971) 55 Cr App Rep
280
mortgages, frauds involving: *Stevens and others* (1993) 14 Cr App R
(S) 372

obscene articles, having for publication for gain: *Emmerson* (1977) 65
Cr App R 154; *Holloway* (1982) 4 Cr App Rep (S) 128; and see
Littleford (1984) 6 Cr App Rep (S) 272 for importation

obscene exhibitions: *Farmer and Griffin* (1973) 5 Cr App R (S) 229

pilfering by employees: *Dhunay* (1986) 8 Cr App Rep (S) 107

pornography, commercial exploitation of: *Holloway* (1982) Cr App R (S) 128

rape: *Billam* (1986) 82 Cr App Rep 347; *Roberts and Roberts* (1982) 4 Cr App R (S)·8

rape by husband: *Stephen W* (1993) 14 Cr App R (S) 246

riot and unlawful assembly: *Caird* (1970) 54 Cr App Rep 499; *Pilgrim* (1983) 5 Cr App Rep (S) 140

robbery (but not mugging): *Turner* (1975) 61 Cr App Rep 67; *Daly* (1981) 3 Cr App Rep (S) 340; *Gould* (1983) 5 Cr App Rep (S) 72

sentences, explaining effect of to defendant: *Practice Direction* of 23 January 1998, Times Law Reports, 24 January 1998

sentences, mitigation when a custodial sentence is otherwise justified: *Howells and others* [1998] Crim LR 836

social benefit frauds: *Livingstone-Stewart* (1987) 9 Cr App Rep (S) 135

unlawful sexual intercourse with girl under 16: *Taylor* (1977) 64 Cr App Rep 182

witness refusing to give evidence: *Montgomery* (1995) 16 Cr App R (S) 274

References

Advisory Council on the Penal System (1970) *Non-custodial and semi-custodial penalties*, Her Majesty's Stationery Office, London

Advisory Council on the Penal System (1978) *Sentences of Imprisonment*, Her Majesty's Stationery Office, London

Aquinas, T (1270 ca) *Summa Theologica, Part I* (1952 trans), Benton, Chicago

Ashworth, A J (1983) *Sentencing and Penal Policy*, Weidenfeld and Nicolson, London

Ashworth, A J (1992) *Sentencing and Criminal Justice*: Weidenfeld and Nicolson, London

Ashworth, A J (1993) 'Victim impact statements and sentencing' in *Criminal Law Review*, 498ff

Atkin, Lord (Chairman) (1924) *Report of the Committee on Insanity and Crime*, Cmd 2005, HMSO, London

Baxter, R and Nuttall, C (1975) 'Severe sentences no deterrent to crime?' in *New Society*, *31*, 11ff

Bean, P (1981) *Punishment: a Philosophical and Criminological Inquiry*, Martin Robertson, Oxford

Beccaria, C (1764) *Dei Delitti e delle Pene*, trans e.g. by H Paolucci, 1963, Bobbs-Merrill, New York

Benn, C (1996) 'Forgiveness and Loyalty' in *Philosophy, 71*, 27 369ff

Bentham, J (1789) *An Introduction to the Principles of Morals and of Legislation*, Payne, London

Blackstone, W (1765–9) *Commentaries on the Laws of England*, Clarendon Press, Oxford

Bottoms, A E (1998) 'Five Puzzles in von Hirsch's Theory of Punishment' in *Fundamentals of Sentencing Theory*, ed A J Ashworth and M Wasik, Clarendon Press, Oxford

Bottoms, A E and Brownsword, R (1983) 'Dangerousness and Rights' in *Dangerousness: Problems of Assessment and Prediction*, ed J Hinton, Allen and Unwin, London

Bracton, H de (1250ca) *De Legibus et Consuetudinibus Angliae*, ed Woodbine, 1915, Yale University Press, Oxford University Press

Braithwaite, J and Pettit, P (1990) *Not Just Deserts: a Republican Theory of Criminal Justice*, Clarendon Press, Oxford

Brongersma, E (1980) 'The meaning of "indecency" with respect to moral offences involving children', in *British Journal of Criminology, 20*, 1, 20ff

Burgh, R (1987) 'Guilt, Punishment and Desert' in *Responsibility, Character and the Emotions*, ed R Schoeman, Cambridge University Press

Butler, Lord (Chairman) (1975) *Report of the Committee on Mentally Abnormal Offenders*, Cmnd 6244, Her Majesty's Stationery Office, London

Cadogan, Sir A (Chairman) (1938) *Report of the Departmental Committee on Corporal Punishment*, Cmd 5684, Her Majesty's Stationery Office, London

Card, C (1972) 'Mercy' in *Philosophical Review, 81*, 182ff

Coke, E (1644) *Institutes of the Laws of England, Third Part*, Society of Stationers, London

Covarrubias a Leyva, D (1558) *In varios pontifici ac civilis juris titulos relectiones*, Leyden

Cox, E (1877) *Principles of Punishment as applied to the Criminal Law by Judges and Magistrates*, Law Times Office, London

Criminal Law Revision Committee (1980) *Offences against the Person* (Fourteenth Report), Cmnd 7844, HMSO, London

Cross, R (1971) *The English Sentencing System*, Butterworths, London

Crown Prosecution Service (1994) *Code for Crown Prosecutors.* Obtainable from the Crown Prosecution Service, London

Dalton, K (1960) 'Menstruation and accidents' in *British Medical Journal, 2,* 1425ff

Daube, D (1956) 'The Defence of Superior Orders in Roman Law' in *Criminal Law Review,* 494ff

Davis, M (1983) 'How to make the punishment fit the crime' in *Ethics, 93,* 726ff

De Waal, F (1982) *Chimpanzee Politics: Power and Sex among Apes,* Jonathan Cape, London

Duff, R A (1986) *Trials and Punishments,* Cambridge University Press

Duff, R A (1996) *Criminal Attempts,* Clarendon Press, Oxford

Dworkin, R (1977) *Taking Rights Seriously,* Duckworth, London

Edwards, S M (1984) *Women on Trial: a study of the female suspect, defendant and offender in the criminal law and criminal justice system,* Manchester University Press, Manchester

Estrada-Hollenbeck, M (1996) 'Forgiving in the face of injustice: victims' and perpetrators' perspectives' in *Restorative Justice: International Perspectives,* ed B Galaway and J Hudson, *Criminal Justice Press,* Monsey, New York

Fallon, P (Chairman) (1999) *Report of the Committee of Inquiry into the Personality Disorder Unit, Ashworth Special Hospital,* Cm 4194–11, Her Majesty's Stationery Office, London

Farrington, D P and Morris, A (1983) 'Sex, sentencing and reconviction' in *British Journal of Criminology, 23,* 229ff

Filangieri, G (1785) *La Scienza della Legislazione,* trans by W Kendall, 1792, Robinson, London

Fingarette, H (1972) *The Meaning of Criminal Insanity,* University of California Press, Berkeley

Fletcher, G (1978) *Rethinking Criminal Law,* Little, Brown, Boston, Massachusetts

Flood-Page, C and Mackie, A (1998) *Sentencing Practice: an examination of decisions in magistrates' courts and the Crown Court in the mid-1990s,* Home Office Research Study 180, Her Majesty's Stationery Office, London

Floud, J and Young, W (1981) *Dangerousness and Criminal Justice,* Heinemann, London

Gardiner, Lord (Chairman) (1972) *Living it Down: the problem of old convictions*, Stevens and Sons, London

Glannon, W (1998) 'Moral responsibility and personal identity' in *American Philosophical Quarterly, 35*, 3, 23 1ff

Glanville, R de (1180ca) *De Legibus et Consuetudinibus Regni Angliae*, ed G D Hall 1965, Oxford University Press

Gordon, G H (1978 edition) *The Criminal Law of Scotland*, Green, Edinburgh

Green, T (1976) 'The jury and the English law of homicide' in *Michigan Law Review, 74*, 413ff

Green, T (1985) *Verdict according, to Conscience*, University of Chicago Press

Gross, H (1992) 'Preventing impunity', in *Jurisprudence: Cambridge Essays*, ed H Gross and R Harrison, Cambridge University Press

Hale, M (1736) *Historia Placitorum Coronae*, Nutt and Gosling, London

Harrison, R (1992) 'The equality of mercy' in *Jurisprudence: Cambridge Essays*, ed H Gross and R Harrison, Clarendon Press, Oxford

Hart, H L A (1968) *Punishment and Responsibility*, Clarendon Press, Oxford

Hart, H L A and Honore, A M (1959) *Causation in the Law*, Clarendon Press, Oxford

Hawkins, W (1716) *A Treatise of Pleas of the Crown*, Nutt and Gosling, London

Hedderman, C and Hough, M (1994) *Does the Criminal Justice System treat Men and Women Differently?* Research Findings No. 10, Home Office, London

Hedderman, C and Gelsthorpe, L (1997) *Understanding the Sentencing of Women*, Home Office Research Study No 170, Her Majesty's Stationery Office, London

Hedderman, C and Vennard, J (1998) 'Analysis of serious incidents reported to have occurred between January and July 1997', attached to Home Office Probation Circular 71/1998

Hegel, G W F (1854) *Philosophie des Rechts* trans as *Philosophy of Right* by T M Knox, 1942, Oxford University Press

Hill, T E Jnr (1992) *Dignity and Practical Reason in Kant's Moral Theory*, Cornell University Press, Ithaca and London

Home Office (1996) *The Victims' Charter: a statement of service standards for the victims of crime*, Home Office Communications Directorate, London

Home Office (1996) *Protecting the Public: the Governments Strategy on Crime in England and Wales*, Cm 3190, Her Majesty's Stationery Office, London

Home Office (1997) *No More Excuses: a new approach to tackling youth crime*, Her Majesty's Stationery Office, London

Home Office Inspectorate of Probation (1998) *Exercising Constant Vigilance: the Role of the Probation Service in protecting the public from sex offenders: report of a thematic inspection*, Home Office, London

Home Office (1998) *Third Report of the Working Group on Confiscation: Criminal Assets*, obtainable from the Home Office, London

Horder, J (1992) *Provocation and Responsibility*, Clarendon Press, Oxford

Hough, M and Roberts, J (1998) *Attitudes to Punishment: findings from the British Crime Survey*, Home Office Research Study 179, Her Majesty's Stationery Office, London

House of Commons' Home Affairs Committee (1992–3) *Third Report: Domestic Violence*, 2 vols., Her Majesty's Stationery Office, London

Hume, D (1750) *A Treatise of Human Nature*, 1978 ed, Clarendon Press, Oxford

Ingleby, Viscount (1960) (Chairman) *Report of the Committee on Children and Young Persons*, Cmnd 1191, Her Majesty's Stationery Office, London

Jackson, R M (1967) *Enforcing the Law*, Sweet and Maxwell, London

Kant, I (1796–7) *Rechtslehre*, trans as *Philosophy of Law* by W Hastie, 1887, Clarke, Edinburgh

Kean, A W (1937) 'The history of the criminal liability of children' in *Law Quarterly Review, CCXI*, July, 364ff

Kennedy, H (1992) *Eve was Framed*, Chatto and Windus, London

Kilmuir, Earl of (1964) *Political Adventure: the memoirs of the Earl of Kilmuir*, Weidenfeld and Nicholson, London

Kupperman, J (1991) *Character*, Oxford University Press

Law Commission (1989) *A Criminal Code for England and Wales*, Her Majesty's Stationery Office, London

Lemert, E (1969) *Human Deviance, Social Problems and Social Control*, Prentice-Hall, New Jersey

Lewis, C S (1953) 'The Humanitarian Theory of Punishment', in *Res Judicatae*, Vol 6, Victoria, Australia (republished in 1954 in *Twentieth Century*, London)

Locke, J (1690) *An Essay concerning Human Understanding*, Basset, London

Longford, Lord (1961) *The Idea of Punishment*, Chapman, London

Macfarlane, A (1995) 'Law and custom in Japan: some comparative reflections' in *Continuity and Change, 10*, 3, 369ff

Mackay, R D (1995) *Mental Condition Defences in the Criminal Law*, Clarendon Press, Oxford

Magistrates' Association (1993) *Sentencing Guidelines*, Magistrates' Association, London

Magistrates' Association (1997) *Sentencing Guidelines*, Magistrates' Association, London

Milgram, S (1963) 'A behavioral study of obedience' in *Journal of Abnormal and Social Psychology*, 67, 371ff

Mitchell, B (1997) 'Diminished responsibility manslaughter' in *Journal of Forensic Psychiatry, 8*, 1, 101ff

Moberly, E (1978) *Suffering, Innocent and Guilty*, Society for the Propagation of Christian Knowledge, London

Moberly, W (1968) *The Ethics of Punishment*, Faber and Faber, London

Molony, T F (Chairman) (1927) *Report of the Committee on the Treatment of Young Offenders*, Cmd 2831, Her Majesty's Stationery Office, London

Moore, M (1987) 'The moral worth of retribution' in *Responsibility, Character and the Emotions* (ed F Schoeman) Cambridge University Press

Moore, M (1990) 'Choice, character and excuse' in *Crime, Culpability and Remedy*, ed E F Paul et al, Blackwell, Oxford

Moxon, D (1988) *Sentencing Practice in the Crown Court*, Home Office Research Study 103, Her Majesty's Stationery Office, London

Murphy, J and Hampton, J (1988) *Forgiveness and Mercy*, Cambridge University Press

Murphy, P (ed) (1998 ed) *Blackstone's Criminal Practice*, Blackstone, London

North, P (Chairman) (1988) *Road Traffic Law Report*, Her Majesty's Stationery Office, London
Nozick, R (1981) *Philosophical Explanations*, Clarendon Press, Oxford

Parole Board for England and Wales (1997) *Report of the Parole Board for 1996/97*, Her Majesty's Stationery Office, London
Percy, Lord (Chairman) (1957) *Report of the Royal Commission on the Law relating to Mental Illness and Mental Deficiency*, Cmnd 169, Her Majesty's Stationery Office, London

Radford, J and Kelly, L (1997) 'Self-preservation: a proposal for a new defence for those charged with murder in the context of domestic violence': a paper for the Cropwood Conference on *Rethinking the Homicide Act 1957*. Institute of Criminology, Cambridge
Rawls, J (1973) *A Theory of Justice*, Oxford University Press
Reed, J (Chairman) (1994) *Report of the Department of Health and Home Office Working Group on Psychopathic Disorder*, Department of Health, London
Robinson, P H and Darley, J M (1995) *Justice, Liability and Blame: Community Views and the Criminal Law*, Westview Press, Oxford
Rutherford, A (1997) 'A presence to be reckoned with: Lord Bingham talks to Andrew Rutherford', in *New Law Journal*, 12 September, 725ff

Sebba, L (1977) 'The pardoning power: a world survey' in *Journal of Criminal Law and Criminology, 68*, 83ff
Shoeman, F (ed) (1987) *Responsibility, Character and the Emotions*, Cambridge University Press
Shapland, J (1981) *Between Conviction and Sentence: the process of mitigation*, Routledge and Kegan Paul, London
Shaw, R (1991) 'Supervising the dangerous offender' in *National Association of Senior Probation Officers News, 10*, 4, 3ff
Shute, S (1998) 'The place of public opinion in sentencing law', in *Criminal Law Review*, 465ff
Smart, A (1968) 'Mercy' in *Philosophy, 43*, 345ff.
Smith, J C (1989) *Justification and Excuse in the Criminal Law*, Stevens, London

Smith, S (1846) *Collected Works, Vol I*, Longman, London

Stallybrass, W T (1945) 'A comparison of the general principles of criminal law in England with the *Progetto Nuovo di uno Nuovo Codice Penale* of Alfredo Rocco' in *The Modern Approach to Criminal Law*, ed L Radzinowicz and J W C Turner, Macmillan, London

Street, R (1998) *The Restricted Hospital Order: from court to the community*, Home Office Research Study 186, Her Majesty's Stationery Office, London

Taylor, P and Gunn, J (1999) 'Homicides by people with mental illness: myth and reality', in *British Journal of Psychiatry, 174*, 9ff

Ten, C L (1987) *Crime, Guilt and Punishment*, Oxford University Press

Thomas, D A (1979 edition) *Principles of Sentencing in the Court of Appeal*, Heinemann, London

Thomas, D A (1979) *Constraints on Judgment*, Institute of Criminology Occasional Series No 4, Cambridge

Thomas, D A (1982, but with frequent loose-leaf updating) *Current Sentencing Practice*, Sweet and Maxwell, London

Thomas, D A (ed) *Sentencing News*, Sweet and Maxwell, London

Thorpe, B (1840) *Ancient Laws and Institutes of England, Vol I*, Commissioners on the Public Records of England, London

Turner, J W C (1961) (ed) *Russell on Crime (12th edn)*, Stevens, London

Uglow, S (1998) 'Criminal Records under the Police Act 1997', in *Criminal Law Review*, 235ff

Ussher, J (1989) *The Psychology of the Female Body*, Routledge, London

von Hirsch, A (1993) *Censure and Sanctions*, Clarendon Press, Oxford

von Hirsch, A and Jareborg, N (1987) 'Provocation and culpability' in *Responsibility, Character and the Emotions*, ed F Schoeman, Cambridge University Press

von Hirsch, A and Jareborg, N (1991) 'Gauging criminal harms: a living-standard analysis' in *Oxford Journal of Legal Studies, 11*, 1ff

von Hirsch, A and Wasik, M (1997)'Civil disqualifications attending conviction: a suggested conceptual framework' in *Cambridge Law Journal, 56*, 3, 599ff

Walker, N (1969) *Crime and Insanity in England, Vol I*, Edinburgh University Press

Walker, N (1985) *Why Punish?* Oxford University Press

Walker, N (1985) *Sentencing Theory, Law and Practice*, Butterworth, London

Walker, N and McCabe, S (1972) *Crime and Insanity in England, Vol II*, Edinburgh University Press

Walker, N and Marsh, C (1984) 'Do sentences affect public disapproval?' in *British Journal of Criminology, 24,* 1, 27ff

Walker, N and Padfield, N (1996 ed) *Sentencing Theory, Law and Practice*, Butterworth, London

Wilkinson, G (1995 ed) *Road Traffic Offences*, ed P Halnan and J Spencer, Oyez Longman, London

Wolfgang, M and Sellin, T (1963) *Constructing an Index of Delinquency*, University of Pennsylvania Press, Philadelphia

Index